CRIMES
AND
VICTIMS

FRANK SMYTH

BARNES & NOBLE BOOKS
NEW YORK

This edition published by Barnes & Noble Publishing, Inc., by arrangement with Bookmart Ltd

2005 Barnes & Noble Books

M 10 9 8 7 6 5 4 3 2 1

ISBN 0-7607-7423-4

Every effort has been made to contact the copyright holders for the pictures.
In some cases they have been untraceable, for which we offer our apologies.
Thanks to the following libraries and picture agencies which supplied pictures:

Associated Press, AP Worldwide, AGIP, Black Museum, Cavendish Press, Corbis, Culver Pictures,
Jack Hickes Photography, Fairfax Ltd, Getty Images Editorial, Illustrated London News,
Hulton-Deutsch Collection, Mary Evans Photo Library, Mirrorpix, News Ltd of Australia,
Popperfotos, Press Assocation, Rex Features, Frank Spooner Pictures,
Syndication International, Suddeutscher Verlag, Topham, UPI/Bettmann

The Authors
Frank Smyth is the consultant editor of *Crimes and Victims* and also wrote the chapters *Crimes of Horror*
and *Crimes of Passion*. He began his career as a crime reporter in Yorkshire,
and has since written numerous books on all aspects of crime, including
Detectives in Fact and Fiction, I'm Jack: The Police Hunt for Jack the Ripper and
Cause of Death: A History of Forensic Science.

J. Anderson Black wrote the chapters *Murder Most Foul* and *Organized Crime*.
He is a fine arts graduate from Edinburgh University.
He has been a professional writer for more than twenty-five years,
and his published work covers a wide range of topics from art to crime,
as well as three novels and several screenplays for feature films.

Contents

CRIMES AND VICTIMS

THE RANGE of human folly, delusion and evil seems to be endless. Just when we think we have read or heard of some atrocity or outrage that marks the limit, along comes another, even more appalling. Sometimes it seems that we live in a world that must surely collapse under the weight of its own corruption and violence. Passions appear to rage unchecked, vices breed like disease, people have no control over their most primitive instincts. Yet the world goes on, despite the litany of horror and scandal that follows it like a shadow.

It is that shadow, and the terrible damage it inflicts, that is the subject of this book. We investigate that many-headed creature called crime, telling in vivid detail the stories of the atrocities, deceptions and heartbreaks it has left in its wake.

From acts of murder, gang-land intimidation, financial corruption, drug-dealing and much more a picture of terror and degradation looms out from these pages. From serial killers to men and women driven insane by thwarted love, and from mobsters gripped in fantasies of megalomania to businessmen seduced by dreams of wealth beyond comprehension, we see the crimes and we count the cost.

For the grim truth is that there is no such thing as a victimless crime. Criminals and victims are locked together in the most gruesome of relationships, like two sides of a coin. And while the guilty may pay the price for their misdeeds, it is all too often the forgotten victims who are the real story. They are the innocent ones who lose their money, their welfare or even their lives, yet they sink back into obscurity while the criminals live on forever in the Hall of Infamy to shock and haunt the imagination.

MURDER
MOST
FOUL

Dr CRIPPEN
Hen-pecked Killer

Dr Crippen is notorious as the first murderer to be arrested with the help of Marconi's newly invented wireless telegraphy. This quiet little patent-medicine salesman was hanged in 1910 for poisoning a wife who had treated him shamefully

Early in 1900 a slight, modest gentleman enquired about an flat in Shore Street, Bloomsbury. He had a high-domed, bald head, a large sandy moustache, and greyish eyes which bulged behind a pair of gold-rimmed spectacles. With him, and seeming to loom over him, was his wife, a florid, full-figured woman in garish silks.

The oddly assorted pair were American, they explained. They had just arrived on the boat from New York, she to make a name on the music-hall stage, he to manage a patent medicine firm. Their names were Dr Hawley Harvey and Mrs Cora Crippen, and they were to become almost synonymous with twentieth-century murder.

THE MEDICAL MAN

Hawley Crippen was born in 1862, the son of a dry goods merchant in Coldwater, Michigan, who had ambitions for his son to be a doctor. In 1879, when he was just seventeen, the young Crippen embarked on his medical training.

In subsequent years he was to be reviled as an out-and-out quack, or defended as a highly qualified medic who was simply unlicensed to practise in England. The truth lies somewhere in between.

He received a general scientific

Above: *Mrs Cora Crippen, an extravagant woman who totally dominated her husband.*

Opposite: *Dr Hawley Harvey Crippen, the mild-mannered purveyor of patent medicines who was driven to murder.*

Left: *39 Hilldrop Crescent, Kentish Town, the Crippen family home where the murder was committed.*

Above: *39 Hilldrop Crescent, London.*

background at the California University, Michigan, and then went on to study medicine at the Hospital College in Cleveland, Ohio. Probably, though not certainly, he left without a degree.

In 1883 he sailed for England and spent some time attending lectures at Guy's and St Thomas's hospitals in London, before returning to New York and enrolling at the Opthalmic Hospital there, gaining a diploma in 1885.

While in Santiago in 1887 he met and married a woman named Charlotte Bell, and the following year their son, Otto Hawley Crippen, was born. This boy was to spend his life in Los Angeles.

The Crippens moved to Salt Lake City, where, in 1890, Charlotte died. Hawley drifted back to New York. Two years later he met a striking young woman of seventeen who called herself Cora Turner and was the mistress of a rich stove manufacturer.

Crippen fell in love with her, and for her part she seemed to like the idea of being a doctor's wife. In 1893 he married her and took her with him to St Louis, where he was working as consultant physician to an optician. There he learned that his wife's real name was Kunigunde Mackamotzki. She was the daughter of a Russian Polish father and a German mother.

Despite the strong prejudice then current among 'White Anglo-Saxon Protestants' against mid-European Catholics, the revelation did little to affect Crippen's passion for Cora.

For her part, Cora was growing dissatisfied with Crippen's earnings as an orthodox doctor, pointing out that there was much more money to be made in the world of 'patent' medicines. One of the best-selling of these was 'Professor Munyon's Pills for Piles'. In 1897, Crippen joined the firm in New York and parted company with the mainstream of medicine for ever.

When Munyon's opened an office in Shaftesbury Avenue, London, Crippen was appointed first manager. The summer of 1900 saw him and Cora taking the lease on the flat in Shore Street, Bloomsbury.

AMBITIONS

Bloomsbury was at the heart of the London music hall world. Cora lost no time in introducing herself into the pubs and restaurants in which the music-hall artistes met, and even hired herself an agent, 'billing' herself under the stage name of Belle Ellmore.

She looked the part. Cora was pretty enough, with dark eyes and raven hair. Her looks, together with her American accent, described as 'twangy', and the stagey clothes she affected reeked of the American vaudeville theatre of which she claimed to have been a part.

The trouble was that Belle Ellmore could not sing – at least she could not project her voice to reach the far corners

Left: *Cora Crippen had a passion for the music hall and a taste for garish fashion.*

WOULD-BE MUSIC-HALL ARTISTE CORA WAS BOOED FROM THE STAGE — PARTLY FOR STRIKE-BREAKING AND PARTLY FOR BEING DREADFUL

Below: *Cora hired herself out as an artiste's agent under her stage name of Belle Ellmore.*

of a theatre. Once, during a music-hall strike, she obtained work at the Euston Palace. But she was hissed and booed from the stage, partly for being a 'blackleg', and partly for being dreadful. After that distressing experience, Cora's active theatrical days were over.

Despite this she remained friendly with such artistes as Marie Lloyd. She also became a member and later honorary treasurer of the Music Hall Ladies' Guild, a charitable organization. And she took to wearing expensive jewellery, which she bullied Hawley Crippen into buying.

In 1901, urged on by Cora to 'better' himself, he took an appointment as consultant to a dubious firm of ear specialists named the Drouet Institute. Its bookkeeper-secretary was a seventeen-year-old named Ethel Neave who shared with Cora a dissatisfaction with her surname and called herself LeNeve. Two years after Crippen joined, the Institute was bankrupted after a charge of negligence was levelled against it – the charge did not involve Crippen. By this time he had fallen in love with Ethel.

Under any name, Ethel LeNeve does not seem to have been particularly prepossessing. Despite her pretty face she was a mousey child with a slight limp who suffered from chronic catarrh.

But, like Cora, she had a strong dominant trait which seemed to appeal to Crippen. And there is no doubt that she loved the by-now infatuated doctor as much as he loved her.

She followed him, as secretary, to the Sovereign Remedy Company, which failed, then to the Aural Company, which also failed, and then back to Professor Munyon's, where he took up his old post as manager.

Later, she became secretary to a dental practice which Crippen set up as an extra source of income at Albion House, New Oxford Street, with a dental surgeon named Dr Rylance.

HEN-PECKED HUSBAND

In 1905, the Crippens left Shore Street and moved north to a leased semi-detached villa at 39 Hilldrop Crescent, off the Camden Road in Kentish Town. By this time Crippen was making money,

Below: *Ethel LeNeve, Dr Crippen's lover, thinly disguised as a boy for their flight to America.*

most of which was spent on entertaining Cora's friends and on buying Cora's dresses and jewellery. However, by now the couple slept in separate bedrooms and were polite to each other only in company. Cora openly had men friends, and occasionally took them to bed in the afternoons when Crippen was at work.

When her interest in the new house waned a little, Cora took in four lodgers. She had an antipathy towards 'living in' domestic servants, so she buckled down to the task of being a landlady herself, with the help of a daily cleaner.

Crippen was ordered up at six in the morning to clean the lodgers' boots, lay and light the fires, and prepare the breakfast – all before he set off for his office at 7.30.

Incredibly, the doctor continued to pay all the household bills, while the lodgers' rents went into Cora's dress and jewellery account.

In December 1906 Crippen came home to find Cora in bed with one of the lodgers, a German. The following day he told Ethel, and for the first time in their four-year relationship she consented to go to bed with him. Their affair was consummated in a cheap hotel one afternoon on Ethel's day off.

Soon after this, Cora tired of the game of being a landlady and dismissed the lodgers. Instead she entertained her friends on two or three evenings a week. For the rest of the time, she and her husband virtually lived in the kitchen. Both of them gave up housework, and cleaning was done only spasmodically.

Over the next four years Crippen continued to live at Hilldrop Crescent, though life with Cora became more and more intolerable. There was no longer any pretence at amiability. Cora mocked him in front of her friends and Hawley Crippen bore it all stoically, buoyed up by his love for Ethel LeNeve.

Cora was by now aware of the affair. At one point Ethel became pregnant and decided to have the baby, thus forcing matters to a crisis. But she miscarried.

Cora's response was to speculate, to a group of her music-hall friends and in her husband's hearing, as to which of Ethel's many lovers was responsible for the child. It may have been at that moment that Hawley Harvey Crippen's patience came abruptly to an end.

THE WORM TURNS

On 1 January 1910 he went to the firm of Lewis and Burrows, wholesale chemists, and ordered seventeen grains of the vegetable drug hydrobromide of hyoscine. It was, he said, on behalf of Munyon's – though the American company did not manufacture in Britain. On 19 January he took possession of the drug, which he had seen used to calm violent patients in mental hospitals. It was also an anaphrodisiac – it killed sexual ardour.

On 31 January the Crippens entertained a couple named Martinetti, theatrical friends of Cora's, to dinner.

During the course of the evening Cora picked a quarrel with her husband because he had not shown Mr Martinetti to the lavatory. It was an odd grudge, even for Cora. But, according to Crippen's later evidence, she took it as a 'last straw' and threatened to leave him.

It is doubtful whether Crippen would have worried overmuch if his wife had simply walked out of his life. But she had access, through their joint account, to his savings, and she would also have taken her valuable jewellery and have had a legal right to their joint property. She had threatened before to leave and take 'her' money – though in fact, apart from the abortive night treading the boards of the Euston Palace, she had never earned a penny in her life.

At 1.30 on the morning of 1 February the Martinettis bade Cora and Hawley goodbye. Cora Crippen was never seen alive again. That afternoon, Crippen called on the Martinettis, as he often did, and remarked that Cora was well.

On 2 February, Crippen pawned for £80 a gold ring and a pair of earrings belonging to his wife. The same evening Ethel LeNeve came to Hilldrop Crescent for the first time and stayed overnight.

The same day a letter arrived at the Music Hall Ladies' Guild office, apparently from their treasurer, Belle Ellmore. It said that she was leaving immediately for America to nurse a sick relative and was therefore tendering her resignation.

On 9 February Crippen pawned more jewellery, this time for £115. At his trial Crippen was to point out indignantly that he had every right to dispose of his wife's

Above: *The SS Negantic is towed into port with Crippen and LeNeve on board. They were initially arrested aboard the SS Montrose.*

Below: *Police accompany Dr Crippen and Ethel LeNeve down the gangway of the SS Negantic after his arrest in 1910.*

jewellery in any way he thought fit, since he had bought it.

On 20 February Crippen carried openness to potentially dangerous lengths when he escorted Ethel LeNeve to the Music Hall Ladies' Guild ball. She was decked out in some of Belle Ellmore's finest jewels – a fact not lost on the Martinettis, among other guests present.

Ostensibly Ethel was still simply Crippen's secretary, standing in for his absent wife at a social occasion. But on 12 March caution was thrown to the winds. Ethel moved in permanently to 39 Hilldrop Crescent.

FAKED DEATH, SUSPICIOUS FRIENDS

On 20 March, with Easter approaching, Crippen wrote to the Martinettis to say that he had heard from his wife and that she was seriously ill with pleuro-pneumonia. He was thinking, he said, of going to the United States to look after her. Contemporary writers have suggested that this may have been his original plan – to go to America and then quietly disappear. But something stopped him, and that something was probably Ethel LeNeve.

At this stage, it seems unlikely that Ethel knew that Cora was dead. But she knew that she was finally with the man

she loved and she was not going to let him leave her, even for a short while.

On 23 March, instead of going to America, Crippen and Ethel took a cross-Channel ferry to Dieppe, where they stayed during Easter week.

But from Victoria station he sent the Martinettis a telegram: 'BELLE DIED YESTERDAY AT SIX O'CLOCK. PLEASE PHONE ANNIE. SHALL BE AWAY A WEEK – PETER.' 'Peter' was a nickname for Crippen used by Belle Ellmore's theatrical friends.

When he returned, Crippen was inundated with enquiries from his wife's friends. Where exactly had she died? Where could they send a wreath? Crippen told them that he was having her cremated in America. When her ashes were shipped back 'we can have a little ceremony then'.

Lil Hawthorne, the well-known music hall comedy singer who had been one of Belle Ellmore's closest friends, was not satisfied. She checked with shipping lines but could find no record of either a Cora Crippen or a Belle Ellmore embarking for the States around the first week in February. Lil and her agent husband, John Nash, had to go to New York on business in March, and their enquiries there also drew a blank.

On his return to London, Nash confronted Crippen. Under questioning, Crippen broke down and sobbed pathetically. Nash, knowing of the doctor's kindly nature and tolerance of what even her friends had to acknowledge as his wife's often outrageous treatment of him, was almost convinced of the truth of Crippen's story.

And yet if Crippen was so distressed, why was his mistress living openly with him? Eventually Nash went to Scotland Yard and, on 30 June, poured out the whole tale.

INTERVIEWED BY THE YARD

A week later, on 8 July, Detective Chief Inspector Walter Dew, accompanied by Detective Sergeant Mitchell, went to call on Crippen at Albion House. Dew was one of the Yard's most experienced detectives. He was impressed, by Dr Crippen's demeanour.

Above: *Crippen arrives at the police station after his arrest in a taxi.*

Below: *Superintendent Frost, head of the Crippen investigation, discusses evidence with his colleagues.*

Asked about his wife's disappearance and alleged death, Crippen immediately confessed that the whole story was untrue. In fact, he said, Belle Ellmore alias Cora Crippen had run off to Chicago with an old prize-fighter lover of hers. Crippen had been so ashamed, and so worried about damaging his medical career with a scandal, that he had invented the story of her fatal illness.

Dew spent all day with Crippen, sitting in the waiting room between Crippen's periodic surgery calls to dental patients.

In the evening, Crippen took the two policemen to Hilldrop Crescent and showed them over the house, from attic to basement. All seemed perfectly normal.

'Of course,' said Dew, 'I shall have to find Mrs Crippen to clear the matter up.'

'Yes,' agreed the doctor, 'I will do everything I can. Can you suggest anything? Would an advertisement be any good?' Dew thought an advertisement in the Chicago papers an excellent idea, and helped Crippen draft one before finally saying goodnight.

In fact, Dew later admitted, the advertisement was unnecessary. He was convinced by that time that Crippen was telling the truth at last, and that the flighty Belle Ellmore had run off.

The investigation was to all intents and purposes finished. However, Crippen had no means of knowing this.

THE FATAL MISTAKE

Despite numerous theories, no one has ever given a satisfactory reason why Crippen, whose nerve had so far held, should suddenly at this point make the mistake of flight. But flee he did.

After carefully putting his affairs in order Crippen and LeNeve took the boat to Rotterdam on the night of 9 July From there they made their way to Antwerp, where they embarked on the SS *Montrose,* bound for Quebec, under the names of Mr and Master Robinson.

Ethel had had her hair cropped short and was wearing cut-down men's clothes, probably Crippen's, and they kept under cover as much as possible before the ship sailed on 20 July.

Even now, the fleeing lovers might have got away but for a fluke. Chief Inspector Dew had forgotten some minor point during his questioning of Crippen. It was not important and there was no urgency. But on Monday 11 July, finding himself in the vicinity of Albion House, he decided to drop in and check it out. There he was told that Crippen had left.

Suddenly alarm bells were beginning to ring, and Dew dashed up to Hilldrop Crescent. All seemed to be in order, but he carried out a thorough search, checking the garden for recent signs of digging and testing the bricks in the empty basement coal cellar with his foot.

All was solid and normal. But Dew was certain that somewhere in this ordinary little house and its garden lay

---

THE TENACIOUS DEW WAS CONVINCED THAT THIS ORDINARY SUBURBAN HOUSE AND GARDEN CONTAINED THE ANSWER TO CORA'S DISAPPEARANCE

Right: *August 1910 – crowds gathered outside Bow Street Court as Crippen stood before magistrates.*

Below: *The trial of Dr Crippen and Ethel LeNeve at the Old Bailey in October 1910 attracted huge public interest.*

the solution to Cora's disappearance.

On the following day he returned with extra men. Again they searched, digging and probing. Again nothing. On Wednesday the 13th they were there again, but towards evening it began to look as if Dew's instinct was wrong. Then, standing in the brick-floored cellar, he probed one of the cracks with a poker and found that the brick was loose. He prised it out, and found loosely packed soil underneath. This time he got a spade, removed the rest of the bricks, and dug. Eight inches down he found what he described at the trial as 'a mass of flesh' wrapped in a striped pyjama top.

On preliminary examination by Dr

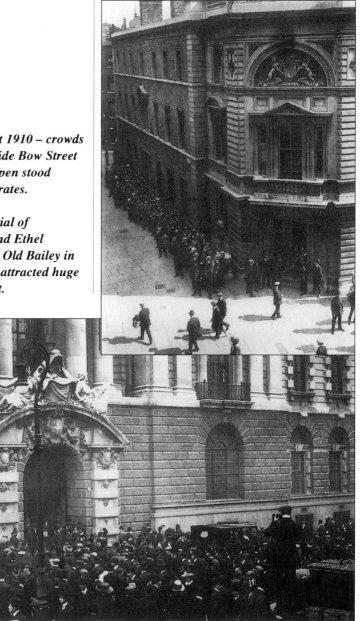

Above: *Dr Crippen in the dock at the Old Bailey during his trial for the murder of his wife.*

THE 'MASS OF FLESH' IN THE CELLAR PROVED TO BE A BODY THAT HAD BEEN FILLETED, WITH SURGICAL PRECISION, JUST LIKE A FISH

IN COURT, THE DISPUTED PIECE OF HUMAN FLESH WAS EXHIBITED TO JUDGE, JURY AND COUNSEL ON A SOUP PLATE

Marshall, the police surgeon, it proved to be a human torso from which the neck and head, arms and legs had been severed. The vagina and uterus had been excised, and the trunk had been neatly filleted – all the bones had been removed – with considerable surgical skill.

On 15 July, Marshall and Dr Augustus J. Pepper, a Home Office pathologist based at St Mary's Hospital, Paddington, removed the remains for further examination. The following day a warrant was issued for the arrest of Crippen and LeNeve.

On 20 July, the westward-bound SS *Montrose* steamed out of Antwerp. Sharing a cabin were a Mr John Robinson and his son, who between them had only one small valise as luggage. The ship's master, Captain Henry Kendal, thought them an odd couple, and kept an eye on them.

Among other things he noticed that 'Mr Robinson' was reading a copy of Edgar Wallace's *Four Just Men*, a famous murder yarn of the time. But he also noticed that the 'son' wore an ill-fitting hat and trousers, which were held together with safety pins at the back, and that the couple held hands in a manner most unusual for a father and son. When he saw a picture of Crippen in a copy of the *Daily Mail* which had been brought aboard just before the *Montrose* sailed, Captain Kendal despatched a wireless message which began: 'Have strong suspicion that Crippen London cellar murderer and accomplice are among saloon passengers....'

The message went out on 22 July, and the following day Dew and Mitchell embarked on the SS *Negantic* at Liverpool just before she sailed. On 31 July, Dew boarded the *Montrose* as she lay at anchor off Father Point, Quebec, and arrested the pair.

Crippen's first words were: 'I am not sorry. The anxiety has been too much.' He was the first murderer to be arrested by wireless telegraphy, for which Marconi had received the Nobel Prize the previous year.

Back in London Dr Pepper, assisted by his colleagues Dr William Willcox and Dr Bernard Spilsbury, had conducted a thorough examination of the remains from the cellar. They contained at least five grains of hyoscine which, as Willcox the toxicologist was to point out, was derived from henbane. When used as a sedative, one-fortieth of a grain had been known to produce 'severe symptoms'.

The defence were to claim that these remains were not those of Belle Ellmore-Cora Crippen, but of some previous murder, coincidentally committed in the house before the arrival of the Crippens. Even this credulity-stretching defence was scotched when pubic hairs on the torso were matched for colouring with Cora's head hair, and Bernard Spilsbury showed that a mark on the skin was not a fold, as alleged by the defence, but the scar of an ovariotomy such as Cora was known to have undergone. At the trial, the piece of flesh and skin showing the scar was handed about, to the judge, jury, defence and defendant Crippen, on a soup plate.

Finally, Crippen was caught out in a direct lie when he claimed that the pyjamas in which the body was wrapped were not his. They were proved to have been bought by him in 1909.

Left: *Ethel LeNeve leaves Bow Street Magistrates Court.*

Below: *Ethel LeNeve, Crippen's lover, was a mousey young woman with a limp and chronic catarrh.*

CRIPPEN'S PATCH

The trial had begun at the Old Bailey on 18 October before the Lord Chief Justice, Lord Alverstone, and the jury took twenty-seven minutes to reach their verdict. Crippen was sentenced to hang, while Ethel LeNeve, tried separately, went free.

Crippen's only concern, after his arrest, had been for the welfare of his mistress. He told Dew: 'She has been my only comfort for the last three years.' In jail at Pentonville his courtesy and pleasant nature almost endeared him to his warders. When he asked the Governor that a photograph and two letters from Ethel LeNeve be buried with him, the Governor readily complied.

Crippen was hanged on 23 November 1910. To this day the graveyard within the walls of Pentonville prison in which he and other executed prisoners were buried is known to staff and inmates as 'Crippen's Patch'.

Exactly when he killed his wife, and how he disposed of the body, remains a mystery. It was most probable that he poisoned her on either the night of 31 January or the following morning. He then cut her up in the bath, and dropped the missing head and limbs overboard in a suitcase during his subsequent trip to Dieppe.

The other abiding mystery is exactly why, after tolerating his apparently intolerable wife for so long, he suddenly decided to kill her. Many theories have been produced over the years, but none have resolved the mystery satisfactorily.

After her acquittal, Ethel LeNeve emigrated to Canada until the fuss died down, and then quietly returned to England in 1916. She took a job as bookkeeper for a company in Trafalgar Square, and married a man who was said to look remarkably like Crippen. They lived in East Croydon.

In 1954, novelist Ursula Bloom published a book entitled *The Woman Who Loved Crippen*. Afterwards, she was approached by an elderly lady who revealed herself to be Ethel. She told Miss Bloom that she had never ceased to love her little doctor. Ethel LeNeve died in 1967, aged eighty-four.

JEREMY BAMBER
An Impatient Heir

The horrific mass killing seemed to be the work of a deranged family member who had then committed suicide. Eventually the real murderer was nailed – but no thanks to the police who jumped to conclusions and destroyed vital evidence

At 3.26 in the morning of 7 August 1985, the duty officer at Chelmsford police station in Essex received a phone call from a young man calling himself Jeremy Bamber. The caller sounded agitated.

He explained to the policeman that he was calling from his home at Goldhanger and that he had just received a frantic call from his father who lived in the nearby village of Tolleshunt D'Arcy. According to Bamber, his father had shouted: 'Come over. Your sister's gone crazy and she's got a gun....'

Bamber had then heard a shot and the line had gone dead. He had tried to call back, but the telephone was off the hook. What should he do?

The duty sergeant told Bamber to go to his father's farm and wait for the police.

Above: *Sheila 'Bambi' Caffell was a pretty young woman but was dogged by psychological problems.*

Opposite: *Jeremy Bamber is consoled by his girlfriend, Julie Mugford, after the funeral of his family.*

Left: *White House Farm at Tolleshunt D'Arcy where the Bamber family were slaughtered.*

Under no circumstances should he enter the building. Within minutes Detective Inspector Bill Miller had assembled an armed squad of forty men which included Special Firearms Unit marksmen.

The police reached White House Farm shortly after 4a.m. There were lights in some of the windows but everything seemed peaceful. Marksmen took up their positions and covered every door and window in the elegant Georgian farmhouse. There was still no sign of life.

Minutes later, Jeremy Bamber arrived at the farm. He was hurried over to Inspector Miller who wanted to know what they were dealing with. Was there

normally a gun in the house?

Yes, Jeremy explained. His father, Nevill Bamber, was a keen shot and kept a rifle, a high velocity semi-automatic .22 Anchutz, which he used for rabbitting.

What about his sister? From the start, Jeremy made it clear that there was no love lost between them. He stressed that they were not really brother and sister, but that they had both been adopted.

'My sister is a nutter,' Jeremy explained. 'She could go mad at any time...She's gone mad before.'

WAITING GAME

The police kept their vigil for a while longer and then made a series of appeals over a loud hailer. There was no response.

Above: *Sheila 'Bambi' Caffell with her adoptive mother, June Bamber, and her two sons, Nicholas and Daniel. All of them died at White House Farm.*

Above right: *Colin Caffell, Sheila's estranged husband, with their two children.*

'MY SISTER IS A NUTTER,' JEREMY BAMBER EXPLAINED. 'SHE'S GONE MAD BEFORE.'

The basic brief in circumstances like these is for police to minimize the risk of loss of life. Since there was a possibility that members of the family were being held hostage, they opted to wait it out.

Bamber, meanwhile, provided police with a detailed picture of the house and family. His adoptive parents, Nevill and June Bamber, both sixty-one, lived there and farmed the surrounding 400 acres. His adoptive sister, twenty-seven-year-old Sheila Caffell, nicknamed 'Bambi', had been staying with them since March with her six-year-old twins, Daniel and Nicholas. Bambi, Jeremy explained, had a long history of depression and had recently come out of mental hospital after a 'nervous breakdown'.

As dawn broke there was still no sign of life in the farmhouse, and the police decided to move in. A squad of ten armed officers inched their way towards the kitchen door. One of the assault team then smashed down the door and the others moved quickly into the building.

But there was no sign of violence – in fact no sign of life at all.

SCENES OF CARNAGE

As the police reached the sitting room, however, they were confronted with a glimpse of the carnage which was to come. The room was a shambles, and lying near the telephone was the body of Nevill Bamber. He had been shot six times in the head, once in the shoulder and once in the arm. He had also been brutally beaten about the head and face.

Other officers moved upstairs. In one of the bedrooms they found the bodies of the twins, Daniel and Nicholas. Both had died from multiple gunshot wounds. They had obviously been murdered while they slept; Daniel was still sucking his thumb.

The master bedroom was the scene of more horror. June Bamber was sprawled in her nightdress on the floor beside the door, a Bible lying open by her side. She had been shot seven times, once directly between the eyes.

And by the window was the body of Sheila 'Bambi' Caffell. She was lying on her back in her nightdress. She had one gunshot wound in the throat and another in her jaw. Across her lap was lying a .22 Anchutz rifle, its butt splintered and its magazine empty.

BERSERK

The forensic team, led by Detective Inspector Ronald Cook, moved into the house together with police surgeon Dr Ian Craig. Craig examined each of the five bodies in turn.

Nevill Bamber had multiple wounds to the head and had probably been beaten unconscious before he was shot. Upstairs, the children and June Bamber were quite obviously victims of a surprise attack.

That left Bambi. Dr Craig examined her two wounds. The shot to her throat had severed her jugular vein. The other had passed through her chin and entered her brain. This would have killed her instantly. Bambi had one impact bruise to her cheek but was otherwise unmarked. Her long fingernails had survived the night of violence unscathed.

Dr Craig went downstairs and joined Detective Inspectors Cook and Miller. There was no sign of a break-in and the

THE SIX-YEAR-OLD TWINS HAD BEEN SHOT WHILE THEY SLEPT — ONE OF THEM WAS STILL SUCKING HIS THUMB

Below: *Whitehouse Farm, a monument to upper-middle class respectability, and scene of one of the worst mass murders of recent times.*

three men agreed that the most obvious scenario was that Sheila Caffell had gone beserk, murdered her entire family and then turned the gun on herself.

They expressed this opinion to Detective Chief Inspector Tom 'Taff' Jones when he arrived at the farm later that morning. Jones was apparently happy to accept their conclusions.

Having 'solved' the case to their own satisfaction, Cook and his forensic team apparently decided that a detailed examination of the house and its contents was surplus to requirements – a decision which would later attract violent criticism from both the press and the judiciary.

The police did remove the rifle and some other items of evidence, but officers failed to wear gloves, and no fingerprints were ever taken of the dead family members, or of Jeremy Bamber, for elimination purposes. The only rooms that were searched were the sitting room and the two bedrooms where the bodies had been found.

Then, in an act of misplaced kindness to Jeremy Bamber, the police destroyed the very evidence they had already failed to examine properly. They washed bloodstains from the walls. Then they removed bedding and carpets from the living room and bedrooms and burned them on a bonfire.

Jeremy Bamber remained outside while his family's bodies were removed from the scene. He remained calm and subdued. The only person he wanted to see was his girlfriend, Julie Mugford. A police officer was despatched to collect her from her home in Colchester.

When Julie was told of the massacre, she looked grim but made no comment. She was driven to White House Farm and she and Jeremy Bamber held each other as they watched evidence being carried from the house and destroyed.

As police moved the focus of their enquiries to neighbours and friends, everything they heard seemed to confirm what they already suspected. The wealthy and eminently respectable Bamber family had died tragically at the hands of a deranged family member.

The suggestion that Bambi might have been involved with drugs was raised by several of the Bambers' neighbours. The

Above: *Police fingerprint Jeremy Bamber's Citroën estate car outside his home at Goldhanger, Essex.*

Below: *A police officer holds up the .22 Anchutz rifle and silencer used in the Bamber murders.*

press were quick to accept salacious village gossip as fact, and this case had everything the tabloids could ask for – a glamorous, drug-crazed heiress had apparently murdered her own children and her adoptive parents.

THE SCEPTICS TAKE ACTION

The police and press had effectively convicted Bambi of murder. Not everyone felt comfortable with that idea, however.

Nevill Bamber's nephew, David Boutflour, had been very fond of his adoptive cousin. He was horrified by the allegations being made against her.

Boutflour said the very idea that Bambi could have carried out the killings was preposterous. He knew from police reports that twenty-five shots had been fired. This would have meant reloading twice in a situation of mayhem, an operation which would have required skill and co-ordination. 'Sheila,' said Boutflour, 'couldn't put baked beans on toast without knocking them over.'

Boutflour's protests fell on deaf ears so he decided it was up to him to obtain evidence which would exonerate Bambi and, he hoped, identify the real killer.

On Sunday, 11 August, while a service for the Bambers was being held at St Nicholas's Church in Tolleshunt D'Arcy, David and his sister, Mrs Christine Eaton, went to White House Farm. They worked their way methodically through the house, looking for possible clues.

Much of the evidence had already been removed or destroyed, but the amateur sleuths found two vital clues. At the back of the gun cabinet David Boutflour discovered a .22 silencer with some specks of blood on it. Christine noticed scratches on the kitchen window-ledge which suggested that the window had been closed and locked from the outside.

Boutflour immediately informed the police of their findings. Detectives were polite but unimpressed, and it was two days before they even bothered to go out to the farm to collect the silencer.

More doubt was cast on the murder-suicide theory two days later by the Home Office pathologist. He reported to detectives involved in the case that, in his opinion, their scenario was absurd.

Firstly it required slender, 5ft 7in Sheila Caffell to bludgeon 6ft 4in Nevill Bamber unconscious. And the 'suicide' shots didn't add up either. The first shot,

Above: *Jeremy Bamber is every inch the grief-stricken son as he follows his father's coffin.*

'SHEILA,' SAID DAVID BOUTFLOUR, 'COULDN'T PUT BAKED BEANS ON TOAST WITHOUT KNOCKING THEM OVER'

THE HOME OFFICE PATHOLOGIST FOUND SEVERAL REASONS WHY SHEILA COULD NOT HAVE FIRED THE GUN, BUT THE POLICE IGNORED HIM

WITH BAMBER AWAY IN FRANCE, JULIE MUGFORD WENT TO THE POLICE AND TOLD A VERY DIFFERENT STORY

Below: *Jeremy Bamber handcuffed to a prison officer as he leaves court in a police van.*

through her jugular vein, would have rendered her incapable of firing the second into her brain. In addition, the second shot had been fired with a silencer, and there was no sign of a silencer near Bambi's body. And if the rifle had been fitted with a six-inch silencer, the weapon would have been so long that Bambi would not have been able to reach the trigger while the muzzle was pressed under her chin. She could not possibly have fired that shot.

Despite these glaring inconsistencies, detectives ignored the pathologist's findings. No mention was made of them at the coroner's inquest, which was held at Chelmsford on 14 August.

The bodies of Nevill and June Bamber were released to Jeremy Bamber. Two days later friends and relatives of the Bambers returned to St Nicholas's church for the funeral service. Then the coffins were driven to Colchester for cremation.

THE TRUTH FILTERS OUT

On 8 September, three weeks after his family's funeral, Jeremy Bamber was arrested – not for murder, but for an unrelated burglary which dated back some six months. He was charged with stealing £980 from a caravan park which he co-owned with his late parents.

The following day, Bamber appeared at Chelmsford court and was refused bail. This was extremely unusual for a first offender accused of a non-violent crime, and it suggests that the police were starting to look at the White House killings in a new light. Jeremy was held in gaol for five days before being released in his own recognizance.

Jeremy left immediately for a holiday on the French Riviera. Surprisingly, he went with a friend, Brett Collins, rather than his girlfriend. This would prove Bamber's most expensive mistake.

A few days after Jeremy left for France, Julie Mugford went to see the Essex police. She told them she was certain that Jeremy had killed his family.

According to Julie, Jeremy had been planning the murders for months. She explained that Jeremy loathed his parents and he resented the fact that he had not been given his inheritance while he was young enough to enjoy it.

Julie said that on the night of the massacre Jeremy had telephoned her and said: 'It's got to be tonight or never.' Julie said she had told him not to be stupid, but that he had hung up. At three the following morning, Jeremy had rung again and said: 'Everything is going well.'

At first, detectives were inclined to believe that they were listening to the bitter rantings of a spurned woman. After all, hadn't Jeremy just taken off to France without her? But, as her story unfolded, they were reminded of the pathologist's findings and the evidence submitted by David Boutflour and Christine Eaton. It was becoming increasingly obvious that they had made a terrible mistake.

On 30 September, police were waiting at Dover ferry terminal when Jeremy Bamber returned from his holiday. He was arrested and charged with murdering Nevill and June Bamber, together with Sheila, Daniel and Nicholas Caffell.

GREED AND EXTRAVAGANCE

On Tuesday, 2 October 1986, more than a year after the massacre at White House Farm, the trial of Jeremy Bamber opened at Chelmsford Crown Court. Bamber had secured one of the country's best criminal solicitors, Sir David Napley, and he in turn had briefed Geoffrey Rivlin QC to conduct the defence. Bamber pleaded not guilty to five charges of murder.

The prosecution, led by Anthony Arlidge QC, opened by describing the massacre in graphic detail. He said that he would prove beyond all reasonable doubt that the perpetrator of the five killings was Jeremy Bamber. His motive, Arlidge claimed, was greed. Bamber knew that if all his family died, he would inherit almost half a million pounds.

The prosecution produced a plethora of evidence and expert witnesses. It all indicated that Sheila Caffell could not have committed the murders, and suggested that Jeremy Bamber might well have done so. The evidence against Bamber was, at best, circumstantial. Mr Arlidge chastised the police for their handling of the case, saying that if they had done their job properly his own job would have been made simpler.

On the morning of 9 October, Arlidge put his star witness on the stand. Julie Mugford wept as she told the jury of the months during which Jeremy Bamber's

Left: *Jeremy Bamber is remanded in custody at Maldon Magistrates' Court.*

IF BAMBER'S WHOLE FAMILY DIED, EXPLAINED THE PROSECUTING COUNSEL, HE WOULD STAND TO INHERIT £500,000

Below: *May 1986 – Jeremy Bamber arrives at Maldon Magistrates' Court for the committal proceedings.*

fantasies of killing his family had threatened to become a horrifying reality. Her answers during cross-examination were precise and consistent, and bore an unmistakeable ring of truth.

On 16 October, Rivlin opened the defence. He set out to prove that Sheila Caffell was a more likely murderer than he was. His argument came unstuck, however, when he was unable to discredit evidence submitted by the ballistics expert and the Home Office pathologist.

The following day, Rivlin put Jeremy Bamber on the witness stand. Bamber denied the killings and claimed to have had a loving relationship with his family. Under cross-examination, however, Bamber displayed a petulant, arrogant streak which did nothing to help his case.

Arlidge went to town on Bamber's character, portraying him as a greedy, vain and idle young man. None of this was very flattering, but it didn't prove that Jeremy Bamber had killed his family. In the final analysis, it all came down to who the jury chose to believe – Jeremy Bamber or Julie Mugford.

In the afternoon of 27 October, the jury retired to consider their verdict. Two days later they returned a verdict of 'guilty' on all five counts by a majority of 10–2.

Sentencing Bamber to five concurrent life sentences, the judge recommended that he should not be released for at least twenty-five years.

REIGN OF TERROR
The Boston Strangler

In 1963 a serial killer stalked the streets of Boston. His female victims were first sexually assaulted, then strangled and left lying in obscene postures. And this demented psychopath left no clues ...

Just before seven o'clock on the evening of 14 June 1962 Juris Slesers, a twenty-five-year-old research engineer, climbed the stairs to his mother's third-floor apartment at 77 Gainsborough Street in Boston. He had arranged to drive her to a memorial service at the Latvian Lutheran church in nearby Roxbury.

Mrs Slesers, a petite fifty-five-year-old divorcee, had fled Soviet-occupied Latvia with her son some twenty years earlier and settled in Boston, where she worked as a seamstress. For the past three months, since Juris had moved out, she had lived alone in this tiny apartment.

Juris knocked on the door and waited. There was no answer. He knocked again, pressed his ear to the metal door and listened. There was no sound from within.

He presumed his mother had popped out to do some shopping and went downstairs. He sat on the front steps and waited. Three-quarters of an hour passed and Juris was becoming concerned. He went back upstairs, hammered on the door and shouted his mother's name. There was still no response.

He put his shoulder to the door, backed

*Opposite: **Albert de Salvo. Was he indeed the Boston Strangler?***

*Below: **Massachusetts State Troopers search for the Strangler.***

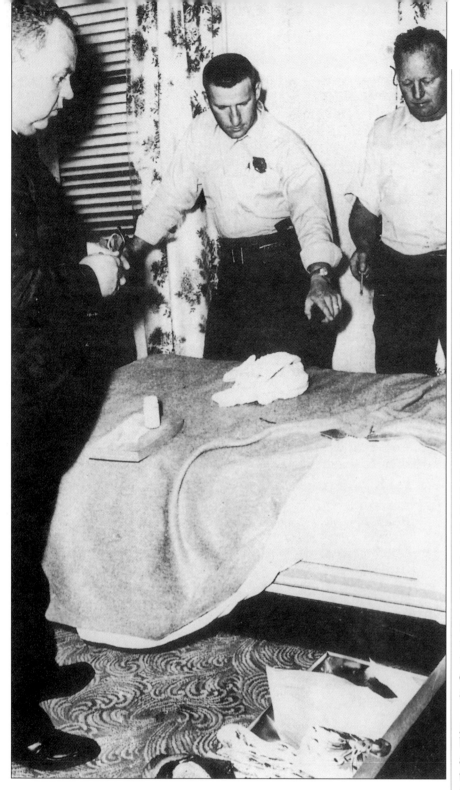

up and then rammed it with all his strength. The door sprang open.

JUST ANOTHER STATISTIC

Inside the apartment it was quite dark, and Juris tripped over a chair which had unaccountably been left in the middle of the narrow hallway. He looked into the living room and the bedroom, both of which were oddly untidy. There was no sign of his mother. He returned to the

Above: *The police search for clues in Helen Blake's apartment.*

THE FIFTY-FIVE-YEAR-OLD WOMAN HAD BEEN RAPED AND THEN STRANGLED WITH HER HOUSECOAT CORD

hallway and headed for the bathroom.

Anna Slesers was lying just outside the bathroom door. She was wearing her blue taffeta housecoat which was spread wide apart at the front, leaving her effectively nude. She lay with her left leg stretched straight out and her right flung at right-angles with the knee bent so that she was grossly exposed. The cord of her housecoat was knotted tightly round her neck and then fastened under her chin in the fashion of a crude bow. She was quite obviously dead.

The police, led by Special Officer James Mellon, arrived on the scene within minutes of receiving Juris Slesers's call.

Despite the fact that there was little sign of disturbance, it was immediately obvious to Officer Mellon that he was dealing with homicide. Mrs Slesers had been sexually assaulted and then strangled.

His initial suspicion was that someone had broken into the apartment with the intention of committing a robbery, had found Mrs Slesers in a state of undress – she looked younger than her years – and was seized by an uncontrollable sexual urge. He had raped Mrs Slesers and then strangled her to prevent her from identifying him.

The police conducted a thorough investigation. House-to-house enquiries were carried out. Relatives and friends were interviewed. A few possible candidates for the crime were picked up and questioned.

But the officers made no headway and, gruesome though the crime was, it soon became just another statistic. Boston averaged more than a murder a week at that time and, with a total lack of clues, the police accepted that their chances of ever finding the man responsible for Anna Slesers's death were very slim.

SEXUAL PSYCHOPATH

At five o'clock on 30 June, two weeks after the murder at Gainsborough Street, Nina Nichols, a sixty-eight-year-old retired physiotherapist, returned home to 1940 Commonwealth Avenue in Boston. She had just spent a pleasant few days in the country staying with friends.

As soon as she got into her apartment Mrs Nichols called her sister, Marguerite Steadman, to say that she was back safely and that she would be over for dinner at six o'clock as planned. The sisters chatted for a while but then Nina Nichols cut their conversation short, saying: 'Excuse me, Marguerite, there's my buzzer. I'll call you right back.'

Mrs Nichols didn't call her sister back, nor did she arrive for dinner at six o'clock. By seven, her sister was becoming concerned and asked her husband, attorney Chester Steadman, to telephone and make sure everything was all right. There was no reply to his call.

Another half an hour passed, and the Steadmans were becoming really alarmed. Maybe she had been been taken ill? Chester Steadman called the janitor of the building, Thomas Bruce. Would he go up to Mrs Nichols's apartment and see if she was still there?

Bruce went upstairs, knocked on the door and, when there was no reply, opened it with his pass-key. He never set foot inside. What he saw from the doorway was enough.

The apartment had obviously been burgled. Drawers had been pulled out, and clothes strewn all over the floor.

But there was worse, much worse. Directly ahead of him, Bruce could see into the bedroom. And on the floor, legs spread wide apart, was the nude body of Nina Nichols. Around her neck, tied so tightly that they cut into her flesh, were a pair of stockings. They were knotted under her chin in a clumsy bow.

Police Lieutenant Edward Sherry was soon at the scene with medical examiner Dr Michael Luongo. The similarities to the Slesers murder were immediately obvious to both men.

Nina Nichols had been sexually molested and then strangled. Both women had been left in a grossly exposed state. And then there were the tell-tale bows in the ligatures. There had been no sign of forceable entry to either apartment. Both had been ransacked but apparently nothing had been stolen in either case, despite the fact that high-value, easily disposable items like jewellery and cameras had been lying around. And there was no reason to

Above: *District Attorney John Burke and homicide officers search the scene where the body of Carrol Anne Donovan, one of the Boston Strangler's victims, was discovered.*

'EXCUSE ME, MARGUERITE,' SAID NINA NICHOLS, 'THERE'S MY BUZZER. I'LL CALL YOU RIGHT BACK.' BUT SHE NEVER DID

believe that the intruder had been interrupted on either occasion.

The police came to the conclusion that the murderer had never intended to commit a robbery – he had merely wanted to give the impression of committing a robbery. So what were they dealing with? Two murders did not constitute a serial, but Sherry and his colleagues had a gut feeling that there was a sexual psychopath at large in Boston.

They did not have to wait long before their fears were confirmed. On 2 July, two days later, police received a call from the neighbours of Helen Blake, a sixty-five-year-old retired nurse.

Helen had not been seen for a couple of days. Her friends had been concerned and borrowed a pass-key from the building supervisor. They had opened the door of her apartment, seen signs of a burglary and been afraid to go in.

The police entered the apartment and found Helen Blake lying face down on her bed. She was naked except for a

'OH GOD,' SAID THE POLICE COMMISSIONER WHEN TOLD OF THE THIRD MURDER. 'WE'VE GOT A MADMAN LOOSE!'

Below: *Mary Sullivan, 19, was found strangled on 5 January 1964 in her Beacon Hill apartment.*

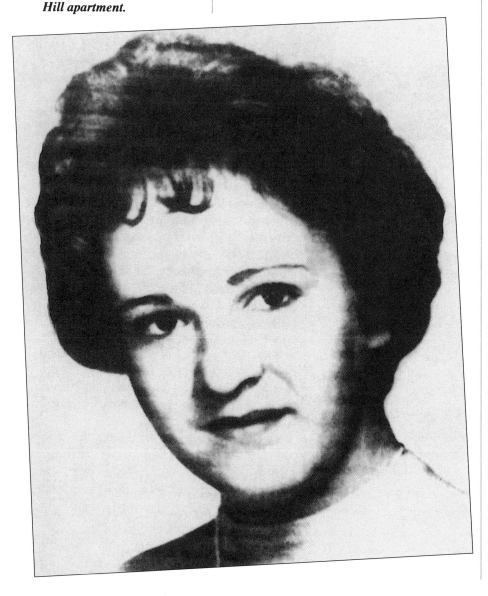

pyjama top, which had been pushed up to her shoulders. She had been sexually assaulted and strangled with a pair of stockings. A brassiere was also tied around her neck, and fastened under her chin in a bow. The medical examiner estimated that she had been dead for about three days.

Police Commissioner McNamara was winding up a conference on the murders of Anna Slesers and Nina Nichols when Lieutenant Donovan told him that Helen Blake's body had been found. As Donovan gave him the details, McNamara expressed the feelings of the whole police department. 'Oh God,' he said. 'We've got a madman loose!'

What McNamara could not know was that these three murders were just the beginning and that, over the next year and a half, a total of eleven women would be strangled and sexually assaulted in Boston. The city would become a town paralysed by terror.

As the public screamed for a solution to the atrocities, the police mounted the greatest man-hunt known in modern crime, using every known detection technique, both natural and supernatural. They would use computers, clairvoyants and psychometrists, psychiatrists with hypnotic drugs and truth serums, psychologists, experts on anthropology, graphology and forensic medicine, as they found themselves confronted by a man whose brutality and insanity were matched by enormous cunning. He appeared to be able to gain access to locked apartments, molest and kill women, and never leave a single clue.

EXHAUSTIVE ENQUIRIES

The day after the discovery of Helen Blake's body, Commissioner McNamara cancelled all police leave. All his detectives were reassigned to homicide. There was a round-up of all known sex offenders. And anyone between eighteen and forty who had been released from a mental institution in the previous two years was investigated.

The police held a press conference during which they appealed to women, particularly women living alone, to keep their doors and windows locked, to admit no strangers, and to report any prowlers, obscene phone calls and letters.

Over the next few weeks the police were deluged with telephone calls and letters conveying tips, suspicions and alarms, both genuine and spurious. Lieutenants Sherry and Donovan, Special Officer Mellon and Detective Phil DiNatale, together with scores of other detectives, spent long hours and weekends covering leads and tracing and picking up possible suspects. The police held identity parades and administered lie-detector tests on scores of men. None of them was the strangler.

By mid-August there had been no more killings, and McNamara was beginning to hope that the strangler had sated his hideous cravings. Then, on 21 August, they found Ida Irga.

A seventy-five-year-old widow, Mrs

Irga had been dead for two days. She had been strangled by human hands, but a pillow case had also been tied round her neck in a bow. Like the other victims, she had been sexually molested and, in her case, the murderer had added an appalling refinement to his attack. He had placed two chairs widely apart and tied one ankle to each in an obscene parody of a gynaecological examination. Again, the apartment had been ransacked yet no property had been removed.

Ten days later, the strangler struck again. His victim was Jane Sullivan, a sixty-seven-year-old nurse. She was found in the bathroom of her apartment; she had been dead for more than a week.

Her body was half kneeling in the tub, her face and arms submerged in six inches of water so that her buttocks were exposed. She had been strangled with two of her own stockings and placed in the bath after death.

UNBRIDLED HYSTERIA

Three months passed without a strangling but, far from relaxing, the people of Boston built themselves up to a state of unbridled hysteria. Every prowler, every flasher, every obscene phone caller was automatically presumed to be the strangler. A housewife in Brockton dropped dead of a heart attack when she found herself confronted with a stranger

Above: *Police remove the body of Mary Sullivan from her apartment.*

THE FOURTH BODY WAS LEFT LYING IN A POSITION THAT OBSCENELY PARODIED THAT OF A GYNAECOLOGICAL EXAMINATION

ONE HOUSEWIFE DIED OF HEART FAILURE WHEN SHE OPENED THE DOOR TO A STRANGER. HE WAS ONLY SELLING ENCYCLOPAEDIAS

on her doorstep. He turned out to be selling encyclopaedias.

The police, with the help of a host of experts, had built up a complex psychological profile of the strangler. He was, they decided, between eighteen and forty years old, white, highly intelligent but psychopathic. He might well be homosexual or bi-sexual. He probably suffered from schizophrenia. He hated women, particularly older women, and had probably been brought up by a domineering mother. To his actual identity, however, they still had no clue.

When the next killing occurred, on 5 December 1962, even their psychological profile proved at least partially inaccurate. The latest victim, Sophie Clark, could not have been more different from the established strangler 'type'. She was an attractive black student of twenty who shared a flat with two other women. And Patricia Bisset, who was found strangled and sexually assaulted on New Year's Eve, was twenty-three and white.

It was now obvious that the strangler struck at random and no woman in Boston, young or old, black or white, living alone or living with others, was safe from him.

FURTHER GROTESQUE ATTACKS

On Wednesday, 8 May 1963, thirty-three-year-old Oliver Chamberlin called round to see his fiancée, Beverly Samans, a graduate student at Boston University. There was no answer when Chamberlin rang the bell of Beverly's apartment, so he let himself in with his own key.

He saw her at once. She was sprawled on a sofa bed in the living room, naked, her legs spread wide apart. Her wrists were tied behind her back with sequin-studded silk scarves. A bloodstained stocking and two handkerchiefs were knotted around her neck.

Beverly, however, had not died of stangulation. She had been stabbed twenty-two times in the throat and left breast. There was no doubt, however, that this was the work of the strangler, whose body count had now risen to eight.

Three months passed before the strangler struck again. Number nine was a vivacious fifty-eight-year-old divorcee called Evelyn Corbin. Strangled, assaulted and grossly exposed, she was found by a neighbour. Again the police found no clues, save a doughnut on the fire escape outside Mrs Corbin's apartment.

Friday 22 November 1963 is a day that no American will ever forget. President Kennedy was gunned down in Dallas, Texas. The following day, the entire nation was reeling from the blow, but for the strangler it was business as usual. This time his victim was a shy twenty-three-year-old, Joann Graff. He strangled her with her own black leotard and left her nude body on a day bed in her apartment.

Christmas came, and the people of Boston did their level best not to let the strangler ruin the holiday season. Indeed he did not strike over that period. But shortly after New Year Pamela Parker and Patricia Delmore returned from work to find their nineteen-year-old flatmate, Mary Sullivan, brutally murdered. It was the most grotesque and macabre killing so far.

Mary's body – in the words of the police report – was 'on the bed in a propped position, buttocks on pillow, back against headboard, head on right shoulder, knees up, eyes closed, viscous liquid dripping from mouth to right breast, breasts and lower extremities exposed, broomstick handle inserted in vagina...' Knotted round her neck were a stocking and a silk scarf tied together in a huge, comic bow. A bright greetings card which read 'Happy New Year!' was propped against her left foot.

The public outrage was intense, and two weeks later the Attorney General, Edward W. Brooke Jnr, announced that the Attorney General's Office of the Commonwealth of Massachusetts was taking over the investigation.

NO LONGER TOLERABLE

The strangler task force worked tirelessly throughout 1964. There were no further stranglings, but the police force's determination to identify and convict the man responsible was undiminished. But, by the autumn of 1964, the authorities were no nearer catching the strangler. It

*Top: **Newsmen and photographers gather outside the apartment of Strangler victim Mary Sullivan.***

*Above: **Police officers look for clues on the roof of Mary Sullivan's apartment.***

THE ONLY CLUE LEFT BY THE STRANGLER AT THE SCENE OF HIS NINTH MURDER WAS A DOUGHNUT DROPPED ON THE FIRE ESCAPE

was now nine months since he had struck and there was a feeling that the killer might have moved from the area, committed suicide or merely quit.

Then, on 27 October, the police in Cambridge, Massachusetts received a complaint from a young housewife. It was destined to open a whole new avenue of enquiry.

She told detectives that she was dozing in bed, after seeing her teacher husband off to work, when a man appeared at the bedroom door. He was about thirty, of medium build, wearing green slacks and large sunglasses.

The man had come slowly towards her and said: 'Don't worry, I'm a detective.' The young woman had yelled at him to get out, but the man had leaped forward, pinned her to the bed and held a knife to her throat. 'Not a sound,' he had commanded, 'or I'll kill you.'

The intruder had gagged his victim with her underwear, then tied her ankles and wrists to the bedposts so that she was spread-eagled. He had proceeded to kiss and fondle her body. Suddenly he had stopped, got to his feet and loosened her bonds slightly.

'You be quiet for ten minutes,' he said. 'I'm sorry,' he added and then fled from the apartment.

After she had finished giving her statement to detectives, the young woman spent several hours with a police artist trying to establish a likeness of her attacker. Between them they did a good job. One of the detectives recognized the face immediately. 'That,' he said, 'looks like the Measuring Man.'

THE MEASURING MAN

This was a character well known to the Boston police. He had been convicted and gaoled in 1960 for breaking and entering and indecently assaulting young women. He had gained his nickname because he had a habit of posing as an artist's agent, calling on young women and taking their measurements for supposed employment as models. The Measuring Man's real name was Albert H. De Salvo.

Thirty-three-year-old maintenance man De Salvo was picked up and brought to the police headquarters at Cambridge. He denied assaulting the young woman, but she identified him immediately. De Salvo was charged and taken into custody. As a matter of routine, the Cambridge police teletyped De Salvo's picture to neighbouring states. The response was astounding.

Messages poured in from New Hampshire, Rhode Island and Connecticut to say that De Salvo had been identified by scores of women as being the man who had sexually assaulted them. In some areas he was known as the Green Man because of his penchant for green trousers.

De Salvo denied everything and refused to answer any questions until he had spoken to his German-born wife, Irmgard. She was duly delivered to him and detectives watched them as they whispered together.

The police got the impression that Irmgard knew her husband had been 'up to something with women'. She confirmed their suspicions by saying aloud: 'Al, tell them everything. Don't hold anything back.'

De Salvo heeded his wife's advice and told detectives: 'I have committed more than four hundred breaks [breaking and entering], all in this area, and there's a couple of rapes you don't know about.'

As the investigation widened,

Below: *Police Commissioner McNamara with the special tactical squad he formed to catch the Boston Strangler.*

detectives soon realized that De Salvo was not exaggerating. They estimated that in the past two years he had committed sexual assaults on more than three hundred women.

De Salvo was shipped to Boston State Hospital for observation while he awaited trial for the Green Man offences. Doctors found him to be 'overtly schizophrenic and potentially suicidal', and on 4 February 1965 Judge Edward A. Pecce ordered him to be committed to a hospital for the criminally insane 'until further orders of the court'.

Al De Salvo should really have been caught up in the 'strangler dragnet' three years earlier. But, because of an administrative anomaly, he had been listed on the computer as a breaking-and-entering man rather than as a sex offender. So he had been overlooked when Boston police were conducting routine questioning early in the case. Now they wanted to know if he was involved.

Below: Store which DeSalvo held up, for which he was later arrested and convicted.

But De Salvo was horrified at the suggestion that he might be connected with the killings. 'No, no' he wept, 'I've done some terrible things with women – but I've never killed anyone.' Detectives were initially inclined to believe him. De Salvo didn't fit their profile of the Strangler, and he simply wasn't smart enough to have got away with it.

In hospital, De Salvo befriended a convicted killer named George Nassar. Soon he was using him as a confidant.

He did not come straight out and say he was the strangler, but his hints were sufficiently pointed for Nassar to get a distinct impression that he might be. A $110,000 reward had been offered to anyone giving information which led to the capture and conviction of the strangler, and Nassar saw this as a perfect chance to make a fast buck. He informed his attorney, F. Lee Bailey.

Bailey went to see De Salvo and recorded his confession to all eleven Boston stranglings, plus another two killings which the police had not previously connected with the strangler. Bailey turned a copy of his tape over to the police and the Attorney General's Office.

At first everyone was sceptical about

De Salvo being the strangler. Not only did he not fit their profile, he had also gained a reputation as a braggart.

But when he was questioned at length, he started to disclose facts about the killings that only the strangler could have known – facts that had been deliberately kept secret to catch out the 'confessors'. De Salvo drew diagrams of the various apartments where the killings had taken place, and under hypno-analysis described the actual stranglings in gruesome detail.

Finally, the authorities were forced to accept that he might indeed be the Boston Strangler.

NO CASE

It was now the spring of 1965. The man-hunt, now in its third year, was wound down, and the investigation team was reduced to two men. Assistant Attorney General John Bottomley spent the next seven months interviewing De Salvo, talking him through each crime in minute detail. De Salvo proved to have an incredible memory and his descriptions of the various murders left Bottomley in absolutely no doubt that Albert De Salvo and the Boston Strangler were one and the same person.

Bottomley had his confession, but he had no one to corroborate it. De Salvo's victims could not testify against him and there were no eye-witnesses to identify him, and in America no one can be convicted solely by their own uncorroborated testimony. After all that effort, the state still had no case.

De Salvo had committed other crimes, however, for which the police had ample evidence. On the last day of June 1966 Albert De Salvo attended a hearing at Middlesex County Courthouse in East Cambridge, which was designed to determine whether he was mentally fit to stand trial for the Green Man offences.

It was his first public appearance since he had been committed to the institution at Bridgewater on 4 February 1965. Everyone in the court knew that De Salvo was probably the Boston Strangler, yet that case was not allowed to be mentioned.

Dr Mezer and Dr Tartakoff appeared as expert witnesses for the prosecution. They said that in their opinion Albert De Salvo was suffering from a committable mental illness, but was quite capable of standing trial.

Dr Robey, however, who had originally committed De Salvo to Bridgewater, disagreed completely: 'He is suffering from schizophrenic reaction, chronic undifferentiated type with very extensive signs of sexual deviation...My opinion is that I cannot – repeat – cannot consider him competent to stand trial....' Dr Robey added that, in his opinion, De Salvo would react to cross-examination by getting 'in such a state that he would not be making sense'.

Ten days later Judge Cahill accepted the prosecution argument and found Albert De Salvo competent to stand trail. The following year De Salvo was tried and convicted of armed robbery, breaking and entering, theft, assault and sexual crimes against four women, all of whom were lucky enough to live to identify their attacker. He was sentenced to life imprisonment.

While Albert De Salvo was never to stand trial as the Boston Strangler, the system had made sure he would never be free again. As it turned out, the length of his sentence was academic. On 26 November 1973, Albert De Salvo was found dead in his cell in Walpole State Prison. He had been stabbed sixteen times. The identity of his killer has never been established.

Above: *Women of all ages crowd into the Middlesex Superior Courtroom, hoping to catch a glimpse of the Strangler.*

GEORGE HAIGH
Acid-Bath Murders

The dapper thirty-nine-year-old charmed the ladies of a London hotel – until one of them disappeared. The suspicions of her best friend led to the conviction of one of the most shocking murderers of the century. Not content with robbing his victims, he also did sickening things to their bodies

Mr John George Haigh was something of an odd-man-out at the Onslow Gardens Hotel in South Kensington. In 1949 this genteel establishment in a fashionable part of London was the haunt almost exclusively of elderly, well-heeled, upper-class ladies.

Not that Mr Haigh's presence was in any way resented by the other permanent residents of the hotel. On the contrary, for the most part they found the dapper thirty-nine-year-old engineer handsome, charming and meticulously well-mannered.

One of his particular fans was Mrs Helen Olivia Robarts Durant-Deacon, a well-preserved, buxom sixty-nine-year-old widow. She was quite smitten with 'young Haigh' and confided in him freely.

Mrs Durant-Deacon's husband, a colonel in the Gloucester Regiment, had died some years earlier and left her a legacy of £40,000. It was enough to allow her to live in some comfort for the rest of her life. But, as she explained to Haigh, she wasn't the sort of person to sit around doing nothing.

She was thinking of starting a business, designing and manufacturing artificial fingernails. She had already made some paper prototypes, but she knew absolutely nothing about the technical side of things. Perhaps Mr Haigh, as an engineer, could give her some pointers?

Above: The .38 revolver used by Haigh to kill Mrs Durant-Deacon.

Left: .38 bullets found by the police at the scene of the crime.

Opposite: George Haigh took elaborate precautions while handling the acids he used to dissolve his victims' bodies.

Below: Mrs Durant-Deacon's handbag was one of many clues found by police at Haigh's workshop.

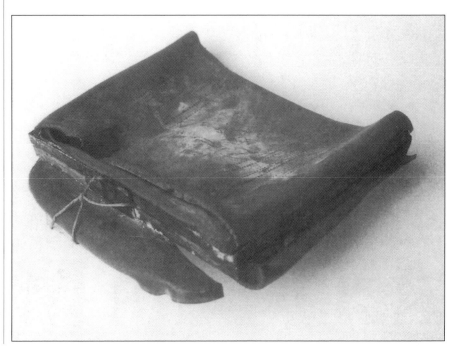

APPOINTMENT WITH DEATH

In reality, Mrs Durant-Deacon's idea was a commercial non-starter in ration-bound post-war England. But Haigh feigned enthusiasm. Of course he would be delighted to help. Perhaps she would like to come out to his factory in Essex some time, and they could look at some possible materials from which the nails could be made.

At about 3p.m. on Friday, 18 February 1949, Haigh picked up Mrs Durant-Deacon and drove her down to a factory in Crawley, Sussex. He did not, as he had claimed, own the factory, but he did know the owner, and had the use of a storeroom for his 'experimental work'.

The grimy brick shed was cluttered with bottles, vats and drums. It was not what Mrs Durant-Deacon had expected, but Haigh reassured her. Experimental laboratories were always chaotic.

Mrs Durant-Deacon took his word for it and reached for her handbag, which held her designs. As she turned away from Haigh, he pulled a .38 Enfield revolver from his jacket pocket. He calmly shot her through the nape of the neck, killing her instantly.

Haigh then kneeled by his victim's body and made an incision in her neck with a knife. He collected a glassful of her still coursing blood and drank it.

Having quenched this gross thirst, Haigh gathered Mrs Durant-Deacon's valuables – a Persian lamb coat, rings, a necklace, earrings and a gold crucifix – and stowed them in his car.

Now it was time to get rid of the body. The very clutter which had offended Mrs Durant-Deacon was, in fact, the paraphernalia of her destruction. There were vats of sulphuric acid, a specially lined metal drum, rubber gloves and a rubber apron, a gas mask and a stirrup pump. Haigh needed all these things to dissolve his victim's body. He knew precisely what to do. He'd done it before.

He laid the forty-five gallon drum on its side and pushed Mrs Durant-Deacon's head and shoulders inside. Then he righted the drum so that the whole body slumped down to the bottom. He donned his rubber apron and gloves, his wellington boots and gas mask and

> LEAVING THE BODY TO DISSOLVE IN A DRUM FILLED WITH SULPHURIC ACID, HAIGH DROVE TO A RESTAURANT TO EAT SOME POACHED EGGS

Below: *Haigh's apron found in the Crawley workshop.*

proceeded to pour concentrated sulphuric acid into the drum.

Using the stirrup pump, Haigh adjusted the level of acid to cover the entire body. Once satisfied, all he had to do was wait for the flesh and bone to dissolve. He knew this would take at least two days. So, tired and hungry after his exertions, he drove to Ye Olde Ancient Priors restaurant in Crawley for a little supper, before driving back to London.

NAGGING SUSPICIONS

At breakfast the following morning several residents of the Onslow Court Hotel remarked on Mrs Durant-Deacon's

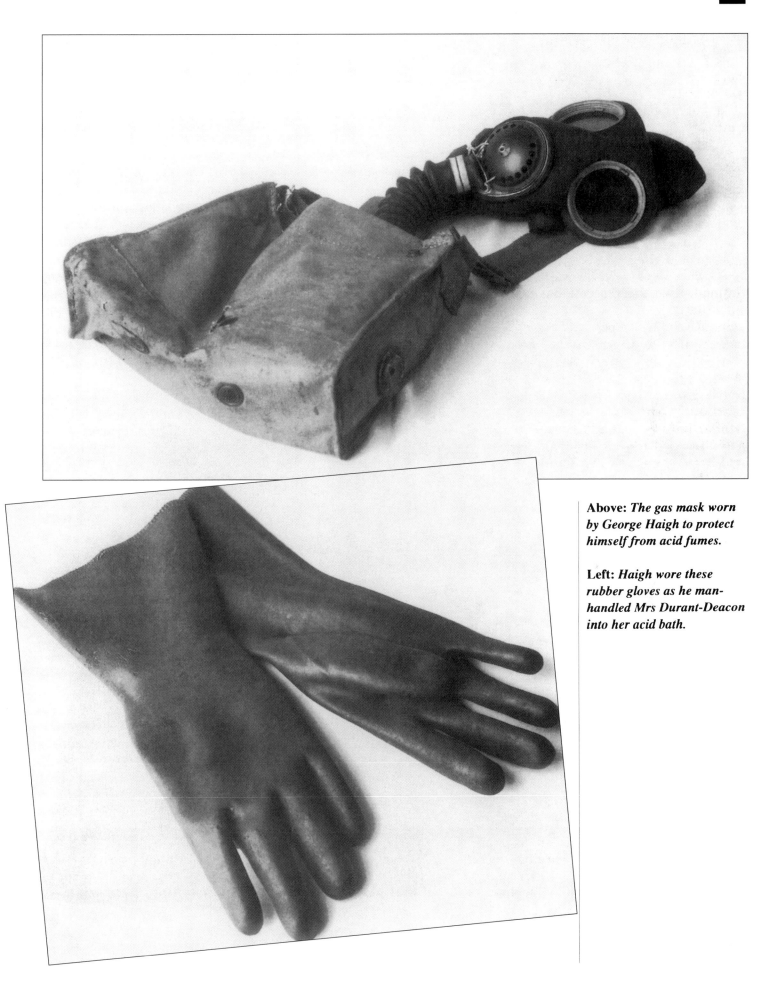

Above: *The gas mask worn by George Haigh to protect himself from acid fumes.*

Left: *Haigh wore these rubber gloves as he man-handled Mrs Durant-Deacon into her acid bath.*

absence. Her closest friend at the hotel, Mrs Constance Lane, was particularly concerned and started to make some discreet enquiries. The chambermaid told Mrs Lane that Mrs Durant-Deacon's bed had not been slept in.

Later that morning Mrs Lane was approached by John Haigh who solicitously enquired about Mrs Durant-Deacon's whereabouts. He said that he

Below: *The barrel used by Haigh to dissolve his victim's body.*

had had an appointment with her the previous day, and that Mrs Durant-Deacon had failed to show up.

Mrs Lane already knew about the trip to Crawley. She had seen her friend just as she was about to leave the hotel. She couldn't understand how Mrs Durant-Deacon could have 'failed to show up'. Mrs Lane had never liked Haigh. He was too oily for her taste, and his involvement with Mrs Durant-Deacon had always made her uneasy. Now she had a creeping feeling that something awful had happened to her friend.

Mrs Lane toyed with the idea of going to the police. But she was afraid that there might be some perfectly good reason for Mrs Durant-Deacon's absence and was anxious not to embarrass her friend – or to make a fool of herself. She decided to wait.

The following morning there was still no sign of Mrs Durant-Deacon. Mrs Lane was at breakfast, pondering her next move, when she was again approached by Haigh, expressing concern. Mrs Lane was suddenly galvanized into action. She told Haigh that she was going down to the police station, and that she would like him to go with her. Haigh had little choice but to agree, so he drove her to Chelsea Police Station.

The report Haigh made to the police was plausible enough. He had arranged to meet Mrs Durant-Deacon outside the Army and Navy Stores in Victoria Street at 2.30p.m. on 18 February. He had waited there until 3.30. Mrs Durant-Deacon had never materialized, and he had driven down to his workshop in Crawley alone.

He was, of course, extremely concerned about Mrs Durant-Deacon's welfare, and would do anything he could to help them locate her. The police thanked Haigh for his cooperation and said that they would be in touch if they thought of anything else.

Haigh drove Mrs Lane back to the Onslow Court and hoped against hope that that was the last he would hear of the matter. It wasn't. Four days later, on Thursday, 24 February, Woman Police Sergeant Alexandra Lambourne went to the hotel to gather additional background information on Mrs Durant-Deacon. She

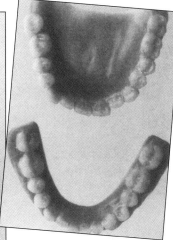

Above: *Haigh's acid bath failed to dissolve Mrs Durant-Deacon's dentures.*

Above left: *Home office pathologist Keith Simpson immediately identified three round 'pebbles' as Mrs Durant-Deacon's gallstones.*

Below: *George Haigh's diary was scrutinized by police.*

interviewed Haigh at some length.

Like Mrs Lane, she was immediately repelled by his superficial charm and his unctuous concern for the well-being of the missing widow. She was an experienced police officer and was convinced that Haigh was lying.

WPS Lambourne had no evidence to support her gut feeling, but she felt strongly enough about it to mention it in her report to her divisional Detective Inspector, Shelley Symes. 'Apart from the fact I do not like the man Haigh and his mannerisms,' she wrote, 'I have a sense that he is "wrong", and there may be a case behind the whole business.'

Symes had sufficient respect for Sergeant Lambourne's judgement to ask the Criminal Record Division at Scotland Yard to run a check on Haigh. Within a matter of hours, they came back to him with a file which showed that John George Haigh had been jailed three times, twice for obtaining money by fraud and once for theft. Further enquiries in London and Sussex showed that he owed substantial sums of money – to the Onslow Court Hotel, among others.

On Saturday, 26 February, Sergeant Pat Heslin of the West Sussex Constabulary, accompanied by Police Sergeant Appleton, went to see Mr Edward Jones, owner of Hurtslea Products, a small engineering company located on Leopold Street in Crawley. Jones told the police that he had known John George Haigh

for some years. Over the past few months he had let him use a store-house at the back of the factory for a nominal rent. Haigh had been using the premises for 'experimental work', but had never said precisely what that entailed.

The police were anxious to look round the shed, but Jones told them that Haigh had the only set of keys. So Heslin picked up a steel bar and prised the padlock off the door. At first glance, the whitewashed interior looked ordinary enough. There was the usual clutter – paint pots, old bits of wood, a couple of work benches, vats of chemicals, protective clothing.

Then something caught the sergeant's eye. On one of the workbenches there was a small hatbox and an expensive leather briefcase. They simply didn't belong.

Heslin looked through the case. He found a variety of papers and documents, including ration books and clothing coupons. The contents of the hatbox were even odder. It contained several passports, driving licences, diaries, a cheque book and a marriage certificate, none of which bore the name of Haigh. At the bottom of the box was the most alarming find of all, a .38 Enfield revolver and a small white envelope containing eight bullets.

Above: *The basement flat in Kensington where Haigh is believed to have killed Dr and Mrs Archibald Henderson.*

Below: *Police search a cellar in Gloucester Road for clues in the Haigh murders.*

The following evening, 27 February, Haigh was invited back to Chelsea Police Station to answer further questions. He appeared totally unconcerned as he was led into an office and given a cup of tea. He had dozed off by the time Detective Inspector Shelley Symes, Inspector Albert Webb, and Superintendent Barratt arrived to interview him at 7.30.

They came at him well-armed with evidence. Not only did they have the obviously stolen documents from the Crawley workshop, they had also traced Mrs Durant-Deacon's jewellery to a dealer in Horsham, Sussex. His description of the seller matched John George Haigh precisely. As did that of a dry-cleaner to whom he had taken Mrs Durant-Deacon's Persian lamb coat.

THE AWFUL TRUTH EMERGES

Confronted with this, Haigh was barely ruffled. Puffing on a cigarette, he said, 'I can see you know what you're talking about. I admit the coat belonged to Mrs Durant-Deacon and that I sold her jewellery.'

'How did you come by the property?' asked Symes, 'And where is Mrs Durant-Deacon?'

Haigh thought for a while before replying. 'It's a long story,' he confided. 'It's one of blackmail and I shall have to implicate many others.'

Just then the telephone rang, and Symes and Barratt were summoned from the room. Left alone with Inspector Webb, the most junior of his interrogators, Haigh changed his tack. 'Tell me frankly,' he asked. 'What are the chances of anyone being released from Broadmoor?'

Webb's immediate reaction to Haigh's extraordinary question was to caution him and advise him of his rights. Haigh dismissed the warning with a wave of the hand. 'If I told you the truth,' he continued, 'You would not believe it. It is too fantastic for belief. I will tell you all about it....

'Mrs Durant-Deacon no longer exists. She has disappeared completely and no trace of her can ever be found. I have destroyed her with acid. You will find sludge that remains at Leopold Road. Every trace has gone. How can you prove a murder if there is no body?' Haigh added, obviously pleased with himself.

Webb's first reaction was to disbelieve Haigh's confession. It was simply too fantastic, too grotesque. Haigh was obviously setting himself up for an insanity plea. After all, he had already mentioned Broadmoor.

When Symes and Barratt returned to the interview room, Webb asked Haigh to repeat what he had said. Haigh did so. Symes cautioned him again, but there was no stopping Haigh now. He talked for two-and-a-half hours. And Inspector Symes wrote it all down.

He described the events of Friday, 18 February, in meticulous detail. He told how he had shot Mrs Durant-Deacon, how he had drunk her blood, put her in the acid bath, and then gone to the Ancient Priors for tea and poached eggs. He explained how, on Monday, he had disposed of her jewellery for £110. Then he had returned to Crawley and emptied the sludge – Mrs Durant-Deacon's decomposed body – out of the drum with a bucket, and poured it on to some wasteground at the back of the shed.

The police said nothing as Haigh told his terrible story of murder and theft, vampirism and genteel cups of tea. When he had finished the story of Mrs Durant-Deacon's death, Haigh moved back in time. By the early hours of 1 March he had confessed to five additional murders.

The first, he claimed, had been committed on 9 September 1944. The victim had been an old acquaintance, William McSwan. He had killed him at a basement flat in Gloucester Road. A year later, he had lured William's parents, Donald and Amy McSwan, to the same flat. There he had beaten them to death.

He had forged Donald's signature to gain power of attorney over the McSwans' estate. While selling one of their properties in February 1948, he had met Dr Archibald Henderson and his wife Rosalie. He had killed them in a storeroom in Giles Yard.

In each case, he had acquired money or other property belonging to his victims by skilful forgery and deception. Years after he had disposed of their remains, he had written forged personal and business letters, 'successfully staving off enquiries from relatives, friends and associates.'

Haigh added that he had destroyed all the bodies by his acid bath method – after drinking a glass of their blood.

The arrest of John George Haigh caused an immediate public sensation. His remand at Horsham magistrates court drew huge crowds – predominantly of jeering women.

BUT WHERE IS THE PROOF?

On 4 March, after being transferred from the Chelsea police cells to Lewes Prison, Haigh sprang more surprises. He asked to see Inspector Webb, with whom he clearly felt some sort of affinity. He confided in the young detective that he had committed three murders which he hadn't mentioned in his earlier statement – a woman and a young man in West London, and a girl in Eastbourne. This brought his total to nine.

The police, however, were having their time cut out establishing a case against Haigh for the murder of Mrs Durant-Deacon. Even though he had admitted to the crime, to be certain of a conviction, the prosecution needed proof that the woman was, in fact, dead, and that Haigh really had killed her.

The Home Office pathologist, Dr Keith Simpson, first carried out routine blood tests at the workshop in Crawley. He

Above: *Rosalie Henderson – she died at Haigh's hands along with her husband Archibald.*

THE PATHOLOGIST SEARCHED FOR THE HUMAN 'SLUDGE' ON WASTEGROUND NEAR HAIGH'S LABORATORY OF DEATH

---

established that blood stains found there were of the same group as Mrs Durant-Deacon. He then turned his attention to the wasteland where Haigh claimed to have deposited the 'sludge' from his acid bath. Soon he found a stone 'the size of a cherry'. It was a gallstone.

Simpson soon found more human remains, including fragments of a left foot. He managed to reconstruct it and cast it in plaster. The cast fitted one of Mrs Durant-Deacon's shoes perfectly.

He discovered other, non-human remains – the handle of a handbag, a lipstick container, a hairpin and a notebook. All of these could be traced back to the victim. His most sensational find, however – the clincher – was a set of dentures which were positively identified as having belonged to the missing woman.

In Lewes Prison, Haigh was well aware of the forensic evidence being amassed against him, but he still remained optimistic. He was certain that he could escape the gallows by convincing a jury that he was insane. And on being told that the eminent barrister Sir Maxwell Fyfe was to represent him, Haigh was delighted. He wrote: 'I'm very glad to see we have got old Maxy. He's no fool.'

THE MIND OF A KILLER

The trial of John George Haigh for the murder of Mrs Durant-Deacon – that was the only charge ever brought against him – opened at Lewes Assizes on 18 July 1949 and lasted less than two days.

There was no real question as to whether Haigh had killed Mrs Durant-Deacon. The case rested on whether or not he was sane. The defence called Dr Henry Yellowlees, a consultant psychiatrist at St Thomas's Hospital, as an expert witness.

Dr Yellowlees was no doubt an able man in his field, but he was a rotten witness. He was a pompous windbag. 'In the case of pure paranoia,' Yellowlees explained, 'it really amounts, as it develops and gets a greater hold, to practically self-worship, and that is commonly expressed by the conviction in the mind of the patient that he is in some

summoned the black cap and condemned him to death. Haigh was taken to Wandsworth Prison to await execution.

While there was no expression of pity for him from the press, there was a great deal of editorial speculation. How was it, they wondered, that an intelligent boy from a good home – his parents were members of the Plymouth Brethren – could grow into a monster like Haigh?

Haigh himself went some way to answering them. He wrote from prison: 'Although my parents were kind and loving, I had none of the joys, or the companionship, which small children usually have. From my earliest years, my recollection is of my father saying "Do not" or "Thou shalt not". Any form of sport or light entertainment was frowned upon and regarded as not edifying. There was only condemnation and prohibition....

'It is true to say that I was nurtured on Bible stories but mostly concerned with sacrifice. If by some mischance I did, or said, anything which my father regarded as improper, he would say: "Do not grieve the Lord by behaving so." '

On 24 July, five days after his trial ended, Haigh's mother sent him a fortieth birthday card, but he rejected any suggestion that she visit him in prison.

mystic way under the control of a guiding spirit which means infinitely more to him and is of infinitely greater authority than any human laws or rules of society.'

Dr Yellowlees rambled on in this vein for some considerable time. He was frequently interrupted by both Sir Travers Humphry, the judge, and Sir Hartley Shawcross, counsel for the prosecution, neither of whom had the faintest idea what he was talking about.

As for the jury, he had lost them after the first few sentences. It took them only fifteen minutes to return a verdict of Guilty on John George Haigh. Sir Travers Humphry was equally speedy as he

Top and above: *George Haigh leaves Horsham Court with his police escort. Haigh is besieged by photographers as he leaves court.*

Right: *Dr Keith Simpson, the Home Office pathologist, was the greatest forensic scientist of his day.*

As the day of his execution approached, Haigh's apparently limitless poise began to crumble. He started to suffer from depression and complained of recurrent nightmares about blood.

Despite his depression, Haigh maintained his sense of theatre. He bequeathed his favourite suit and tie to Madame Tussauds, ensuring himself a place in the Chamber of Horrors. He even requested his model should show at least one inch of shirt cuff.

Then Haigh became concerned about the hanging itself. He contacted the prison governor, Major A.C.N. Benke, and requested to rehearse his own execution. 'My weight is deceptive,' Haigh insisted, 'I have a light springy step and I would not like there to be a hitch.'

The governor turned down his request, assuring him that the executioner was highly experienced and that there would be no hitches.

On 9 August, the eve of his execution, Haigh wrote a letter to his parents. It began: 'My dearest Mum and Dad, Thank you for your very touching letter which I received this morning and which will, I suppose, be your last....'

He went on to say that he had found parts of his upbringing very restrictive: 'There was much that was lovely.... We cannot change the inscrutible predictions of the eternal.... I, that is my spirit, shall remain earthbound for some time: my mission is not yet fulfilled....'

Haigh did not go on to explain what he thought his mission was, nor expressed any remorse for his terrible crimes. In the end, the ultimate mystery of Haigh's life – what was going on inside his mind? – would go to the grave with him.

At 9a.m. on 10 August, John George Haigh was executed. His depression had left him and he was his old self, all swank and swagger, as he faced the gallows. He was buried the same day inside the prison walls, as is the custom in cases of execution.

Below: *10 August 1949. A crowd gathers outside Wandsworth Prison as John George Haigh is executed.*

SNYDER & GRAY
Momsie and Loverboy

The mousey little underwear salesman wanted a passionate woman to dominate him. The blonde good-time girl was after a man whom she could control utterly. It seemed the perfect match – but after sex came murder

They were an odd couple. He was a submissive traveller in ladies' underwear; she was a domineering good-time girl. Dubbed 'Putty Man' and 'Granite Woman', they fulfilled a need in each other and, while their relationship was always faintly ludicrous, it was also to prove ultimately deadly.

ATTRACTION OF OPPOSITES

Judd Gray and Ruth Snyder first met in June 1925 at Henry's, a small Scandinavian restaurant in New York City. It was a blind lunch date set up by two of Ruth's friends, Karin Kaufman and Harry Folsom.

Judd and Ruth hit it off from the start. It was an attraction of opposites. She was an attractive twenty-eight-year-old blonde, an extrovert who enjoyed drinking, dancing and sex. He was thirty-one, slight, shy and myopic. He too had a thirst for excitement which he had never had either the courage or the opportunity to slake. In Ruth he saw the chance for a passionate affair, an escape from the drudgery of his bourgeois life.

Judd and Ruth spent their first three hours together in the restaurant booth swapping personal and marital histories. She explained that she was married with a seven-year-old daughter, Lorraine, and lived in the suburb of Queens with her husband, Albert, who was much older than she. Art editor with *Motor Boating* magazine, he was a great outdoors man and spent most of his time and money on boating and fishing.

In fact, he was away on one of his trips as they spoke. She didn't care for the outdoor life. She preferred dining in good restaurants and dancing – not that Albert cared. In all, she painted her marriage in fairly grim terms with herself as the grass widow to a selfish and insensitive man.

What she neglected to mention to Judd Gray was that he was merely the latest in a long string of 'men friends' whom she had cultivated to compensate herself for her marital dissatisfaction.

Judd responded by saying that he too was married with a daughter and lived in East Orange, New Jersey. He described his wife Isabel as a good mother and a

Opposite: *'Granite Woman', Ruth Snyder was a good-time girl who liked to dominate the men in her life.*

Below: *Judd Gray, 'Putty Man', was an ineffectual underwear salesman who lusted after excitement. He found it in Ruth Snyder.*

Above: *The Snyder house in East Orange, New Jersey.*

Opposite: *In her younger years, Ruth Snyder cut a glamorous figure.*

meticulous housekeeper, but made it plain that she did not provide the excitement he wanted from life.

The one bright spot in his otherwise dull existence was his job. As a travelling salesman for the Bien Jolie Corset Company, he spent much of his time on the road. The company's headquarters were in New York and so he came to the city on a regular basis. Would Ruth like to meet him again? Yes, she would.

By the time Ruth and Judd parted company on the sidewalk outside Henry's it was after 4p.m., and both of them had found what they had been searching for: Judd, a passionate affair in which he could be led and dominated; Ruth, a man she could control utterly.

CONSUMMATION ON THE OFFICE FLOOR

Despite this obvious mutual attraction, it was almost two months before the couple met again for their first real date. On 4

August, Judd called Ruth and asked if she would care to join him for dinner at 'their place' – Henry's Swedish restaurant. After the meal Judd, fortified with copious quantities of rye whiskey, invited Ruth back to the Bien Jolie offices on Fifth Avenue. 'I have to collect a case of samples,' he explained lamely.

Once inside the empty office, Judd made his move. 'You really ought to try one of the new glamour corsets,' he suggested. 'I'll fit it for you if you like.'

Ruth took off her coat. 'Okay,' she said. 'You can do that. And from now on you can call me Momsie.'

And so, on the floor of the Bien Jolie Corset Company, Ruth Snyder and Judd Gray consummated their affair, an affair which was to burn with increasing ardour for almost two years. Soon after their first tryst, Judd and Ruth started to meet regularly, spending nights – or parts of nights – together in Manhattan hotel bedrooms. While Judd needed no excuse to be away from home, Ruth would tell

Albert that she was visiting girlfriends. Despite the fact that the meetings became increasingly frequent, Albert suspected nothing – or perhaps he didn't care.

As the relationship developed, its true nature became more apparent. Ruth became increasingly dominant and Judd became correspondingly more besotted. He would sink to his knees and caress her feet and ankles. 'You are my queen, my Momsie!' he would simper, gazing up into her imperious face. 'And you are my baby, my Bud, my Lover Boy,' she would reassure him.

By the end of 1925 the couple had abandoned the last vestiges of discretion and Judd started to visit Ruth at home. Ruth took little Lorraine on her visits to New York, leaving her in the care of the hotel concierge while she went upstairs to spend a few hours with her Lover Boy.

From their first meeting, Ruth had made it clear that her marriage was not happy. As time passed she amplified this point with frequent references to Albert's cruelty, claiming that he beat and humiliated her. When she spoke of these things, she always made a point of saying how wonderful things would be if only she and Judd were both free and could be together all the time.

'ACCIDENTS'

Ruth did not come right out and say that she wished her husband was dead, but she was soon sowing the seeds of the idea in her lover's mind. Just before Christmas 1925, Ruth told Judd about a series of strange 'accidents' which had befallen her husband in recent months.

On one occasion, while he had been changing a tyre, the jack had slipped and the car had almost crushed him to death. A few days later, he had been in the garage stretched under the car with the engine running. Ruth, the ever-dutiful wife, had brought him a glass of whiskey and, not thinking, had closed the garage door after her. A few minutes later Albert had felt very dizzy, and he had just managed to escape from the garage before being asphyxiated by exhaust fumes.

Albert might have seen nothing ominous about these incidents, but Judd

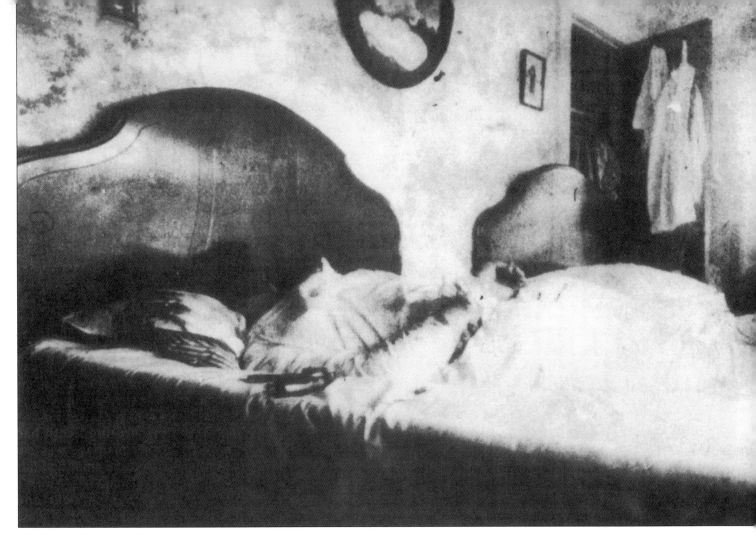

Above: *Beaten, smothered, gagged and bound, Albert Snyder lies dead on his own bed.*

Gray certainly did. 'What are you trying to do?' he asked, horrified. 'Kill the poor guy?'

Ruth pouted: 'Momsie can't do it alone. She needs help. Lover Boy will have to help her.' They had both been drinking heavily and Judd wrote off this first suggestion of murder as alcoholic bravado.

The next time the couple met, however, Judd realized that she was deadly serious. 'We'll be okay for money,' Ruth said. 'I've just tricked Albert into taking out some hefty insurance. He thinks it's for $1000, but it's really for $96,000 with a double indemnity clause.'

Judd made light of the idea and changed the subject, but Ruth was not about to be dissuaded. Over the next few months she gradually chiseled away at Judd's resistance.

In December she told him that Albert had bought a gun and was threatening to kill her. She appealed to Judd directly to help her kill Albert. When he refused, she said she would do it by herself.

> TIRED OF HER LOVER'S NON-COMPLIANCE IN HER MURDER PLANS, RUTH ORDERED HIM TO BUY SOME CHLOROFORM AND PICTURE WIRE

THREATS AND BULLYING

Finally Ruth tired of trying to persuade and cajole her lover into action. It was time, she decided, to capitalize on her dominant position in the relationship and to give a few outright orders.

In February 1927 the couple spent the night together in the Waldolf-Astoria Hotel. Ruth instructed Judd to purchase some chloroform, a sash weight and a length of picture wire. These, she explained, were to be their murder weapons: 'That way,' she explained gleefully, 'we have three means of killing him. One of them must surely work.'

But again Judd baulked at the idea of becoming involved in murder. Ruth flew into a rage and threatened him: 'If you don't do as I say, then that's the end of us in bed. You can find yourself another Momsie to sleep with – only nobody else would have you but me!'

Cowed by the prospect of losing Ruth and returning to his old, dull life, Judd reluctantly agreed to help. Two days later, while passing through Kingston in

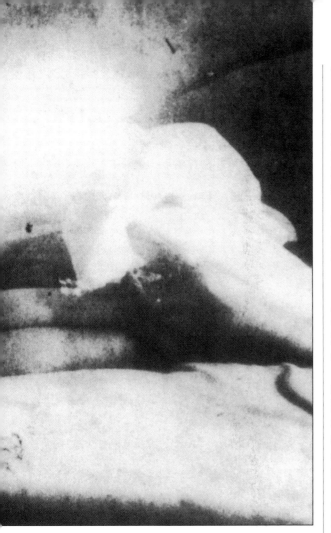

following night.

He told Haddon that he had an assignation with a lady in New York. Would he cover for him? He asked Haddon to 'muss up' his bedclothes and to hang a 'Do Not Disturb' sign on the bedroom door. Haddon readily agreed to this 'manly' conspiracy.

Having thus established his alibi – and, in the process, established the premeditation of his crime – Judd set off by train for New York City.

He arrived at Grand Central Station at 10.20p.m. on the evening of 19 March. After stopping briefly at the Pullman window to purchase a return ticket to Syracuse on the morning train, he walked out on to 42nd Street.

It was raining, but Judd chose to walk the four miles to Queens rather than risk being recognised by a cab driver. He made frequent stops along the way to drink from his hip flask, and he was already quite drunk when he reached his destination.

Judd reached the Snyders' three-storey, clapboard house shortly after midnight. He knew that Ruth and her family would be out at a party until very late, and he let himself into the house by a side door, using a key that Ruth had hidden for him. He went upstairs and into the spare bedroom. Keeping on his buckskin gloves, he removed his hat and coat and hung them in the wardrobe. Then he felt under the pillow and retrieved the sash weight, chloroform, picture wire and a bottle of whiskey which had been left there by Ruth. He laid these props on the bed along with various other items which he had brought with him – a handkerchief, some cheesecloth and an Italian newspaper he had found on the train.

Judd opened the whiskey, took a long slug and settled down to wait.

At about 2am, Judd was woken from his drunken sleep by the sound of the Snyders' car pulling up outside. He heard the front door open, and then footsteps on the stairs. He recognized the voices of Ruth and Lorraine. Ruth slipped into the room where Judd was hiding.

She kissed him and whispered: 'Have you found the sash weight?' Judd nodded. 'Good,' she said. 'Keep quiet and I'll be right back.'

JUDD'S ALIBI HAD ANOTHER, LESS DESIRABLE EFFECT: IT ESTABLISHED THAT THE MURDER OF RUTH'S HUSBAND WAS PREMEDITATED

New York State, he bought a bottle of chloroform in a drug store. He then walked a few doors further along the street to a hardware store and bought a foot-long, lead sash weight and a coil of picture wire.

The next day, Judd returned to New York City and met Ruth at Henry's Restaurant. There he handed over a parcel containing his purchases. Despite the fact that Ruth had brought her daughter with her she was anxious to get on with things, and so the couple discussed the murder of Lorraine's father by exchanging notes scribbled on table napkins. By the time they got up from the table, a date for the killing had been set – Saturday, 19 March.

THE PLAN TAKES SHAPE

On Friday the 18th, Judd Gray registered at the Hotel Onondaga in Syracuse, New York State. In the lobby he bumped into an old friend, Haddon Gray (no relation). Judd saw this as a piece of good fortune and decided to use him as an alibi for the

She returned a few minutes later in her negligee. 'He's just brushing his teeth.' she said, and slipped away again. And so the farce continued for half an hour with Ruth toing and froing, updating Judd on the status in the master bedroom.

'He's getting undressed now.... He's in bed but he's still awake.... I think he's dropped off, but we'd better leave him to settle for a while....'

It was almost 3a.m. before Ruth decided the time was right and joined Judd in the bedroom. He was sitting on the floor and, having almost finished the bottle of whiskey, was very drunk.

'You are going through with it tonight, aren't you?' Ruth asked him.

'I don't know whether I can or not. I'll try.' he replied. Ruth helped him to his feet. 'Now,' she said.

Judd removed his buckskin gloves and pulled on a pair of rubber housegloves in their place. He picked up the sash weight with one hand and with the other took Ruth's arm. And so the odd couple picked their way along the darkened corridor towards the master bedroom.

Ruth led Judd over to the bed where Albert was sleeping. Judd lifted the sash weight above his head and brought it down with all the force he could muster. The blow should have smashed Albert's skull but Judd's aim was off. The weight only glanced the side of Albert's head and crashed into the wooden bedhead.

Albert sat bolt upright and started lashing out at his unseen assailant. Judd hit him again, harder this time, but Albert continued to struggle. Judd dropped the weight and climbed on to the bed, trying to smother his victim with the bedclothes. Albert managed to get his hands round Judd's throat and started to throttle him. Judd screamed at Ruth: 'Momsie, Momsie, for God's sake help me!'

Ruth picked up the sash weight and smashed it into her husband's skull, time and time again. Once Albert stopped struggling, Judd climbed off the bed and watched Ruth put the finishing touches to the job. She tied Albert's hands and feet with a towel and a tie and stuffed his mouth and nostrils with cotton rags soaked in chloroform. Then, just for good measure, she garotted him with the length of picture wire.

'HE'S CLEANING HIS TEETH... HE'S GETTING UNDRESSED... HE'S IN BED BUT HE'S STILL AWAKE...'

'MOMSIE, MOMSIE, FOR GOD'S SAKE HELP ME!' CRIED THE INCOMPETENT WOULD-BE MURDERER AS HIS VICTIM STARTED TO THROTTLE HIM

There was blood everywhere, and Ruth and Judd spent the next half-hour cleaning themselves up. Ruth changed nightdresses and Judd borrowed one of Albert's shirts to replace his own, which was ripped and bloodstained.

Ruth then reminded Judd that they had agreed to ransack the house to make it look like a robbery. They overturned furniture in the living room and scattered the contents of various drawers around the floor. Ruth took all the money out of Albert's wallet and gave it to Judd, and then offered him her jewellery. He refused, and suggested she hide it under the mattress.

In an equally futile attempt to destroy the evidence, Ruth went down to the cellar. There she burned the bloodstained shirt and nightdress in the furnace, and hid the sash weight in a tool box.

Satisfied that everything was just so, Ruth gave Judd another bottle of whiskey for the journey, and told him to knock her out, so that it would look as if she too had been a victim of a robbery.

Judd could not bring himself to do this, but tied her hands and feet and gagged her with a piece of cheesecloth. He left her on the spare bed, with the Italian newspaper – his idea of a false clue – by her side.

As he left, he looked back at Ruth and

Below: *Ruth Snyder and her defence team. Their argument failed to convince the jury.*

was momentarily overcome with disgust and guilt. 'It may be two months,' he said, 'it may be a year, and it may be never before you see me again.'

CLUMSY LIES, SCATTERED CLUES

The murder of Albert Snyder must have been a noisy affair, but little Lorraine Snyder apparently slept through the whole thing. She was woken at 7.45 by a knocking at her bedroom door. She opened the door and found her mother, bound and gagged, lying on the floor in the hallway.

Lorraine undid the cheesecloth gag, and her mother told her to run and get help. Minutes later, the child returned with Louis and Harriet Mulhauser, their friends and neighbours.

'It was dreadful, just dreadful!' Ruth screeched at the Mulhausers. 'I was attacked by a prowler.... He tied me up.... He must have been after my jewels.... Is Albert all right?' Louis Mulhauser crossed the hall and went into the master bedroom. Seconds later, he returned with the awful news. Albert had been battered to death.

Ruth Snyder repeated her version of events twice more that morning, elaborating a little with each successive version. 'He was a big, rough-looking

Above: *Huge crowds gathered outside the court hoping to gain access to the Snyder-Gray trial.*

'IT MAY BE TWO MONTHS, IT MAY BE A YEAR, AND IT MAY BE NEVER BEFORE YOU SEE ME AGAIN'

SHE HAD POWER OVER ME. SHE TOLD ME WHAT TO DO AND I JUST DID IT

---

guy of about thirty-five with a black moustache,' she told Dr Harry Hansen. 'He was a foreigner, I guess. Some kind of Eyetalian.'

Dr Hansen was not convinced by her story, and nor were the police when they arrived. Police Commissioner George V. McLaughlin, heading the investigation, had investigated enough robberies to know the real thing when he saw it. And this definitely was not the real thing.

It had all the hallmarks of an inside job, carried out with the help of an accomplice, probably a man.

A clue to that man's identity came when one of the detectives found a tiepin with the initials JG on the floor of the master bedroom. Then another detective found Ruth's address book which contained the names of twenty-eight of her men friends; the most recent entry was one Judd Gray. Then they found a cancelled cheque made out to Gray by Ruth Snyder in the amount of $200.

By this time, other detectives had discovered the bloodstained sash weight in the cellar and Ruth's jewellery stuffed under the mattress in the spare bedroom. They also found insurance policies taken out on Albert Snyder's life to a total of $96,000.

After twelve hours of questioning, Ruth caved in and admitted that she had been present at her husband's murder, but she denied playing any part in the actual killing. That was all Judd's doing. She was shipped off to the Jamaica Precinct police station and charged.

Acting on information from Ruth Snyder, police arrested a snivelling and terrified Judd Gray at the Onondaga Hotel later that evening. They brought him back to New York City by train.

By the time they arrived, Judd too had confessed to being a party to the murder, but he did not cover up for Ruth. 'I would never have killed Snyder, but for her,' he wept as he completed his statement. 'She had power over me. She told me what to do and I just did it.'

GOOD NEWS FOR THE TABLOIDS

From then on, the case against Snyder and Gray proceeded with all the implacability of the law. Their trial opened on 18 April at the Queens County Courthouse and lasted eighteen days.

The central issue at stake for the jury was not whether the defendants were guilty of killing Albert Snyder. They had both confessed to being present and playing a part in the murder. What had to be decided was whether the crime was premeditated, and whether or not it had been executed for financial gain. Both these factors would have a bearing on the eventual sentencing.

The two defence teams tried to push the blame on to each other's clients to a point where the case became not so much the State v Snyder & Gray as one of Ruth Snyder v Gray. This did nothing for the cases of the two defendants.

On 9 May, Snyder and Gray were duly found guilty of murder in the first degree and sentenced to die in the electric chair at Sing Sing prison in upstate New York.

CHANGED CHARACTERS

Immediately after sentencing, both teams of defence lawyers filed appeals. Ruth's appeal was heard on 27 May, Judd's on

---

FROM THE CONDEMNED CELL RUTH TOLD A REPORTER: 'I ALWAYS WANTED AN ELECTRIC HEATER, BUT MY HUSBAND WAS ALWAYS TOO STINGY TO BUY ME ONE'

'I NEVER SAW ANYTHING MORE TERRIBLE,' SAID RUTH'S LAWYER. 'I CANNOT DESCRIBE HER AGONY, HER MISERY, HER TERROR'

Below: *Ruth Snyder being followed by jail matron, Mrs Irene Wolf.*

---

10 June. On 23 November both appeals were rejected and Snyder's original sentence was upheld.

With all legal means for clemency now closed to her, Ruth started writing her autobiography, My Own True Story – So Help Me God! which was syndicated by the Hearst newspaper chain.

She also promoted herself in the media by granting audiences to press men from her condemned cell. She even managed moments of black humour. Talking of her forthcoming execution, she told reporter Jack Lait: 'I always wanted an electric heater, but my husband was always too stingy to buy me one.'

While awaiting execution, Ruth had a regular flow of fan mail. It included 164 proposals of marriage, mainly from men desperate to take Judd Gray's place as her slave.

For all her bravado, however, the 'Granite Woman', as the press had dubbed her, was terrified of dying. Screams could be heard coming from her Sing Sing cell at night.

Judd Gray, in contrast, appeared totally resigned to his fate. He spent much of his time writing letters to his family and friends. When he was not busy with his correspondence, he studied the Bible and discussed religious matters with the prison chaplain.

The execution was set for 11 p.m. on 12 January 1928. At 7.30 p.m., Ruth Snyder was moved to her death cell, 30 feet from the execution chamber.

Shortly before the evening meal she was visited by her lawyer, Edgar Hazleton. Her condition was pitiful, he recalled. 'She was too far gone to know what she was doing. I never saw anything more terrible. I cannot describe her agony, her misery, her terror.'

A little later Samuel Miller, Judd Gray's attorney, visited him in his death cell, a few feet away from that of his erstwhile lover. Miller painted a very different picture of his client to that of Hazleton. 'He is absolutely resigned and courageous,' Miller said. 'He indulges no self-pity. He realizes the enormity of his act.'

A few minutes before 11 p.m. twenty-four witnesses, most of them reporters, were shown into the death chamber.

Among those who took their seats opposite the electric chair was a young photographer, Thomas Howard. Cameras were strictly forbidden in the chamber, but Howard had managed to smuggle in a tiny one strapped to his ankle.

At precisely 11 p.m. Ruth Snyder, her head shaved, was led from her cell by two female warders. As she was strapped to the chair, she wept: 'Father, forgive them, for they know not what they do.' Seconds later the state executioner, Robert Elliot, threw the switch and a massive surge of electricity shot through Ruth's body. At precisely that moment, Thomas Howard released the shutter of his hidden camera, recording the death of Ruth Snyder on film and

guaranteeing for himself a place in journalistic folklore.

At 11.10, after Ruth Snyder's body had been removed to the nearby autopsy room, Judd Gray was brought into the death chamber. He stood between two warders, calm and composed. A priest stood by him as he was strapped into the chair, and they recited the Beatitudes together. Gray continued to pray as the electrodes were fitted and a mask was pulled over his face.

Ten minutes later, Judd Gray was reunited with Ruth Snyder for the first and last time since the fateful night of Albert Snyder's murder. This time they lay side-by-side on a slab in the Sing Sing prison morgue.

Above: *Ruth Snyder at the moment of her death in the electric chair: taken by a camera smuggled into the death chamber strapped to the photographer's leg.*

GRAY CONTINUED TO PRAY EVEN AS THE ELECTRODES WERE FITTED AND A MASK WAS PULLED OVER HIS FACE

HAROLD SHIPMAN
Doctor Death

Until recently Britain's worst serial killer was Victorian serial poisoner, Mary Ann Cotton, who murdered an estimated 21 people in the 1870s. Now that dubious distinction is claimed by Dr. Harold Shipman.

Dr Shipman ran a one-man practice in Hyde in the north of England. Most of Harold Shipman's patients were elderly women, living alone and vulnerable. They adored their doctor, Harold 'Fred' Shipman, and even when their contemporaries began dying in unusually high numbers, patients remained loyal to the murderous M.D. It seemed that as long as he spared them, his victims loved their doctor – to death.

A KILLER'S CHILDHOOD

Harold Frederick Shipman was born into a working class family on June 14, 1946 and was known as Fred or Freddy. His childhood, however, was far from normal. He always kept a distance between himself and his contemporaries – mainly due to the influence of his mother, Vera. The reason for this distance was to become clear in later years.

It was Vera who decided who Harold could play with, and when. For some reason she wanted to distinguish him from the other boys – he was the one who always wore a tie when the others were allowed to dress more casually. His sister Pauline was seven years older, his brother Clive, four years his junior, but in his mother's eyes, Harold

'VERA WAS FRIENDLY ENOUGH, BUT SHE REALLY DID SEE HER FAMILY AS SUPERIOR TO THE REST OF US. NOT ONLY THAT, YOU COULD TELL HAROLD (FREDDY) WAS HER FAVOURITE — THE ONE SHE SAW AS THE MOST PROMISING OF HER THREE CHILDREN.'

was the one she held the most hope for.

Shipman was comparatively bright in his early school years, but rather mediocre when he reached upper school level. Nonetheless, he was a plodder determined to succeed, even down to re-sitting his entrance examinations for medical school.

Funnily enough, he had every opportunity to be part of the group – he was an accomplished athlete on the football field and the running track. In spite of this, his belief in his superiority appears to have prevented him from forming any meaningful friendships.

There was something else that isolated him from the group – his beloved mother had terminal lung cancer. As her condition deteriorated, Harold willingly played a major supportive role.

WATCHING VERA DIE

Shipman's behaviour in his mother's final months closely paralleled that of Shipman the serial killer. Every day after classes, he would hurry home, make Vera a cup of tea and chat with

Above: *Dr Shipman's surgery in Hyde, Greater Manchester*

her. She found great solace in his company and always eagerly awaited his return. This is probably where Shipman learned the endearing bedside manner he would later adopt in his practice as a family physician. Towards the end, Vera experienced severe pain, but, because pumps to self-administer painkillers did not exist at that time, Vera's sole relief from the agony of cancer came with the family physician.

No doubt young Harold watched in fascination as his mother's distress miraculously subsided whenever the family doctor injected her with morphine. Ms. Shipman grew thinner and frailer day by day, until on June 21, 1963, the cancer claimed her life. Harold felt a tremendous sense of loss following his mother's death. After all, she was the one who made him feel special, different from the rest. Her passing also left him with an indelible image – the patient with a cup of tea nearby, finding sweet relief in morphine.

This must have made a great impact on the 17-year-old, as it was a scene he would recreate hundreds of times in the future once he became a doctor – with no regard for human life or feeling.

HAROLD THE STUDENT

Two years after his mother died, Harold Shipman was finally admitted to Leeds University medical school. Getting in had been a struggle – he'd had to re-write the exams he'd failed first time around. His grades, however, were sufficient enough for him to collect a degree and serve his mandatory hospital internship.

It is surprising to learn that so many of his teachers and fellow students can barely remember Shipman. Those who do remember claim that he looked down on them and seemed bemused by the way most young men behaved. 'It was as if he tolerated us. If someone told a joke he would smile patiently, but Fred never wanted to join in. It

> HE WAS OFTEN UNNECESSARILY RUDE AND MADE SOME OF HIS COLLEAGUES FEEL 'STUPID' – A WORD HE FREQUENTLY USED TO DESCRIBE ANYONE HE DIDN'T LIKE. HE WAS CONFRONTATIONAL AND COMBATIVE WITH MANY PEOPLE, TO THE POINT WHERE HE BELITTLED AND EMBARRASSED THEM. NOT YET THIRTY, SHIPMAN HAD BECOME A CONTROL FREAK.

seems funny, because I later heard he'd been a good athlete, so you'd have thought he'd be more of a team player.' He was simply remembered as a loner. The one place his personality changed, however, was the football field. Here, he unleashed his aggression and his dedication to win was intense.

Shipman finally found companionship in a girl, Primrose, who was three years his junior. He married her when he was only nineteen years old.

Above: *Primrose, Shipman's wife.*

Primrose's background was similar to Fred's, whereby her mother restricted her friendships and controlled her activities. Being rather a plain girl, Primrose was delighted to have finally found a boyfriend. Shipman married her when she was only seventeen and 5 months pregnant.

By 1974 he was a father of two and had joined a medical practice in the Yorkshire town of Todmorden. At this stage in his life Fred seemed to undergo a transformation. He became an outgoing, respected member of the community in the eyes of his fellow medics and patients.

But the staff in the medical offices where he worked saw a different side of the young practitioner. He had a way of getting things done his way – even with the more experienced doctors in the practice.

ADDICTION

His career in Todmorden came to a sudden halt when he started having blackouts. His partners were devastated when he gave them the reason – epilepsy. He used this faulty diagnosis as a cover-up. The truth soon came to the surface, when the practice receptionist Marjorie Walker came across some disturbing entries in a druggist's controlled narcotics ledger. These records showed how Shipman had been prescribing large and frequent amounts of pethidine in the names of several of his patients, when in fact the pethidine had found its way into the doctor's very own veins.

Not only that, he'd also written numerous prescriptions for the drug on behalf of the practice. Although this was not unusual because drugs were kept for emergencies, the prescribed amounts were excessive.

Following the discovery of Shipman's over-prescribing, an investigation by the practice uncovered the fact that many patients on the prescription list had neither required nor received the drug.

When confronted in a staff meeting, Shipman's way of dealing with the problem was to provide an insight into his true personality. Realizing his

SHIPMAN WAS CHALLENGED IN A STAFF MEETING. THEY PUT BEFORE HIM EVIDENCE THAT HE HAD BEEN PRESCRIBING PETHIDINE TO PATIENTS, THAT THEY'D NEVER RECEIVED THE PETHIDINE, AND IN FACT THE PETHIDINE HAD FOUND ITS WAY INTO HIS VERY OWN VEINS.

career was on the line, he first begged for a second chance.

When this request was denied, he became furious and stormed out, threw his medical bag to the ground and threatened to resign. The partners were dumbfounded by this violent – and seemingly uncharacteristic – behaviour.

Soon afterwards, his wife Primrose stormed into the room where his peers were discussing the best way to dismiss him. Rudely, she informed the people at the meeting that her husband would never resign, proclaiming, 'You'll have to force him out!'

And this was exactly what they had to do. They forced him out of the practice and into a drug rehabilitation centre in 1975.

Two years later, his many convictions for drug offences, prescription fraud and forgery cost him a surprisingly low fine – just over £600. Shipman's conviction for forgery is worth noting, because he was to use this skill later when faking signatures on a patently counterfeit will – that of his last victim, Katherine Grundy.

BACK TO WORK

Today, it is unlikely Harold Shipman would be allowed to handle drugs unsupervised, given his previous track record. However, within two years, he was back in business as a general practitioner in the Donneybrook Medical Centre in Hyde in the north of England. How readily he was accepted demonstrates his absolute self-confidence – and his ability to convince his peers of his sincerity. Again, he played the role of a dedicated, hardworking and community-minded doctor. He gained his patients' absolute trust and earned his colleagues' respect, but perhaps he was not watched carefully enough. In Hyde, Harold Shipman was home free – and free to kill!

A DIARY OF DEATH

Because of the nature of the Shipman case, it may never be possible to document every murder he committed, but it is estimated that he is responsible for the deaths of at least 236 patients over a 24-year period.

KATHLEEN GRUNDY, 81 (RIGHT)

A former mayoress of Hyde and the last victim, Mrs Grundy died on June 24 1998. She was found fully clothed on a settee at home. Dr Shipman killed her with a heroin overdose on a visit to take a blood sample. He has also been found guilty of forging her will and two letters to secure her £386,000 estate, as well as altering his medical records to suggest that the widow was addicted to morphine.

JEAN LILLEY, 58

Mrs Lilley was visited by Dr Shipman on the morning of her death on April 25, 1997. A neighbour became increasingly concerned about the length of time that the GP had been with Mrs Lilley, who was suffering from a cold. She found her friend's body within moments of the doctor leaving her home. An ambulance crew later said Mrs Lilley had been dead for some time, killed by a lethal dose of morphine. She was the only one of the 15 victims to have been married at the time of her death. Shipman contacted her husband by mobile phone to tell him his wife had died.

MARIE WEST, 81

On March 6, 1995, Harold Shipman injected Mrs West, his first victim, with a fatal dose of diamorphine (the medical term for heroine), unaware that her friend was in the next room. Shipman first told Mrs West's son that she had died of a massive stroke, then said it was a heart attack. Mrs West ran a clothes shop in Hyde, a suburb of Manchester, where all the victims came from.

IRENE TURNER, 67

Mrs Turner was found dead fully clothed on her bed by her neighbour, after Dr Shipman had called at Mrs Turner's house on July 11, 1996. Earlier, he had asked the neighbour if she could help pack Mrs Turner's belongings for hospital, but told her to wait for a few minutes before going over. Morphine was later found in Mrs Turner's body.

KATHLEEN WAGSTAFF, 81

Shipman confused Mrs Wagstaff with another patient, Anne Royal, whose daughter was married to Kathleen's son Peter, and called on the wrong person on December 9 1997 to announce she had died. Harold Shipman visited Angela Wagstaff at her workplace to tell her her mother had died, but the dead woman was in fact her mother-in-law Kathleen. After injecting Mrs Wagstaff with morphine, Shipman put her death down to heart disease.

BIANKA POMFRET, 49 (RIGHT)

Mrs Pomfret, a German divorcee, was found dead at her home by her son William on the same day she had been visited by Shipman, on December 10, 1997. Excessive morphine levels were found in her body, but the GP claimed Mrs Pomfret had complained to him of chest pains on the day of her death. He fabricated a false medical history to cover his tracks after killing her.

LIZZIE ADAMS, 77

Mrs Adams, a retired sewing machinist, died at home on February 28 1997. Dr Shipman stated that she had died of pneumonia and pretended to call for an ambulance, although no such call was made.

NORAH NUTTALL, 65

Mrs Nuttall, a widow, died on January 26 1998 after visiting Shipman's surgery for cough medicine. The GP later visited Mrs Nuttall at her home, where her son Anthony found his mother slumped in a chair.

MAUREEN WARD, 57

Mrs Ward, a former college lecturer, died on February 18 1998. Although she had been suffering from cancer, she was not ill at the time of her death. Dr Shipman claimed she died of a brain tumour.

WINIFRED MELLOR, 73

Mrs Mellor, a widow who had been Dr Shipman's patient for 18 years, was found dead on May 11 1998 in a chair at home with her left sleeve rolled up to suggest a heroin habit, following an earlier visit by Dr Shipman. He killed her with a fatal injection of morphine, and then returned to his surgery to create a false medical history to support a cause of death from coronary thrombosis.

JOAN MELIA, 73

Shipman murdered the divorcee on a visit to her home in Hyde on June 12 1998. She was found dead by a neighbour in her living room, having earlier visited Dr Shipman at his surgery about a chest infection. Shipman issued a death certificate stating she had died from pneumonia and emphysema. Her body, later exhumed, was found to contain morphine. The GP also claimed to have phoned for an ambulance, but didn't.

IVY LOMAS, 63

Dr Shipman killed Mrs Lomas at his surgery on May 29 1997 in Market Street, Hyde. He then saw three more patients before telling his receptionist that he had failed to resuscitate her. Morphine was later found in her body. She was such a regular there that Shipman told a police sergeant who was called after her death he thought her a nuisance. He joked that part of the seating area should be reserved for her and a plaque put up.

MURIEL GRIMSHAW, 76

Mrs Grimshaw was found dead at her home on July 14 1997. Shipman, who was called to examine her, said there was no need for a postmortem. Morphine was later found in her body.

MARIE QUINN, 67

Dr Shipman injected Mrs Quinn with morphine at her home on November 24 1997. Shipman claimed she had contacted him complaining of feeling unwell before her death. But her telephone bills showed no such call was made.

PAMELA HILLIER, 68

Shipman gave Mrs Hillier's family a confusing account of how she had died, on Feb 9 1998, saying she had high blood pressure, but that it wasn't high enough to give him major concern, although she had died from high blood pressure. He had in fact given her a lethal dose of morphine.

ANGELA WOODRUFF

In this macabre and still unfinished story, Shipman's former patients are grateful indeed he was finally stopped. The feeling that they could have been next will always haunt them, and there is little doubt that some owe their lives to a determined and intelligent woman named Angela Woodruff.

This lady's dogged determination to solve a mystery helped ensure that, on Monday, January 31, 2000, the jury at Preston Crown Court found Shipman guilty of murdering 15 of his patients and forging the will of Angela's beloved mother, Katherine Grundy.

Following her mother's burial Ms. Woodruff returned to her home, where she received a troubling phone call from solicitors. They claimed to have a copy of Ms. Grundy's will.

A solicitor herself, Angela's own firm had always handled her mother's affairs, in fact her firm held the original document lodged in 1986. The moment she saw the badly typed, poorly worded paper, Angela Woodruff knew it was a fake. It left £386,000 to Dr Shipman.

It was at this time that Angela went to her local police. Her investigation results ultimately reached Detective Superintendent Bernard Postles. His own investigation convinced him Angela Woodruff's conclusions were accurate.

THE TRIAL BEGINS

To get solid proof of Kathleen Grundy's murder, a post mortem was required which, in turn, required an exhumation order from the coroner. By the time the trial had begun, Det. Supt Postles' team would be uncomfortably familiar with the process. Of the fifteen killed, nine were buried and six cremated. Katherine Grundy's was the first grave opened. Her body was the first of the ongoing post mortems. Her tissue and hair samples were sent to different labs for analysis, and the wait for results began.

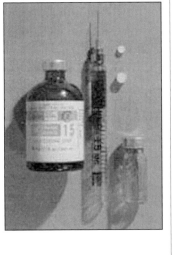

IT WAS DISCOVERED THAT THE MORPHINE LEVELS IN THE DEAD WOMAN'S BODY WOULD UNDOUBTEDLY HAVE BEEN THE CAUSE OF DEATH.

At the same time, police raided the doctor's home and offices. It was timed so that Shipman had no chance of learning a body had been exhumed for a post mortem. Police had to be certain no evidence could be destroyed or concealed before their search. When the police arrived, Shipman showed no surprise; his approach was one of arrogance and contempt as the search warrant was read out.

One item crucial to police investigations was the typewriter used to type the bogus will. Shipman produced an old Brother manual portable, telling an improbable tale of how Ms Grundy sometimes borrowed it. This unbelievable story was to go against Shipman – especially when forensic scientists confirmed it was the machine used to type the counterfeit will and other such fraudulent documents.

The search of his house also yielded medical records, some mysterious jewellery and a surprise. The Shipman home was littered with filthy clothes, old newspapers and, for a doctor's home, it was nothing short of unsanitary. But an even bigger surprise was due.

When toxicologist Julie Evans filed her report on the cause of Ms Grundy's death, Det. Supt Postles was astounded. It was discovered that the morphine level in the dead woman's body would undoubtedly have been the cause of death. Not only that, her death would have occurred within three hours of having received the fatal overdose.

Shipman would claim later that the stylish and conservative old lady was a junkie. Even today psychologists speculate on the possibility that he wanted to be caught. Otherwise, why would he hand them the typewriter and use a drug so easily traced back to him? Others believe he saw himself as invincible, believing that, as a doctor, his word would never be questioned.

The detective realized the case went far beyond one death, and the scope of the investigation was broadened immediately.

THE VERDICT AND SENTENCE

The outcome of all the tests carried out was consistent. In case after case, it was proved that the victims had not died from old age or natural disease. Typically, morphine toxicity was the cause of death.

It took the judge, Mr. Justice Forbes, two weeks to meticulously dissect the evidence heard by the jury. He urged caution, noting that no witness had actually seen Shipman kill, and he also urged the jurors to use common sense in arriving at their verdict.

At 4:43 pm on Monday January 31, 2000, the foreman declared all the jury's verdicts were unanimous – they found Shipman GUILTY on 15 counts of murder and one of forgery.

THE SHIPMAN LETTERS WERE WRITTEN BETWEEN SEPTEMBER 1998 WHEN HE WAS FIRST ON REMAND, AND JANUARY 2000 WHEN HE KNEW HIS TRIAL DEFENCE WAS DOOMED — THESE INTIMATE LETTERS ARE THE ONLY INSIGHT TO THE TRUE THOUGHTS OF DOCTOR DEATH.

Judge Justice Forbes presided in Shipman's trial .

The disgraced doctor stood motionless showing no sign of emotion as he heard the jurors' verdicts read. Wearing black, Shipman's wife, Primrose, also remained impassive. Her boys – one beside her and the other seated behind – looked down and seemed to visibly shrink on hearing the results.

In the public gallery, some gasped as Shipman's previous forgeries were described. The defence counsel asked that sentence be passed immediately.

The judge passed fifteen life sentences for the murders and a four-year sentence for forgery.

Then the Judge broke with the tradition that usually involves writing to the Home Secretary about his recommendations on length of the sentence:

> 'In the ordinary way, I would not do this in open court, but in your case I am satisfied justice demands that I make my views known at the conclusion of this trial . . . My recommendation will be that you spend the remainder of your days in prison.'

Fifteen murders, a mere fraction of the suspected death toll, had been dealt with and the fifty-seven day trial was over. But there was one last life for Shipman to take.

At 6.20 a.m. on Tuesday January 13, 2004, Harold Shipman was found hanging from the window bars in his cell in Wakefield Prison by a ligature made of bed sheets. Staff at the prison tried to revive him but he was pronounced dead at 8.10 a.m.

As Shipman died before his 60th birthday, his widow, Primrose, will receive a pension of £10,000 per year, and a tax-free lump sum reported to be in excess of £100,000. Had he died after 60, the pension would have been halved, with no additional sum. This, it is believed, is the reason for his suicide.

Within hours of his suicide, the word "justice" had been graffitied 12 times across his former Hyde surgery.

TED BUNDY
The Charmer

Serial killer Ted Bundy terrorized young women throughout various American states and claimed the lives of many young women in vicious sexual assaults and killings. Ted Bundy is estimated to have murdered between 35 to 50 young women in almost a dozen states.

As a youth, Ted was terribly shy and was often teased and bullied in his junior high school. Despite this he was able to maintain a high grade average that would continue throughout high school and later into college. Ted was more popular in high school than he was in junior high. Although he was very shy, Ted was thought of as being well dressed and exceptionally well mannered . He was not known to have dated anyone during this period, it seemed his interests lay elsewhere such as in skiing and politics. In fact, it was in high school that Ted's interest in politics began to bloom.

Ted graduated from high school in 1965 and won a scholarship to the University of Puget Sound. In 1966 he transferred to the University of Washington, where he began his intensive studies in Chinese. He worked his way through the university by taking on low-level jobs such as a bus boy and shoe clerk. It was in the spring of 1967, when he began a relationship, that would change his life forever.

Stephanie Brooks was everything

TED WAS A MAN WITH A MISSION AND MOST IMPORTANTLY HE WANTED TO IMPRESS STEPHANIE. HE RE-ENROLLED AT THE UNIVERSITY OF WASHINGTON AND STUDIED PSYCHOLOGY, A SUBJECT IN WHICH HE EXCELLED. BUNDY BECAME AN HONOURS STUDENT AND WAS WELL LIKED BY HIS PROFESSORS AT THE UNIVERSITY.

Ted had ever dreamed of in a woman. She was a beautiful and highly sophisticated woman from a wealthy Californian family. Although they had many differences, they both loved to ski and it was during their many ski trips together that they began to fall in love. Stephanie was Ted's first love and they spent a lot of time together. However, Stephanie was not as infatuated with Ted as he was with her. She believed that he had no real direction or future goals and it appeared she wanted someone who would fit in with her lifestyle. Ted tried too hard to impress her, even if that meant lying, something that she didn't like at all.

In 1968, after graduating from the University of Washington, Stephanie broke off relations with Ted. Ted never recovered from the break-up. Nothing, including school, seemed to hold any interest for him and he eventually dropped out, dumb-founded and depressed over the break-up. Ted was totally obsessed with Stephanie and he couldn't get her out of his mind. It was an obsession that would span his lifetime and lead to a series of events that would shock the world.

A TIME OF CHANGE

Ted re-enrolled at the University of Washington, to study psychology. It was at this time that he met Meg Anders, a woman with whom he would be involved with for almost five years. Meg worked as a secretary and was a somewhat shy and quiet woman. She was a divorcee who seemed to have found the perfect father figure for her daughter in Ted Bundy. Meg was deeply in love with Ted from the start and wanted to one day marry him. She was totally unaware of the infatuation that he still held for Stephanie. Ted, however, was not yet ready for marriage because he felt there was still too much for him to accomplish.

Outwardly, Ted's life seemed to be changing for the better. He was more confident with high hopes for his future. Ted began sending out applications for various law schools, while at the same time he became active in politics. He worked on a campaign to re-elect a Washington governor, a position that allowed Ted to form bonds with politically powerful people in the Republican Party. Ted also did some voluntary work at a crisis clinic on a work-study programme. He was pleased with the path his life was taking at this time, everything seemed to be going in the right direction. He was even commended by the Seattle police for saving the life of a three-year-old boy who was drowning in a lake.

In 1973, during a business trip to California for the Washington Republican Party, Ted met up with his old flame Stephanie Brooks for a night out. Stephanie was amazed at the transformation in Ted. He was much more confident and mature. They met several times, unknown to Meg. During Ted's business trips he romantically courted Stephanie and she once again fell in love with him.

Ted raised the subject of marriage many times during that autumn and winter. But suddenly it all changed. Where once Ted lavished affection upon Stephanie, he was suddenly cold and despondent. It seemed as if Ted had lost all interest in her over the period of just a few weeks. Stephanie was undoubtedly confused as to the sudden change in Ted. In February 1974, with no warning or explanation Ted ended all contact with Stephanie. His plan of revenge worked. He rejected Stephanie as she had once rejected him. Stephanie was never to see or hear from Ted again.

A TIME OF TERROR

On December 6, 1973, a young couple stumbled across the remains of a 15-year-old girl in McKenny Park, Washington. Kathy Devine was last seen by friends on November 25, hitch-hiking to Oregon, trying to run away from home. Shortly after she began her journey Kathy met her death. She had been strangled, sodomized and her throat cut. A month after the discovery of the Devine girl came the attack of Joni Lenz, which was soon followed by an even more gruesome attack.

Left: *Lynda Ann Healy*

Lynda Ann Healy didn't show up for work or for dinner on January 31, 1974. Healy's parents immediately called the police and soon after their arrival, they discovered a mass of blood drenching Lynda Ann's mattress. They also found a nightdress close to the bed with blood on the collar.

During that spring and summer, seven more women students suddenly and inexplicably vanished within the states of Utah, Oregon and Washington. There were striking similarities among many of the cases – all the girls were white, thin, single and wearing slacks, had long hair parted in the middle, and they all disappeared in the evening. Police interviews of college students revealed that they had seen a strange man wearing a cast on either his arm or leg. Others reported a strange man in the campus car park who had a cast and asked for assistance with his car. A man wearing a cast was also spotted in the same area where two of the girls mysteriously disappeared.

Finally, in August of 1974 in Lake Sammamish State Park, Washington State, the remains of some of the

SHE WAS NOT ASLEEP, AS HER ROOMMATES HAD THOUGHT WHEN THEY APPROACHED THE BED OF JONI LENZ ON THE AFTERNOON OF JANUARY 4, 1974. THEY FOUND HER LYING IN A POOL OF BLOOD THAT WAS SEEPING FROM HER HEAD AND FACE.

missing girls were found and two were later identified. It was remarkable that police were able to identify two of the bodies considering what was left. The girls identified were Janice Ott and Denise Naslund who disappeared on the same day, July 14th.

The similarities between the Washington State and Oregon murders caught the attention of local police in Utah, who were frantically searching for the man responsible for these awful crimes. The evidence was slowly mounting and Utah police consulted with Oregon and Washington State investigators. Almost all agreed that it was highly likely that the same man who committed the crimes in Oregon and Washington State had been responsible for the killings in Utah.

When Lynn Banks, a close friend of Meg Anders, saw the account of Melissa Smith's murder in the paper and the composite picture in the paper of the could-be-killer, she knew Ted Bundy must be the man. Meg also had to agree that the sketch of the killer did resemble Ted, yet she couldn't believe the man she loved and lived with could do such horrible things. Hesitantly, she contacted the police on the advice of her friend. Meg was one of five people to have turned in Ted Bundy's name to police. Her report, along with the others, was filed away and forgotten until a few years later. Police were so inundated with tips that when they came to Ted Bundy, an apparently respectable man, they set him aside to investigate other more likely suspects.

It wasn't until November 8, 1974, that police investigators were to get the break in the case for which they had been waiting.

CAROL DARONCH

One rainy night in November 1974, Carol DaRonch was window-shopping in Salt Lake City, Utah when she was approached by a man in his twenties who said he was a policeman. He asked her if she had left her car in the car park and asked for her registration number.

The plain-clothes policeman said a man had been arrested for trying to break into her car and asked if she could come and see if anything had been stolen. But she became suspicious as they walked to the car park because he did not seem to know the way.

The 17-year-old then asked him for proof of his identity and he produced his wallet and showed her what appeared to be a police badge. When they got to the car – and found nothing stolen – he asked her to accompany him to police headquarters to make a statement. He led the way to his own car, an old Volkswagen Beetle, and she

Above: *Ted Bundy drove around in a Volkswagen Beetle and used such ruses as feigning a broken arm to seek help from women. He would then lead his victims into his car and to their death.*

became suspicious again and asked for his name. The man said he was Officer Roseland of the Murray Police Department. He was so convincing that she got into the Beetle and they drove off.

A LUCKY ESCAPE

She began to panic when she smelt alcohol on his breath and realised he was driving in the opposite direction to the police station. When he stopped briefly in a side street, she reached for the door handle and tried to get out. But he was too quick for her and he snapped a handcuff on one wrist but was unable to secure the other one.

She continued to struggle and he pulled out a gun and threatened to shoot her. Then Carol's instincts took over – she pulled the door open, clambered out and began to run. The man began chasing her, but he stopped when a car turned into the street. He got back in his VW and sped off.

Carol had been lucky, but Bundy was determined to claim a victim. Later that night he abducted and murdered 17-year-old Debbie Kent. And she would not be the last of his victims . . .

Bundy's first victim was Lynda Healy, 21, a psychology student at the University of Washington in Seattle, who was abducted from her basement flat.

Five more young women vanished from the Seattle area in the spring and summer of 1974, but the case did not merit national newspaper headlines until July, when two girls disappeared from Lake Sammamish State Park on the same day.

SEATTLE

It had been a sunny day and the park, 12 miles from downtown Seattle, had been crowded with people walking their dogs, sailing boats and enjoying picnics. Several women reported having seen a man, calling himself Ted, with an arm in a sling. He had been asking for help with his boat. Doris Grayling had accompanied him to his

ONE OF THE MOST FEARED SERIAL KILLERS IN AMERICAN HISTORY, TED BUNDY WAS KNOWN IN SOME CIRCLES AS 'THE CHARMER' DUE TO HIS POLITE AND WELL-SPOKEN MANNER.

BUNDY NEARLY ESCAPED DEATH BY THE CHAIR WHEN IT WAS DISCOVERED THAT HE WAS A MANIC-DEPRESSIVE, BUT IN THE END, NOT EVEN THAT COULD SAVE HIM FROM EXECUTION.

brown VW, but then became suspicious and left.

Two other women, however, Janice Ott, 23, and Denise Naslund, 19, must have fallen for Bundy's trick, and they were never seen alive again. The double murder struck terror into women in Seattle but Bundy, having finished his psychology degree, was about to leave the city and move to Salt Lake City to study law.

It wouldn't be long before Bundy continued his murder spree. In October, he claimed his first Utah victim. Three more killings followed that first murder and another happened in the ski resort of Snowmass in neighbouring Colorado.

DISCOVERED BY CHANCE

In the early hours of August 16, 1975, Bundy was stopped while driving without lights in a Salt Lake City suburb. Bundy's evasive answers fuelled the suspicions of Utah Highway Patrolman Bob Hayward, who soon discovered a balaclava, a stocking mask, an iron bar and a pair of handcuffs on the floor of the car.

Bundy was arrested but he remained cool under pressure and explained away the items, saying he needed the balaclava and mask for skiing and had found the handcuffs in a rubbish bin. A search of Bundy's flat uncovered a brochure from a hotel in Snowmass.

Bundy denied having been to Colorado but by now the police were beginning to see through his harmless, self-confident exterior. Bundy was ordered to attend an identity parade and was picked out by Carol DaRonch and two other witnesses. It seemed that Ted Bundy had been caught.

He was convicted of the aggravated kidnapping of Carol DaRonch and was jailed for 15 years. In June 1977 he jumped out of the window of a court building and escaped, only to be recaptured eight days later. The authorities in Colorado were confident they could put him on trial for the murder of Caryn Campbell, the girl who was killed in Snowmass at the height of the skiing season.

But in December 1977 Bundy escaped again – this time by cutting a hole in the ceiling of his cell with a hacksaw blade and this time he would not be caught so easily.

BUNDY ON THE RUN

Bundy fled east and by mid-January was in sunny Florida, 1,500 miles from chilly Colorado. By now he had adopted a new identity. Bundy was no longer the dapper, mild-mannered Republican, he had become an unkempt fugitive from justice, whose murderous urges were out of control.

On January 15 he broke into a sorority house on a university campus in Tallahassee, Florida. He strangled 21-year-old art history student Margaret Brown and beat to death Lisa Levy, 20, after assaulting her. Two other girls who lived in the house had also been beaten with a wooden club but they survived.

A month later Bundy claimed what would be his final victim, 12-year-old Kim Leach. She was abducted from a high school gym, sexually assaulted and strangled. Bundy's days as a free man were, however, numbered.

RECAPTURED

Bundy was finally arrested in the early hours of February 15, 1978, as he drove a stolen car, an orange VW, towards Pensacola, and in June 1979, he went on trial for the sorority house murders. Bundy protested his innocence and conducted his own defence.

The evidence for the prosecution - including evidence from a dentist that his teeth matched bite marks found on Lisa Levy – was overwhelming and the jury found him guilty, sentencing him to death.

Bundy spent the next ten years on Florida's Death Row, using legal tactics to delay his execution and offering confessions to his crimes in exchange for a reprieve. After years of living in denial – insisting his innocence – Bundy finally confessed to the murders of 28 women. However, many believe the number of deaths to be much higher.

No one will ever really know how many women fell victim to Ted Bundy; it would be a number he would take to his grave. After countless appeals, Ted was finally executed on January 24, 1989.

Above: *Theodore R. Bundy (right) is taken from a Pensacola jail by Pensacola police Captain Raymond Harper, following his arrest on February 15, 1978 for driving a stolen car.*

DONALD NEILSON
The Black Panther

For three years police pursued a man who committed sixteen robberies and four murders and terrorized a large part of England. But the real Donald Neilson was very far from the hooded 'Black Panther' image of popular imagination

On the evening of 13 January 1975, seventeen-year-old Lesley Whittle was at home alone and went to bed early. She lived with her widowed mother, but on this particular night Mrs Dorothy Whittle was out for the evening. When she did return to her comfortable home in the village of Highley, Shropshire at 1.30a.m., Mrs Whittle made a point of checking her daughter's bedroom. Lesley was sound asleep.

HOODED FIGURE CLAD IN BLACK

Shortly after Mrs Whittle herself retired to bed, a man forced the lock on the garage door. He was dressed from head to foot in black and was wearing a hood. Working silently and in total darkness, the intruder cut the telephone line and then moved into the house. Passing through the living room, he climbed the stairs and made his way directly to Lesley's room.

Lesley Whittle was woken by a hand shaking her roughly. She looked up to see the black-clad figure standing over her, pointing a sawn-off shotgun in her face. Lesley lay transfixed as the intruder taped her mouth, and indicated that she should get out of bed. He led Lesley downstairs and outside to a waiting car, a green Morris 1300. He laid her on the back seat, bound her wrists and ankles and placed tape over her eyes.

The intruder then removed his hood, got into the driving seat and set off on a sixty-mile trip to his hiding place. He drove down the M6 motorway, turned off at Junction 16 and drove to Bathpool Park, near Kidsgrove. He parked the car alongside the access shaft of the town's drainage system, removed the manhole cover and forced Lesley to climb 65 feet down a rusty ladder.

When they reached a tiny platform, on which he had installed a foam rubber mattress, the kidnapper removed Lesley's dressing gown, placed a wire noose around her neck and clamped it to the wall. Below, the access shaft fell away. If Lesley were to slip she would hang.

The kidnapper then made his next move in an elaborate plan to extort money from his victim's family. He

Above: *Lesley Whittle's disappearance prompted a nation-wide hunt.*

Opposite: *The Black Panther. A model dressed in the outfit adopted by Donald Neilson.*

uncovered Lesley's eyes, proffered a memo machine, and instructed her to read two messages which he had written on a pad.

Lesley did not know her kidnapper. She had never laid eyes on him before in her life. His name was Donald Neilson.

The name would have meant nothing to her. It would have meant little to the police either, even though they had been chasing him for more than three years, during which time he had been responsible for armed robberies and the murder of three sub-postmasters. Yet they only knew him by a nickname.

No one knew it yet, but Lesley Whittle had been kidnapped by the 'Black Panther'.

HOAXES AND MISTAKES

On the morning of 14 January, Mrs Dorothy Whittle woke to find her daughter missing. She was more puzzled than alarmed. Lesley had been safely tucked up in her bed at 1.30. Nothing bad could have happened to her since then. Mrs Whittle checked round the house and then tried to telephone her son, Ronald.

The phone, of course, had been cut. But, assuming it was merely out of order, Dorothy Whittle drove to her son's house at the other end of the village.

Neither Ronald nor his wife Gaynor had seen Lesley that morning. Mrs Whittle was now becoming uneasy.

Gaynor drove back home with Mrs Whittle, and the two women checked the house more carefully in the hope of finding a note. They found a note all right, but it wasn't from Lesley.

In a cardboard box, resting on a flower vase in the lounge, they discovered a long roll of Dymo tape. There were three messages carefully typed into the coloured plastic. The messages were ransom demands.

The first read: 'No police £50,000 ransom to be ready to deliver wait for phone call at Swan shopping centre telephone box 6 p.m. to 1 a.m. if no call return following evening when you answer give your name only and listen you must follow instructions without argument from the time you answer you are on a time limit if police or tricks death.'

Above: *The access shaft to the sewer system at Bathpool Park where Neilson held, and finally murdered, Lesley Whittle.*

Despite the warning in the note, Mrs Whittle did not hesitate to call the police. Within an hour the case was being led by the head of West Mercia CID, Detective Chief Superintendent Bob Booth.

He was in no doubt that this was a professional kidnapping. Lesley was a logical target. Two years earlier she had been the beneficiary of a large and highly publicized inheritance.

Booth advised the Whittle family that their best chance of getting Lesley back alive was to comply fully with the kidnapper's demands.

While Ronald Whittle, who owned a successful coach company, was raising the money, Booth had his own elaborate arrangements to make. He installed taps on the phones at Mrs Whittle's home and the phone box at Kidderminster.

After midday, Booth and his detectives were joined by a team of kidnap specialists from Scotland Yard.

Shortly after 5p.m. Ronald Whittle, armed with a white suitcase full of money, installed himself in the phone box at Kidderminster, and waited.

The police, who were watching Whittle from a discreet distance, hoped to have the whole episode dealt with that night, but it was not to be. A freelance journalist had somehow got wind of the operation and started making a nuisance of himself.

Rather than alerting the kidnapper to the fact that the police were indeed involved, Booth decided to abort the mission.

The following evening, Ronald Whittle returned to the phone box with the money. Shortly after 8 p.m., the police called him out again. They had received a call from a man claiming to be the kidnapper and had been given delivery instructions for the ransom money. The call, however, proved to be a hoax.

Meanwhile, another drama was unfolding. Donald Neilson left his hideout in the drains of Bathpool Park and did a dummy run of the route he had mapped out for the ransom carrier. He travelled to Dudley in Worcestershire, stopping at various telephone boxes to conceal more Dymo tape instructions.

In Dudley itself, he decided to check over the final drop-off point, the Freightliner depot. He was browsing around when he was challenged by the night supervisor, Gerald Smith.

Neilson shot Smith six times. He then ran from the scene, abandoning his stolen Morris car.

When local police investigated the shooting, they failed to check the car. This was a tragic oversight, because the boot of the car was a positive treasure trove of clues.

Amazingly, Gerald Smith survived the shooting – though he died fourteen months later as a result of his wounds – and was able to give the police a description of his assailant. What he told them left police in no doubt that he was the victim of the 'Black Panther'.

At 11.45 p.m. on the night of 16 January, the third day of the kidnap, Leonard Rudd, transport manager of Whittle's Coaches, received a telephone call. On the other end of the line was Lesley Whittle's recorded voice instructing the courier to take the ransom money to a phone box at Kidsgrove.

Ronald Whittle was extensively briefed by Detective Chief Super-intendent Lovejoy of Scotland Yard.

Whittle reached the Kidsgrove telephone box shortly after 3 a.m., and waited there for half an hour before discovering another Dymo message. It read: 'Go up road to Acres Nook sign. Go up Boathouse Road turn right into public footpath deadend go into entry service area. Drive past wall and flash headlights looking for torchlight run to torch instructions on torch. Go home wait for telephone.'

Below: *The boot of Neilson's Morris car yielded a host of clues for police.*

Ronald Whittle got back into his car and followed the directions. After a few minutes he arrived at Bathpool Park. He flashed his headlights and waited for the torch signal. It never came.

Donald Neilson had been watching as Ronald Whittle arrived, and was immediately suspicious. He could smell police.

Certain that he would never now get his hands on the ransom money, he flew into a rage. As soon as Whittle had left he climbed back down the drainage access shaft, pushed Lesley Whittle off her precarious platform and left her to hang by her neck until she died.

By dawn, he was on the train north to his home in Bradford.

VITAL NEW EVIDENCE

Most of Booth's and Lovejoy's efforts now centred around the village of Highly, where the abduction had taken place. Everyone in the village and the surrounding area was interviewed. But this revealed absolutely nothing.

And then, on 23 January, a week after the last abortive attempt to deliver the ransom money, a police constable patrolling the Freightliner depot at Dudley became interested in a green Morris 1300. He noticed it had been parked in the same spot for several days.

The car was towed into the police station and searched. The boot revealed startling new evidence. There were a tape recorder containing a tape of Lesley Whittle's voice, a gun, torches and a foam mattress. A ballistic examination of the gun confirmed that it had been used in the 'Black Panther' raids.

As the days passed, Detective Chief Superintendent Booth felt sure that Bathpool Park was probably the most important location they had encountered in their investigation, and he was determined to search it thoroughly. To this end, he planned an elaborate ruse.

On the evening of 5 March, Booth appeared on a television news programme with Ronald Whittle and the two men acted out a pre-rehearsed confrontation. Whittle described how he had gone to Bathpool Park on the night of 16 January. Booth, pretending this was

Above: *A press conference given by the police during the hunt for the 'Black Panther'.*

the first he had heard of the abortive rendezvous, flew into a rage and stormed out of the studio. The effect was to make Booth look extremely foolish. In fact, the deception gave him the excuse he had been looking for to search the park.

At dawn the following day, the police moved into Bathpool Park. At first their search yielded nothing. But then, two schoolboys came forward with a torch they had found there a few weeks earlier. Wrapped around the handle was a strip of Dymo tape which read: 'Drop suitcase into hole.'

On the next day, Friday, 7 March, Police Constable Paul Allen removed the manhole cover of the drainage system and climbed slowly down. He had descended about twenty feet when he paused and shone his torch downwards.

He was confronted with the grisly spectacle of Lesley Whittle's naked body, hanging from its wire noose.

UNITED AGAINST THE PANTHER

Up to this point, different teams of police had been working on 'Black Panther' murders in Accrington, Harrogate and Langley, as well as the team investigating the kidnap of Lesley Whittle. There had been close cooperation between the forces, but now it was decided to form a single 'Black Panther' task force under Scotland Yard's murder squad.

The murder squad took over Kidsgrove police station, and 800 officers were drafted in to interview every one of the town's 22,000 population.

In an attempt to solicit help from the public, a local actor was dressed in black and drove the green Morris along the route thought to have been taken by the Panther. The reconstruction was shown on national television and attracted more than a thousand phone calls. Scores of names were submitted but the name Donald Neilson was not among them.

Nine months passed, and the murder squad were no nearer identifying the 'Black Panther'.

On Thursday, 11 December, Donald Neilson finally obliged them. It was 11 p.m. and Constables Stuart McKenzie and Tony White were sitting in their Panda car in Mansfield Woodhouse, Nottingham, when they caught sight of a man with a hold-all loitering outside the Four Ways public house.

McKenzie did a U-turn and pulled up alongside Neilson. White got out of the car and asked him what his name was, and what he was doing. Neilson smiled, gave them a name and a local address, and said he was on his way home from work. Still suspicious, White asked him to write down his particulars.

Suddenly Neilson produced a sawn-off shotgun from under his coat. He forced White into the back seat of the Panda car and got into the front passenger seat himself. He instructed McKenzie to drive to Blidworth, a village six miles away.

As they drove, White in the back noticed the shotgun waver away from his partner's side. He lunged forward and grabbed the barrel of the gun. McKenzie slammed on the brakes; the shotgun went off, blowing a hole in the roof of the car.

The Panda screeched to a halt outside a fish and chip shop, which was still open. As the two constables wrestled with Neilson, two customers, Keith Wood and

Above: *Police sniffer dogs search for clues in the murder of Lesley Whittle.*

As White grabbed the gun barrel his partner slammed on the brakes - the shotgun blew a hole in the car roof

Above: *The diminutive figure of Donald Neilson, head covered, is led away from the committal proceedings.*

THE JURY WATCHED IN OPEN-MOUTHED HORROR AS THE DEFENDANT RELATED HIS GHASTLY CRIMES IN MATTER-OF-FACT DETAIL

Roy Morris, rushed over to help.

Despite his diminutive stature, Neilson fought ferociously and it took all four of them to subdue him. A few minutes later, other police cars arrived on the scene. Donald Neilson was driven the 70 miles to Kidsgrove police station.

Neilson was questioned for twelve hours before he finally admitted to the abduction of Lesley Whittle.

The burning question for the police was, just who was this man Donald Neilson? For a man who had terrorized an entire region, he did not cut a very impressive figure – forty years old, 5 ft 4 ins tall, and slightly built.

Yet, over the previous ten years, he had committed more than four hundred robberies – sixteen on sub-post offices – and had killed four people. All this, and he had never so much as been questioned by police.

The secret of his 'success', the police were to discover, was discipline and meticulous planning, qualities he had developed courtesy of Her Majesty's armed forces. In 1955–7 Neilson had spent his National Service in the King's Own Yorkshire Light Infantry, where he rose to the rank of lance corporal and served in Kenya, Aden and Cyprus.

At the time of his arrest, Neilson lived a quiet life with his wife Irene and their fifteen-year-old daughter Kathryn at their terraced house on the outskirts of Bradford. He made a modest living as a jobbing carpenter and, according to his neighbours, had no enemies and few friends.

WHEN LIFE MEANS LIFE

The trial of Donald Neilson began on 14 August 1976 at Oxford Crown Court. In addition to the murder of Lesley Whittle, Neilson stood charged with the murder of three sub-postmasters – Donald Skepper of Harrogate, Derek Askin of Accrington and Sidney Gray-land of Langley – all of whom had been shot to death in 1974. He was defended by Gilbert Gray QC and entered a plea of Not Guilty to all four charges.

Neilson's behaviour in court was nothing short of extraordinary. He maintained his military posture throughout the trial, standing smartly to attention and answering questions with a brisk 'Yes, sir,' or 'No, sir'.

Neilson seemed to have the idea that by being calm, precise and matter-of-fact he could persuade the court that he was the victim of a ghastly misunderstanding. At no time did he show one iota of sadness or remorse.

When it came to the murder of the three sub-postmasters, Neilson again tried to portray himself as the victim of misfortune. On all three occasions, he claimed, the gun he was carrying had gone off accidentally.

All in all, it was one of the most feeble defences ever presented to a British criminal court, and the jury wasted no time in returning a verdict of Guilty on all charges.

Sentencing Donald Neilson to life imprisonment, Mr Justice Mars-Jones would not set a minimum number of years. 'In your case,' he said, 'life must mean life. If you are ever released from prison it should only be on account of great age or infirmity.'

CRIMES
OF
HORROR

PETER SUTCLIFFE
The Yorkshire Ripper

In the 1970s Yorkshire women were terrorized by a serial killer who, like the notorious Jack the Ripper, inflicted hideous mutilations on his victims. Was Peter Sutcliffe a paranoid schizophrenic, or just 'a wilfully evil bastard'?

Late on the afternoon of 22 May 1981, a dark-haired, bearded, scruffy little man rose to his feet in the dock beneath the dome of Number One Court at the Old Bailey to hear judgement passed upon him.

Found guilty of murdering thirteen women, and attempting to murder seven others, thirty-five-year-old Peter William Sutcliffe, 'The Yorkshire Ripper', was sentenced to life imprisonment with a recommendation that he should serve at least thirty years.

AN ORDINARY MURDER

The Ripper murders began in 1975 in the rundown Chapeltown area of Leeds. A milkman spotted a frosted bundle of what appeared to be rags on the white-rimmed grass. He went and peered at it. It was a woman's body.

She lay on her back, her dyed blonde hair dark and spiky with dried blood. Her jacket and blouse had been torn open and her bra pulled up, revealing breasts and abdomen, and her trousers were round her knees, though her pants were still in position. Her torso had been stabbed and slashed fourteen times, after her death from two crushing hammer blows to the back of the skull.

The dead woman's name was Wilma McCann. She was twenty-eight years

old, and what the police classed as a 'good time girl'. Because Mrs McCann's purse was missing, West Yorkshire Metropolitan Police treated the case as murder in the pursuance of robbery. Despite the brutality of the attack there seemed no other motive. Yet, when another murder was committed just over two and half months later, the similarities convinced the police that they were dealing with a double murderer.

ANOTHER GOOD TIME GIRL

Emily Jackson, like Wilma McCann, came to Chapeltown only once or twice a week to sell herself on a casual basis.

Her body was discovered in the early

Left: *Peter Sutcliffe at seven years old.*

Opposite: *Peter Sutcliffe, the Yorkshire Ripper, on his wedding day.*

THE MILKMAN THOUGHT THE PILE OF RAGS WAS AN ABANDONED GUY FAWKES FIGURE – WHEN HE LOOKED, HE SAW IT WAS A WOMAN'S BODY

Below: *Peter and Sonia Sutcliffe with friends on holiday.*

morning of 21 January 1976. She had also been killed from behind by two blows from a heavy hammer. Her breasts were exposed and her trousers pulled down, though again her pants were in place. On her right thigh was stamped the impression of a heavily ribbed wellington boot. The only solid clue the police had so far was that the perpetrator took size seven in shoes.

SERIAL KILLER ON THE LOOSE

No progress was made on either case, and a year passed by. Then, on 5 February, 1977, the killer struck again. Another 'good-time girl', twenty-eight-year-old Irene Richardson, was discovered by a jogger on Soldiers' Field, not far from Chapeltown. She was lying on her face and had died from three hammer blows to the back of her skull. Her killer had stripped her from the waist downwards. Her neck and chest had been subjected to a frenzied knife attack. The pattern of wounds now left no doubt that the police were dealing with a serial killer.

This alarmed the street-girl population, and their numbers in Chapeltown declined. Not so, however, in the red light district of Bradford, some ten miles away, where 'Tina' Atkinson lived and worked. On Sunday, 24 April, Tina's friends called for her at her flat, but got no answer. She had been out boozing the night before, and the door was ajar so they went in. Tina lay naked on her bed, the back of her head crushed by four hammer blows. Seven knife wounds had lacerated her stomach, and her side had been slashed open.

Any doubts about the killer's identity were dispelled by a clue found imprinted on the bottom bedsheet. It was the mark of a size seven wellington boot, identical with the imprint found on Emily Jackson's thigh.

The police believed that the killer was specifically targeting prostitutes and so began touring the red light districts, questioning street girls about any regulars who might have acted suspiciously. But, it soon became clear

*Above: **Police examine the scene where Emily Jackson was murdered.***

IT WAS WOUNDED MALE PRIDE THAT HAD LED SUTCLIFFE TO CARRY OUT HIS FIRST 'REVENGE' ATTACK ON A PROSTITUTE

Below: *Assistant Chief Constable George Oldfield and Superintendent Richard Holland at a 'Ripper' press conference.*

that the Yorkshire Ripper regarded any woman out alone at night as fair game.

THE RIPPER SPREADS HIS NET

On Sunday, 26 June 1977, a sixteen-year-old girl named Jayne MacDonald was found slumped and dead in a street on the fringes of Chapeltown. She had sustained at least three hammer blows to the head. She had been stabbed once in the back and several times through the chest. But she was no prostitute or good-time girl. A fortnight later, a Bradford housewife, Maureen Long, was struck down near her home but miraculously survived.

The police stepped up their enquiries. Three hundred and four officers were assigned to the case. And to hear them, veteran detective George Oldfield, Assistant Chief Constable (Crime), came out from behind his desk at administrative HQ in Wakefield.

The next time the Ripper struck he changed his location and killing pattern, but left a vital clue.

On 1 October 1977, Jean Bernadette Jordan, was picked up near her home in Moss Side, Manchester and driven by her murderer to the Southern Cemetery two miles away. She demanded £5 in advance and was paid with a crisp new note, which she stored in her purse.

As she climbed from the Ripper's car on to allotment land adjoining the large cemetery, Mrs Jordan was knocked to the ground with a hammer blow and beaten eleven times more. Then she was pulled into a clump of bushes. Disturbed by a car, the killer then fled.

The £5 note had been given to Sutcliffe in his wage packet two days before the attack. He realized that it might be a valuable clue, so eight days later returned to the scene. He searched in vain for the handbag, then attacked the decaying body with a shard of glass.

Below: *Police search the alley where the body of Barbara Leach was discovered.*

Bottom: *Police search for clues in their hunt for the Yorkshire Ripper.*

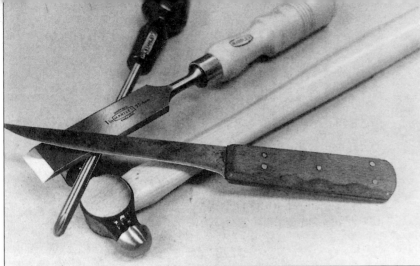

Two days after the second attack, Mrs Jordan's remains were discovered along with the missing handbag which had fallen among the bushes. The £5 note, serial number AW51 121565, was traced to the wage packets of the road haulage firm T. and W. H. Clark. One of their drivers was Peter Sutcliffe, who had worked there since October 1976.

LIVING VICTIMS

Detectives visited Sutcliffe at his home. He seemed a steady, quiet man, and the officers left, satisfied that he was not the Ripper.

But had they had time and reason to do so, they would have discovered from old Bradford City Police files that Peter Sutcliffe had once been questioned by police regarding an attack back in August 1969. This first attack was not quite motiveless. Earlier that summer he had suspected his girlfriend Sonia of seeing another man. To 'get even', he had approached a Bradford prostitute, but had been unable to maintain an erection. The woman had laughed at him, taken his £10, and got her pimp to chase him away.

In August he had seen her in the St Paul's red light district, crept after her, and hit her violently on the back of the head with a stone in a sock. The woman had noted the number of his van, and Sutcliffe had been traced. But because he had no record, he had been let off with a caution.

Since then he had left five women damaged but alive. Each of these living victims had tried to describe their attacker. One described him as thirtyish,

Above left: Peter Sutcliffe's murder weapons could have been bought at any local hardware store.

Above: The bus stop at Leeds' Arndale Shopping Centre where Jacqueline Hill was accosted and murdered by the Yorkshire Ripper.

about 5 ft 10 ins tall, and bearded. Another had described him accurately as having a black, crinkly beard.

On the evening of 21 January 1978, a twenty-two-year-old 'career' prostitute named Yvonne Pearson was seen in Bradford, climbing into a car driven by a man described as having a dark beard and black, piercing eyes - it was Sutcliffe. He took her to waste ground in Arthington Street, killed her with a club hammer and jumped on her chest until her ribs cracked. He then piled an old abandoned horsehair sofa on top of her. About a month later, when the body remained undiscovered, Sutcliffe returned and placed a current copy of

The Daily Mirror under one of her mouldering arms. Between this killing and the newspaper incident he had also paid a visit to Huddersfield.

On the snowy night of Tuesday, 31 January 1978, Sutcliffe picked up Helen Rytka. They went into a timber yard under railway arches near the centre of the town and, uncharacteristically, Sutcliffe managed to have intercourse with her before killing her in his usual fashion.

Immediately after this murder, the police were optimistic. Helen's abduction had taken place in the early evening on a busy street. But despite tracing a hundred passers by, and with all but three cars and one man eliminated, there was no real result.

The police were convinced that the Ripper lived in the locality of Leeds or Bradford, but they little realized that, by the end of 1978, they had interviewed him no fewer than four times. Apart from two visits concerning the £5 note clue, they had called at his home because routine checks had turned up Sutcliffe's car registration in red light areas. They also called to check on tyre tracks to compare them with some found near the scene of Irene Richardson's murder.

But they did not check two vital clues they knew about the Ripper against Sutcliffe. The Ripper was a B secretor – a rare blood type. And he took size seven boots – very small for a man.

Above: *Peter and Sonia Sutcliffe's house in Garden Lane, Heston, Bradford.*

On the night of 16 May 1978, two months after Yvonne Pearson's body was found, Sutcliffe killed Vera Millward, a forty-one-year-old prostitute. He then waited eleven months before he killed again. His next victim was nineteen-year-old Josephine Whittaker, a clerk in the Halifax Building Society headquarters. She was attacked and killed with sickeningly familiar ferocity.

TAUNTS AND HOAXES

Between Josephine's death and September of the same year there was another lull. This time it was filled by a brutal hoax which almost certainly cost three women their lives.

Since March 1978 George Oldfield had received two letters supposedly

OBSESSED WITH THE 'SUNDERLAND CONNECTION', THE POLICE DISREGARDED ONE OFFICER'S DEEP SUSPICIONS OF SUTCLIFFE

Left: *Police dig up Peter Sutcliffe's garden shortly after his arrest on suspicion of being the Yorkshire Ripper.*

from the Ripper. Shortly before the Whittaker murder a third letter came, mentioning Vera Millward's death. All three letters were postmarked from Sunderland. On the third, traces of engineering oil, similar to traces found on Josephine Whittaker's body, were discovered. This seemed to confirm that the letters were written by the Ripper.

When, on 18 June 1979, a tape recording addressed in the same handwriting as the letters was received, West Yorkshire police were convinced that this was their man. The tape, a taunting message to Oldfield, was in a broad Geordie accent. Therefore, the West Yorkshire police became convinced that anyone without a Geordie accent could be eliminated from their enquiry. This, of course, put Sutcliffe temporarily in the clear.

In July Sutcliffe was visited by Detective Constable Laptew, who had noticed that his car had been spotted in one red light area on thirty-six separate occasions. Laptew was deeply suspicious of Sutcliffe but he went unheeded by his superiors who were convinced their killer was a Geordie. As a result, Sutcliffe went on to kill three more times.

On 1 September 1979 Sutcliffe ambushed and killed a social sciences student named Barbara Leach.

On 18 August 1980 his victim was forty-seven-year-old civil servant Margaret Walls. Because she had been bludgeoned and strangled, but not mutilated further, the Ripper Squad were reluctant to add her to their list of victims. But there was no question of the authenticity of his thirteenth and final slaying.

Below: *There was tight security as a crowd assembled to watch the arrival of Peter Sutcliffe at Dewsbury Magistrates' Court.*

Left: *Police help Sonia Sutcliffe as she enters Dewsbury Court for her husband's hearing.*

SUTCLIFFE CLAIMED THAT A VOICE IN A GRAVEYARD HAD ORDERED HIM TO GO OUT AND KILL PROSTITUTES

Below: *Peter Sutcliffe after being attacked in prison.*

Twenty-year-old Jacqueline Hill, a language student at Leeds University, was walking home when she was dragged by Sutcliffe on to waste land and savaged with a hammer, a knife and a screwdriver. This brutal death caused a backlash of frustration among the public and police.

The Home Office set up a 'super squad' of four outside detectives and a forensic scientist. The idea was that this team should review the evidence. They did make some progress, but eventually, it was by chance that Peter Sutcliffe was caught. On 2 January 1981, two police officers were cruising along Melbourne Avenue, Sheffield – a haunt of prostitutes – when they saw a girl getting into a Rover V8 3500. They stopped the driver, a short, bearded man, who gave his name as Peter Williams. It was discovered that his number plates were false and had been stolen from that town.

The bushes in Melbourne Avenue were searched, and officers found a ball-pen hammer and a knife, which eventually were to be matched to the Ripper's crimes. Then Sutcliffe finally confessed to the Dewsbury police. 'I'm glad it's all over. I would have killed that girl if I hadn't been caught.'

What made him do it? Some experts argued that he was a paranoid schizophrenic who had little control over the delusions and impulses that haunted him, while one of the Home Office pathologists who worked on the case echoed the thoughts of the general public: 'He was quite simply a wilfully evil bastard.'

While awaiting trial in Armley gaol, Leeds, Sutcliffe was overheard by a warder planning with his wife Sonia that he would fake 'madness' and 'be out in ten years'. As it was, his plot failed. He was sent to Parkhurst maximum security prison on the Isle of Wight.

Peter Sutcliffe's mental condition did begin to deteriorate, and in March 1984 he was moved to Ward One of Somerset House, Broadmoor Institution for the Criminally Insane, where he remains.

IAN HUNTLEY
Child Killer

The mother of Holly Wells could not have known that when she took the picture of her 10 year-old daughter with best friend Jessica Chapman at just after 5p.m. on Sunday, August 4 2002, in their beloved Manchester United football shirts, it would be a photo which would dominate front pages of both national and international newspapers for weeks to come – used first in the search for two missing girls and then in the hunt for their murderer.

The truth of exactly what horror befell Jessica Chapman and Holly Wells after leaving Holly's house on that fateful day may never be completely revealed.

'TEENAGERS SCREAMING'

There were just two confirmed sightings of the girls before they simply vanished. The first, at 6.17pm, was CCTV footage, which showed them walking happily together across the car park of the Ross Peers sports centre in Soham. The second, and last, sighting was at 6.30p.m. when they were seen walking along Sand Street by somebody who knew them. A jogger claims to have heard what he believed to be 'teenagers screaming' between 10 and 11p.m. in the Warren Hill area near to Newmarket, but did not report it to the police until two days later.

The alarm was raised at 7.30 p.m. by Holly's parents when they realised that the girls were not upstairs playing, as they had originally thought. Consequently, at the break of dawn the following morning, police and volunteers began the search for the girls in Soham, and by midday, following the broadcast of a national appeal, the search was on not only in

Above: The last ever photograph of Holly Wells and Jessica Chapman alive. After the photograph was taken, they changed into trousers and set off on a walk from which they were never to return

Above: Reward posters for Holly Wells and Jessica Chapman are shown outside St. Andrew's Church in Soham, Cambridgeshire

Below: Parents of murdered Soham schoolgirls Holly Wells and Jessica Chapman, Kevin and Nicola Wells and Leslie and Sharon Chapman hold a press conference

Soham but across the country. By the end of the day, the girls' parents had attended a press conference in which they appealed for information regarding their daughters' safety and whereabouts. The police search continued into the night.

NATIONWIDE SEARCH

The girls' disappearance triggered one of the biggest police searches in British history. Hundreds of local people, friends and neighbours had joined the police in the search for the girls, and amongst the volunteers was 29 year-old Ian Huntley, the caretaker at Soham Village College, which occupied the same site as the primary school that the girls attended. He not only helped in the search, but also informed the police that he too had seen the girls on the day they went missing. He told them how the girls had come to his door, 'happy' and 'giggly', and he had watched them walk away and continue down the road. He spoke to the media and even sought out Holly Wells's father, 'Kev' as he called him, to offer his condolences.

On Tuesday August 6, the football star David Beckham joined the parents and families of the girls in appealing for Holly and Jessica to come home, and a reconstruction of the girls' last confirmed movements was filmed on Saturday August 10.

The news that everyone had been dreading came a week later, on August 17. Two naked and decomposing bodies had been found in a ditch in Lakenheath, Suffolk, approximately 10 miles from the village of Soham where the girls lived. The nation's worst fears were confirmed when the police announced that these were indeed the bodies of Holly and Jessica. The following week, the burnt remains of the clothing that the girls had been wearing when they disappeared was discovered by police in a bin in the Soham Village College.

THE CARING CARETAKER

It had very quickly become clear to the police that Ian Huntley, the Soham caretaker who had been so helpful with their enquires and who had been happy to talk to the media, was one of the last people to see the girls alive. They arrested him on the day the bodies of the two girls were found, and three days later he was charged with both of their murders. His girlfriend, Maxine Carr, a temporary teaching assistant in Holly and Jessica's class, was also arrested, although charged not in connection

Holly sat on the edge of the bath while he dampened a tissue to hold to her face. However, as he approached her with the tissue, he stumbled and bumped into her, causing her to fall backwards into the bath, already filled with approx 45cm of water. She banged her head as she fell which caused Jessica to begin screaming at Huntley accusing him of pushing her friend. To stop Jessica screaming, Huntley placed his hand over her mouth, where it remained until he realised that instead of simply calming the second little girl, her body was now limp and no longer supporting itself. As he let go of Jessica, her body slumped to the floor. He turned to the bath, where Holly's lifeless body lay. He checked her pulse, no longer beating, and then put his face close to Jessica's, where there was no longer breath. He said he 'panicked and froze' when he realised what had happened, unable even to attempt to revive them. His next memory of the events was being sat on the carpet in his bathroom, next to a pile of his own vomit. He knew he should call the police, he said, but also knew that they would never believe that such a tragedy had occurred when he failed to believe it himself.

Above: A cordoned off search area in Warren Hill, Suffolk. The area was investigated when a jogger claimed to have heard 'teenagers screaming' there on the night of the girls' disappearance

Left: The burnt remains of one of the red Manchester United shirts belonging to the two murdered ten year old girls which were found along with traces of Huntley's hair in the school grounds where he worked

with the murder of the girls, but for lying to the police and perverting the course of justice in providing a false alibi for Huntley's whereabouts on the day of the murder. Both denied the charges against them.

'PANICKED AND FROZE'

The court-case which lasted over a year, made headline news nationally and worldwide, and in it, Huntley did finally admit that the girls had died in his house. However, he denied murder. Rather, he claimed that the deaths of both girls were the result of a tragic sequence of events. He claims to have been outside his house washing his dog when the girls passed by, and he noticed that Holly was suffering with a nose bleed. He therefore invited the girls into his house and took them up to his bathroom, where he intended to curb the flow of blood from Holly's nose.

'ONE DIED AS A RESULT OF MY INABILITY TO ACT AND THE OTHER DIED AS A DIRECT RESULT OF MY ACTIONS'

He pleaded guilty to manslaughter only, but went on to concede all the other given facts of the case – that he had bundled the bodies of Holly and Jessica into his car, bending their legs to make them fit, cut the clothing from them - their red Manchester United shirts, trousers, underwear, the bra which Holly's mother had bought for her only the day before - and left the corpses to burn in a remote ditch

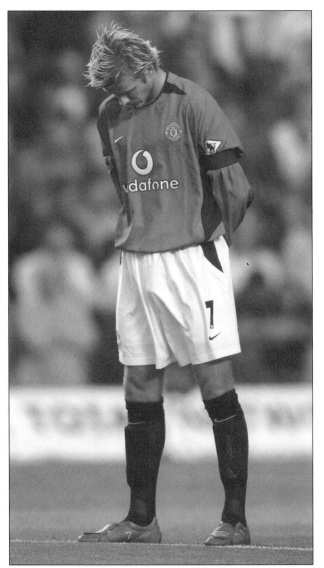

Above: Holly and Jessica's football hero, David Beckham, looks to the ground during the minute silence during the Barclaycard Premiership match between Chelsea and Manchester United in London on August 23, 2002, a tribute to the two murdered school children

Right: Flowers laid down in memory of Jessica and Holly

where the nettles grew thickly. He had then taken the girls' clothing and deposited it in a bin at Soham Village College.

Prosecutor Richard Latham supported this with forensic evidence that hairs, proven to be Huntley's, were found amongst the charred remains of the clothes in the bin, and that his fingerprints were present on the bin liner. He also presented evidence regarding Huntley's car. All four tyres on the car had been replaced the day following Jessica and Holly's disappearance. Latham claimed that this was to prevent his car being traced in any way to the girls' bodies.

Latham went on further to claim that Huntley's primary motive had been sexual. He asserts that the girls were lured into Huntley's house, possibly in the belief that Maxine Carr

was inside, and that when his advances towards one or the other had been rejected, both girls had had to die. 'They had to die in his own selfish self-interest. Each were potential witnesses - he was quite merciless.'

Huntley's version of events, that the death of the two girls had simply been the result of a tragic accident, was believed neither by the public, nor the jury who found him guilty on two counts of murder, the most serious of all the charges he could have faced, and when trial judge Justice Moses sentenced him to two life imprisonments a hushed 'yes' echoed around the courtroom. Moses told Huntley that he was '...the only person who knows how you murdered them.', and said that he displayed 'no regret' after the murders, even increasing the pain of the families by continuing to lie and deceive the police and investigators.

CATALOGUE OF OFFENCES

Information regarding Huntley's past had to be kept private during the trial in order not to influence the court, but on the conclusion of his case, a dark and disturbing catalogue of offences against children and teenagers was made public. It

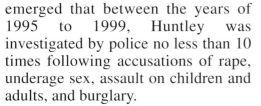

emerged that between the years of 1995 to 1999, Huntley was investigated by police no less than 10 times following accusations of rape, underage sex, assault on children and adults, and burglary.

Current regulations state that anybody applying to work with or around children has to undergo local police checks to ensure their suitability. Huntley's past went undetected by two police forces, Cambridgeshire and Humberside. Humberside, where the alleged offences had been reported, defended themselves by saying that the data protection act declares it unlawful to hold data concerning allegations which did not lead to a conviction. They have faced criticism from other police forces who believe this to be too strict an enforcement of the act. Perhaps aware of these regulations anyway, Huntley had changed his name when applying for the job in

Soham to Ian Nixon - his mother's maiden name.

Much is still not known about what actually happened inside Huntley's house. It is reported that Huntley and Carr had cleaned the house of every DNA trace of the girls. There were no hairs, blood or saliva and not a single fingerprint. The clean-up operation had centred around the dining room, although what happened to the girls in that room has never emerged.

'LOVELY GIRLS'

Maxine Carr, although not present on the day of the girls' deaths, was living with Huntley in the house where the girls died. On that fateful Sunday, she was in fact visiting her parents in Grimsby, although told police that she had been at home with Huntley all day in order to protect him. On August 20, she was charged with lying to the police. She appeared in

Above: Court drawing by artist Sian Frances. Ian Huntley and Maxine Carr stand to hear the verdict being read out December 17, 2003 in London

Above left: Police photograph of Maxine Carr following her arrest in August 2002. She was found guilty of conspiring to pervert the course of justice, but cleared of helping an offender

court on charges of assisting an offender and perverting the course of justice. In response to the first charge, she claimed that she had no knowledge of what had actually transpired in the house, and had only lied to protect Huntley, believing him to be innocent. She was found not guilty. She was therefore, found guilty of the second, less serious, charge of perverting the course of justice and received a sentence of three and a half years imprisonment. By the time the trial had concluded though, she had already served 16 months in prison, almost half of her sentence, and was later released on probation on May 10, 2004. During the trial she spoke of Holly and Jessica as 'lovely girls', and referred to Huntley as 'that thing', saying that she would not take the blame for his actions, and had been feeling guilty for long enough believing that she could have prevented Holly and Jessica's deaths had she been in the house on the Sunday. The judge proclaimed her imminent release to be a sentence in itself, and that she would lead a terrible existence, forever looking over her shoulder.

For her involvement with Ian Huntley, Carr is now a hate figure and considered to be at such a risk from the public that she is to be issued with a new identity. Threats have already been made on her life, some claiming

Above: Queen's Council for the prosecution Richard Latham arrives at the Old Bailey on December 12, 2003 in London

How did it feel to carry Jessica's dead body down the stairs?" Huntley did not reply. "Well?" "Not good," said Huntley in a low voice

that she would be dead within a week of her release from prison. Consequently, on her release from Foxton Hall Prison in Derbyshire, Maxine Carr was moved to a secret location pending her official release.

As a result of speculation by British newspapers on whether Carr would be given plastic surgery, or sent to live abroad, an injunction was granted by London's High Court preventing any photographs of Carr, or details of her whereabouts, treatment or new life, being published. Her movements may be protected by the courts for the rest of her life. This was granted for reasons of her health and safety, and also to enable the Probation Service to supervise her and ensure that she settles back into society and doesn't re-offend.

However, documents containing full details of her release and new identity were stolen from the car of a Home Office official parked in Hampstead Heath just days before her release date. In spite of this, the Home Office confirmed that her release had

Right: Parents of Holly Wells and Jessica Chapman arrive for the first day of the murder trial. They sat together in the courtroom, remaining silent. They were commended for their strength and dignity throughout the proceedings.

not been compromised and would go ahead as planned. They stated that there was nothing in the stolen documents which could give away her new location and identity.

Ian Huntley is no safer in prison than Maxine Carr is out of it. Knocked unconscious by another inmate who is now considered a 'hero' by fellow prisoners, Huntley has reportedly become the target of a deadly 'race' between two prison gangs to murder him. Bets have been placed on which will succeed, and prison guards are on 'extra high alert' for his safety. Rumours have leaked to the prison authorities that plans are first to disfigure Huntley by throwing boiling water on him, and then to kill him. An unnamed source described Huntley as a 'scared rabbit' in prison. He had previously been rushed to hospital in a 'life-threatening condition' having taken an overdose in an attempt to take his own life.

HUNTLEY'S HOUSE OF HORROR

The house, 5 College Close, owned by the local education authority, is due to be pulled down, along with the hangar at the Soham Village College in which the burned clothing was discovered. Until recently, for legal reasons, the house could not be touched, but lawyers for Huntley have given their consent to demolition, stating that no further evidence from the house would need to be used in any appeal. Plans for the sites are to be discussed with the relatives of Jessica and Holly.

Above: Candles are lit in remembrance of Holly Wells and Jessica Chapman inside St Andrew's Church August 18, 2002 in Soham, Cambridgeshire

YOUR RIGHT TO GROW, TO MATURE AND PLAY
SO CRUELLY DENIED IN A SINISTER WAY
ATTENTIVE AND CARING, A PARENT'S DELIGHT.
BUT SO YOUNG AT HEART, NEEDING COMFORT AT NIGHT.

- First verse of a poem written and read by Kevin Wells, in a service to celebrate the girls' lives at Ely Cathedral

DENNIS NILSEN
A Quiet Civil Servant

Was it fear of desertion that caused Dennis Nilsen to become a mass murderer in the most gruesome of circumstances? And was he merely evil, or was he himself one of life's victims – a schizophrenic?

At 6.25 on the morning of 8 February 1983, Michael Cattran parked his Dyno-Rod van outside 23 Cranley Gardens in the north London suburb of Muswell Hill. It was a routine call. Jim Allcock, one of the residents of No. 23, had phoned to say that the drains had

Above: *A police constable stands guard at the back of 23 Cranley Gardens, Muswell Hill, where Dennis Nilsen rented an attic flat.*

AT THE BOTTOM OF THE STINKING SHAFT WAS A GLUTINOUS, GREYISH-WHITE SUBSTANCE

Left: *The front of 23 Cranley Gardens.*

been blocked for five days. After a quick examination of the interior plumbing, Cattran decided the problem lay outside the house itself. He walked round to the side of the house and removed the manhole cover.

The smell was nauseating as Cattran climbed down the 12-foot inspection shaft. At the bottom he found a glutinous greyish-white mass.

Cattran told Jim Allcock that it was nothing serious and that he would be back shortly to straighten things out. When he called his boss, however, he voiced his real suspicions. The matter which was clogging the drains at 23 Cranley Gardens was, in his opinion, human flesh.

Cattran and his boss returned to Muswell Hill the following morning. To Cattran's surprise, the glutinous mass had vanished. He knew that, even though it had been raining the previous day, the drains could not possibly have cleared themselves. Cattran reached deep into the drainpipe and pulled out several pieces of meat and a number of bones.

Cattran explained the mystery of the missing sludge to Jim Allcock and another tenant, Fiona Bridges. They told

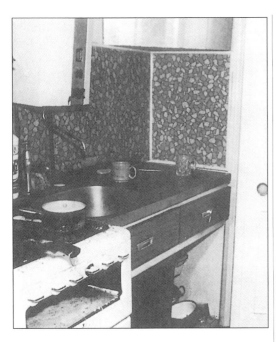

him they had heard someone moving the manhole cover in the early hours of the morning. They thought it might be Mr Nilsen who lived above them in the attic flat. Cattran and his boss decided it was time to call the police.

Detective Chief Inspector Peter Jay arrived on the scene shortly after 11a.m. and collected the meat and bones for forensic examination. At Charing Cross Hospital, it took pathologist Professor David Bowen only minutes to confirm that the meat was indeed human flesh and that the bones were from a man's hand.

THE TENANT OF THE ATTIC FLAT

Police attention immediately focused on the occupier of the attic flat, Dennis Andrew Nilsen, an executive officer at

Above left: *The stove in Nilsen's kitchen was caked with grease. Forensic examination determined that this was human fat.*

Above: *Black plastic bags in Nilsen's wardrobe contained the remains of two bodies.*

Right: *Two bodies had been dissected in Nilsen's bath, and the remains of Stephen Sinclair had been hidden under it.*

Below: *A cooking pot used by Nilsen to simmer the head of one of his victims.*

the Kentish Town Jobcentre, who lived alone with his dog, Beep. The other tenants had seen him leave for work that morning at his usual time of 8.30.

Peter Jay, together with Detective Inspector McCusker and Detective Constable Butler, waited outside 23 Cranley Gardens for Nilsen to return.

When he walked up to the front door at 5.40, Peter Jay intercepted him. Nilsen, a polite, quietly spoken man in his late thirties, seemed surprised but not alarmed when Jay introduced himself and his colleagues as police officers.

The four men went inside the house and climbed the stairs to Nilsen's tiny flat. Once inside, Jay told Nilsen about the human flesh which had been found in the drain outside. Nilsen feigned horror, but Jay was not remotely convinced. 'Stop messing about,' he said. 'Where's the rest of the body?'

Nilsen didn't even bother to protest his innocence. 'In two plastic bags in the wardrobe. I'll show you,' he said, unlocking the doors. The awful stench from the cupboard confirmed that Nilsen was telling the truth.

He arrested Nilsen, charged him with murder and shipped him off to Hornsey Police Station.

En route, Inspector McCusker asked Nilsen if there was anything he wanted to say. Nilsen replied, 'It's a long story. It goes back a long time. I'll tell you everything. I want to get it off my chest.'

'Are we talking about one body or two?' McCusker asked Nilsen.

'Fifteen or sixteen,' Nilsen replied calmly. 'Since 1978.... Three at Cranley Gardens and about thirteen at my previous address, 195 Melrose Avenue in Cricklewood.'

CONTENTS OF A WARDROBE

Detective Chief Inspector Jay returned to 23 Cranley Gardens with Detective Chief Superintendent Chambers and the pathologist, Professor Bowen. They removed the two stinking black plastic bags from Nilsen's wardrobe and took them to Hornsey mortuary.

When Bowen opened the first he found it contained four smaller shopping bags. In the first of these was the left-hand side of a man's chest with the arm attached. The second contained the right-hand side of a chest. The third held a torso, and the fourth an assortment of human offal.

In the other black bag, Bowen found two human heads and another torso with the arms attached but missing the hands. One of the heads had most of the flesh boiled away.

Nilsen told the police that one of the heads belonged to a young drug addict called Stephen Sinclair. The second he knew only as 'John the Guardsman'. He could put no name to a third victim whose remains were later found in a tea chest at his flat.

Nilsen seemed willing, even anxious, to help the police. On 11 February, three days after his arrest, he accompanied Peter Jay to the ground-floor flat at 195 Melrose Avenue which he had occupied from 1976 to 1981.

'ARE WE TALKING ABOUT ONE BODY OR TWO?' ENQUIRED THE POLICEMAN. 'FIFTEEN OR SIXTEEN,' WAS THE CALM REPLY

Below: *Nilsen's obsession with death was already evident during his days in the National Service.*

He told Jay that he had cut up the bodies and burnt them on a series of huge bonfires in the back garden. He even pointed out where the fires had been and where they should look for human remains.

Using this information, forensic teams started the laborious task of sifting through the earth for evidence. A day later they had found enough human ash and bone fragments to establish that at least eight people had been cremated in the garden.

Despite his willingness to cooperate with the police, Nilsen was unable to identify many of his early victims. None of them had ever been more than casual acquaintances. They had been, for the most part, young, homeless homosexuals – social misfits, drug addicts or alcoholics, men who could simply disappear without anyone knowing or caring. However, based on dates and

physical descriptions given by Nilsen, and comparing them with missing persons' records, the police were eventually able to identify six victims with reasonable certainty.

The question now for the police and Nilsen's lawyer was not if Nilsen was a mass murderer, but rather why he had killed more than a dozen young men. On this point, Nilsen could not help. 'I am hoping you will tell me that,' he said.

FOUR YEARS OF CARNAGE

Nilsen was questioned for the next few weeks, during which time he gave a meticulous account of his four years of carnage. It was a story so monstrous and grotesque that it made even case-hardened police interrogators physically ill to listen to it.

It had all started on New Year's Eve 1978. Nilsen had met a young Irish boy in a pub in the West End and taken him back to his flat in Melrose Avenue. After seeing in the New Year, the two men had gone to bed together. They were both stupefied with drink, and no sex took place between them.

In the morning, according to Nilsen, he woke to find the young Irishman still asleep beside him. He was suddenly overcome with terror that the boy would want to leave as soon as he too awoke. Nilsen desperately wanted him to stay, and could only think of one way to ensure that he did so.

Nilsen picked up a tie from the floor, straddled the boy's chest, placed the tie around his neck and pulled. The boy woke and a mighty struggle ensued before he finally passed out.

But he was not dead yet. So Nilsen went to the kitchen, filled a bucket with water and held the boy's head under the water until he drowned.

Nilsen then bathed the boy's body, dressed it in clean underwear and socks, took it back to bed with him and masturbated. For the next week, Nilsen went off to work as usual. He returned each evening to his dead companion who would be sitting in an armchair, waiting for him.

After eight days, Nilsen prised up some floor boards and hid the corpse. It

Above: *After a brief stint with the police, Nilsen, aged 28, spent three months working as a security guard.*

Below: *In the winter of 1975, Nilsen moved into a ground floor flat at 195 Melrose Avenue. It was here that he committed a dozen murders.*

remained there for seven months before Nilsen dissected it and burnt it on a bonfire in his back garden.

On the evening of 3 December 1979, almost a year later, Dennis Nilsen was cruising the gay bars of Soho when he met a twenty-six-year-old Canadian tourist, Kenneth Ockendon. Ockendon, who was staying at a cheap hotel in King's Cross, was due to fly home the following day.

Nilsen persuaded him to accompany him back to Melrose Avenue for a meal. He could stay the night if he wanted, and pick up his things from the hotel the following morning.

By the early hours of the morning the two men were in Nilsen's sitting room, both much the worse for drink. Nilsen was watching Ockendon as he listened to music through a set of headphones.

His feelings of imminent desertion were similar to those he had experienced a year earlier.

So Nilsen walked behind Ockendon's chair, grabbed the flex of the headphones and strangled him with it. Again he

*Above: Police remove
human remains from
Nilsen's flat at Melrose
Avenue.*

washed the body, dressed it in clean underwear, placed it next to him in bed and went to sleep.

Ockendon's corpse remained his constant companion for the next two weeks. Nilsen spent the evenings watching television with the body in an armchair next to him. When he was ready for bed, he would wrap it in a curtain and place it under the floorboards for the night.

Unlike the Irish boy, Ockendon's disappearance caused a considerable stir. Several of the tabloids carried his picture and Nilsen felt sure that his days were numbered. But the police didn't come. And over the next eighteen months eleven more young men were destined to die at Melrose Avenue.

By the end of 1980, Nilsen had accumulated six bodies. Three were stowed under the floorboards, while the others were cut up, stuffed in suitcases and stored in a garden shed.

At the beginning of December, Nilsen

EVERY EVENING NILSEN WOULD WATCH TELEVISION WITH OCKENDON'S BODY IN AN ARMCHAIR NEXT TO HIM

WITH NO FLOORBOARDS AND NO GARDEN, HOW WAS NILSEN GOING TO DISPOSE OF HIS VICTIMS AT HIS NEW ADDRESS?

---

built an enormous bonfire which was constructed in part from human remains wrapped in carpet. He crowned the fire with an old car tyre to disguise the smell of burning flesh.

At the end of 1981, Nilsen was planning to move. By this time he had accumulated a further five bodies and, shortly before he left, he had another massive fire.

No. 23 Cranley Gardens, Nilsen's new home, presented some real problems for a mass murderer of his ilk. It was an attic flat with no floorboards and no garden – in fact nowhere decent to hide a body at all. But this didn't stop him.

Within weeks of his move to Muswell Hill, Nilsen strangled John Howlett with an upholstery strap and then drowned him. Graham Allen was the next to die. Nilsen couldn't actually recall killing him, but thought he had strangled him with a tie while he was eating an omelette.

On 26 January Nilsen met his last victim. Stephen Sinclair, a drug addict and petty criminal, was wandering the streets of Soho looking for a hand-out. Nilsen offered to buy him a hamburger and then persuaded him to go back to Cranley Gardens with him.

Two weeks later, Michael Cattran of Dyno-Rod found what was left of Stephen in the drain outside 23 Cranley Gardens.

NO EMOTION, NO REMORSE

On 24 October 1983, Dennis Andrew Nilsen stood before Mr Justice Croom-Johnson at No. 1 Court in the Old Bailey. He was charged with six murders and two attempted murders.

There was no doubt that Nilsen had committed the offences. What the court had to evaluate was Nilsen's mental state at the time when he committed them.

If Nilsen had pleaded Guilty, as he originally intended, he would have saved the jury a considerable ordeal. Instead, they were forced to spend two weeks listening to detailed evidence of Nilsen's gruesome acts.

Detective Chief Superintendent Chambers spent almost an entire day reading out a transcript of Nilsen's confession. The graphic descriptions of decapitations and dissections, of the boiling and mincing of human flesh, and of necrophilia, sickened and enraged the jury. Nilsen, for his part, sat through the evidence without betraying a single vestige of emotion.

The prosecution called three witnesses to give evidence that Nilsen had attempted to kill them. Paul Nobbs, a university student, told how he had been rescued by Nilsen from the unwanted attentions of another man.

Nilsen had taken him back to Cranley Gardens and had shown him genuine kindness. He had not tried to ply him with drink or force him to have sex. He had even suggested that he call his mother so that she would not be worried. Nobbs had gone to bed alone but had woken in the early hours of the morning with a splitting headache. He had looked in the mirror and had seen that his eyes were completely bloodshot and that there was a bruise around his neck.

Nilsen had feigned concern, saying that Nobbs looked awful and should go straight to a doctor.

At the casualty department of the hospital he went to, Nobbs was told that he had been partially strangled. He had realized that Nilsen must have been his attacker, but had been reluctant to report the incident to the police because he felt sure that he would not be believed.

The defence made much of Nobbs's testimony. It demonstrated that Nilsen could behave perfectly normally one minute and then be possessed of murderous impulses the next, without provocation or reason. It proved, they said, that Nilsen was clearly insane.

If Nobbs's story was difficult to credit, Karl Strotter's encounter with Nilsen was nothing short of fantastic. Strotter had met Nilsen in a pub in Camden Town. He was depressed after the break-up of a relationship and, like Nobbs, described Nilsen's behaviour towards him as sympathetic and undemanding.

They had gone back to Cranley Gardens together and Nilsen had put him to bed in a sleeping bag. Strotter described what happened next: 'I woke up feeling something round my neck. My head was hurting and I couldn't breathe

Above: *Having confessed his crimes, Nilsen is remanded at Highgate Magistrates' Court in north London.*

NOBBS WOKE UP WITH BLOODSHOT EYES AND A SPLITTING HEADACHE. DOCTORS TOLD HIM SOMEONE HAD TRIED TO STRANGLE HIM

---

properly and I wondered what it was.

'I felt his hand pulling at the zip at the back of my neck. He was saying in a sort of whispered shouting voice, "Stay still. Stay still." I thought perhaps he was trying to help me out of the sleeping bag because I thought I had got caught up in the zip, which he had warned me about. Then I passed out.

'...the pressure was increasing. My head was hurting and I couldn't breathe. I remember vaguely hearing water running. I remember vaguely being carried and then felt very cold. I knew I was in the water and he was trying to drown me. He kept pushing me into the water....I just thought I was dying. I thought: "You are drowning. This is what it feels like to die." I felt very relaxed and I passed out. I couldn't fight any more.'

Strotter said he was amazed to awake lying on a sofa with Nilsen massaging him. Nilsen had then helped him to the underground station and wished him luck.

This apparent detachment from reality was echoed in Detective Chief Inspector Jay's evidence as he described Nilsen's behaviour during his interrogation. He was, Jay said, relaxed, cooperative and matter-of-fact. He did not, however, show any remorse. It was as though he was talking about someone else.

Both the prosecution and defence trotted out their 'expert witnesses', a mandatory feature of insanity pleas. Two equally well-qualified psychiatrists proceeded to give directly conflicting evaluations of the mental condition of the accused, thus effectively cancelling one another out in the eyes of the jury.

The judge spent four hours summing up, addressing himself in particular to the question of Nilsen's personality. 'A mind can be evil without being abnormal,' he advised the jury. 'There must be no excuses for Nilsen if he has moral defects. A nasty nature is not arrested or retarded development of the mind.'

The implication of what Mr Croom-Johnson was saying was obvious. Dennis Nilsen was, in his opinion, evil rather than insane, and the jury should therefore find him guilty of murder.

The jury retired on the morning of Thursday, 3 November 1983. Despite the clear guidance given by the judge, they returned the following morning to say that they were unable to reach a

Above: *Two that got away: Douglas Stewart (left); Karl Stotter (right). Both testified at the trial that they had been victims of attacks by Dennis Nilsen. Their evidence was vital for the prosecution as it argued that Nilsen was not technically insane.*

Below: *Nilsen's face bears the scar from an attack by a fellow prisoner.*

consensus about Nilsen's state of mind at the time of the various murders.

Mr Croom-Johnson said that he would accept a majority verdict. At 4.25 that afternoon the jury returned to court with a verdict of Guilty on all six counts of murder, by a majority of ten to two.

The judge condemned Dennis Andrew Nilsen to life imprisonment, with the recommendation that he should serve no less than twenty-five years.

Nilsen spent the first nine months of his sentence in Parkhurst Prison on the Isle of Wight.

In the summer of 1984 Nilsen was transferred to Wakefield Prison. He remains there to this day, sharing his cell with a budgerigar called Hamish.

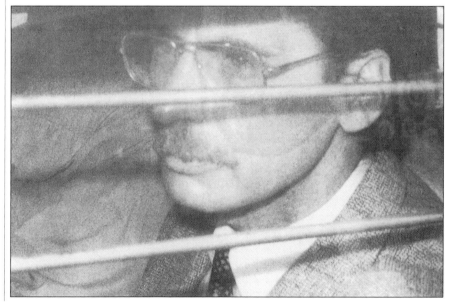

THE WESTS
House of Horrors

On 24 February 1994, police began to dig up the garden at 25 Cromwell Street to look for Heather West, daughter of Rosemary and Frederick West. On 13 December 1994, Frederick West was charged with twelve murders. Rose also received life imprisonment on each of the ten counts of murder.

Young women would go and stay at 25 Cromwell Street, either as nannies, lodgers or friends, but very few of them made it out of the West house alive. It was slowly becoming a House of Horrors.

FRED'S CHILDHOOD

Frederick West was born in 1941 to Walter and Daisy West, who lived in Much Marcle, a village about 120 miles west of London. After Fred, Daisy had another six children during the following ten years.

As Fred grew older, he developed a close relationship with his mother, doing everything she asked. Fred also had a good relationship with his father whom he admired as a role model.

While being a scruffy looking boy, Fred inherited some of his mother's features, a rather large mouth with a gap between his big teeth, resembling the looks of a gypsy.

At school, Fred was always in trouble for which he was frequently caned. His mother, Daisy, would then go to the school and yell at the teacher, which made Fred the victim of many jokes.

Opposite: *Police guarding 25 Cromwell Street as evidence is being removed.*

Right: *Fred and Rosemary West, the happy couple.*

At the age of fifteen and virtually illiterate, Fred left school and went to work as a farm hand. By the time he was sixteen, he had become very aggressive to the opposite sex and persued any girl that took his fancy.

Fred, recognised as a notorious liar, claimed that his father had sex with his daughters using the excuse 'I made you so I'm entitled to have you'. Then at seventeen, he was seriously injured in a motorcycle accident. After a week in a coma, a broken leg and having a metal plate inserted into his head, Fred was left with one leg shorter than the other. This head injury may have resulted in

Fred being prone to sudden fits of rage and the loss of control over his emotions.

After this accident Fred met a pretty 16-year-old called Catherine Bernadette Costello. Nicknamed Rena, she had always been in trouble with the police since early childhood and was an accomplished and experienced thief. They quickly became lovers. The affair ended months later as she returned to Scotland. Then, after plunging his hand up a young woman's skirt while on a fire escape at a local youth group, Fred

Left: *Rosemary as a child.*

fell, banged his head and lost consciousness. It may be that he suffered brain damage due to his two head injuries and this could have been the cause of a lasting impact on Fred's behaviour.

After being fined for theft in 1961, Fred was accused of getting a 13-year-old girl pregnant. He couldn't understand that he had done anything wrong, as this girl was a friend of the family, it caused a scandal and he was told to find somewhere else to live. Working on construction sites, it wasn't long before he was caught stealing and having sex with young girls.

At the age of 20, although he got off without a prison sentence, Fred had become a convicted child molester and petty thief; a complete disgrace to his family.

ROSE'S CHILDHOOD

Daisy Letts was hospitalized in 1953, due to her deepening depression, and trying to cope with a violent husband, three daughters and son, she had electroshock therapy. Shortly after this treatment she gave birth to Rosemary. Rosemary Letts was born in Devon in November 1953. Her mother suffered from severe depression and her father, Bill Letts, was a schizophrenic. Bill

> 'DOZY ROSIE' – AS SHE WAS CALLED, WAS NOT VERY INTELLIGENT ALTHOUGH SHE WAS SMART ENOUGH TO BECOME HER FATHER'S PET, ALWAYS DOING WHATEVER HE WISHED IMMEDIATELY.

was a violent and dominant man, demanding obedience from both his wife and children and enjoyed looking for reasons to beat them. The family was short of money because Bill was not an ideal employee and only maintained a series of unskilled and low paid jobs.

Rose had developed a habit of rocking herself in her cot and as she became older, she would swing her head for hours until she reached semiconciousness. Being quite pretty, if a little chubby, she was called 'Dozy Rosie', although she was smart enough to become her father's pet. But at school, due to cruel jokes and teasing, Rose was recognised as an ill-tempered, aggressive loner.

In her teens she walked around naked after baths, fondled her brother and became sexually precocious. As boys were not interested in her she focused her attentions on the older men of the village.

During 1968 Rose was raped by an older man who had taken advantage of her innocent ways. Then at the beginning of 1969 Daisy, her mother, took 15-year-old Rose and moved in temporarily with one of her other daughters to escape from Bill. At this time Rose began to spend a lot of time out with men. Later that year, Rose moved back home with her father.

As Rose Letts was not a very smart nor good tempered girl she became unfocused towards any productive goal except finding a lover older than herself.

THE FIRST VICTIM

In 1962 Fred was allowed to move back home in Much Marcle. Rena Costello returned from Scotland in the summer and they met up immediately, continuing their relationship. Although Rena was pregnant by an Asian bus driver, she and Fred secretly married and moved to Scotland. Charmaine was born March 1963. They both wrote to Fred's parents, stating that their baby had died at birth, therefore they had adopted a child of mixed race.

Fred's interest for normal sex was small, although he had a voracious appetite for oral sex, bondage and sodomy. As an icecream man, his apparent politeness and sincerity attracted teenagers around his van. This led to many sexual encounters. With his growing number of infidelities, Rena and Charmaine were pushed out of his mind.

FRED AND ROSE

Rena gave birth to Fred's child in 1964, and they named her Anne Marie. During their turbulent marriage, the West's embarked on a friendship with Anna McFall. Then Fred, Rena and their two children, as well as Anna, moved to Gloucester where Fred found work in a slaughterhouse. This is probably where Fred developed a morbid obsession with blood, corpses and dismemberment.

As the marriage fell apart, Rena returned to Scotland alone. When she returned to Gloucester in July 1966, she found Fred living in a trailer with Anna McFall. Due to pressure from Anna to marry her, Fred responded by killing her and her unborn child sometime in July 1967. He slowly and methodically dismembered her and the foetus, cutting off her fingers and toes, and buring her body somewhere near the trailer park.

Rena then moved back in with Fred, earning money as a prostitute, while he began, openly, to fondle Charmaine.

Then in February 1968, due to his mother dying, Fred started a series of petty thefts, which caused him to change his job frequently. In November 1968, while on one of these many jobs,

Left: *Anne Marie daughter of Fred and Rena Costello.*

AT THE AGE OF JUST 16, ROSE LEFT HOME TO LOOK AFTER CHARMAINE, ANNA MARIE AND FRED, WHO WAS CONSTANTLY IN TROUBLE WITH THE POLICE.

Fred met Rose Letts, his future wife.

Although Rose's father did not approve of Fred, she carried on seeing him until she found herself pregnant with his baby. At the age of 16, Rose left home to take care of Charmaine, Anna Marie and Fred.

CHARMAINE

Rose gave birth in 1970 to Heather. While Fred was in jail, Rose was left at home with the all the children whom she treated quite badly. Then one day during the summer of 1971, Charmaine went missing. Although this happened while Fred was in prison, he probably helped to bury her body under the kitchen floor of their home in Midland Road, removing her fingers, toes and kneecaps, only to be discovered 20 years later. It was only a matter of time before Rena came looking for Charmaine. When she found Fred, he got her drunk, then strangled, dismembered her body and buried her as he had done with Anna, cutting off

HE WOULD DISMEMBER THE BODY, CUTTING OFF THE FINGERS, TOES AND KNEECAPS — THEN PUT THE REMAINS INTO BAGS READY FOR BURIAL.

Below: *Leading into the cellar at 25 Cromwell Street.*

her fingers and toes.

Fred and Rose married in Gloucester registry office in 1972, then Rose gave birth to a daughter, Mae West. As the family increased in size, they moved to 25 Cromwell Street, where Rose also had room for her prostitution business.

As the cellar was soundproof, they used it as a 'torture chamber'. Anne Marie, their 8-year-old daughter was the first victim, her mother held her down and her father raped her. The pain was so bad that she could not attend school.

CAROLINE OWENS

The couple hired a nanny, 17-year-old Caroline Owens. They abducted, raped and threatened her but she got away and reported this to the police. There was a hearing. At this time Fred was thirty-one and Rose only nineteen, and they were found not guilty.

LYNDA GOUGH

Lynda Gough, a friend who helped take care of the children, became the next victim. She was dismembered and buried in a pit in the garage, having had her fingers, toes and kneecaps removed.

A terrible pattern was beginning to develop.

CAROL ANN COOPER

In August 1973, Stephen, their first son was born. Fred and Rose abducted 15-year-old Carol in November, abusing her sexually until they strangulated or suffocated her. They dismembered and buried her body at the growing graveyard of 25 Cromwell street.

LUCY PARTINGTON AND THE REST

The cellar was enlarged and the garage was transformed into an extension of the main house, all done by Fred at strange hours of the day. On December 27, 1973, Lucy Partington went to visit her disabled friend but had the misfortune to bump into Rose and Fred. She was tortured for a week and then murdered, dismembered and buried under one of Fred's many construction projects at 25 Cromwell Street.

During the period from April 1974 to April 1975 another three women became victims like Carol and Lucy. They were Therese Siegenthaler 21, Shirley Hubbard, 15 and Juanita Mott, 18. The Wests buried these bodies under the cellar floor. Juanita had been gagged by a ligature made from a pair of white nylon socks, two pairs of tights and a bra, then tied up with plastic covered rope, the type used for a washing line. Tied up so tightly so that she could hardly move, she was probably suspended from the beams in the cellar. As for Shirley Hubbard, her body was wrapped entirely with tape, a plastic tube had been inserted up her nose, allowing her to breathe.

Fred continued to get into trouble with the police with thefts and stolen

> NOT ONLY DID HE KILL HIS MISTRESS AND THEIR UNBORN CHILD, HE SLOWLY AND METHODICALLY DISMEMBERED HER CORPSE AND BURIED HER ALONG WITH HER FOETUS.

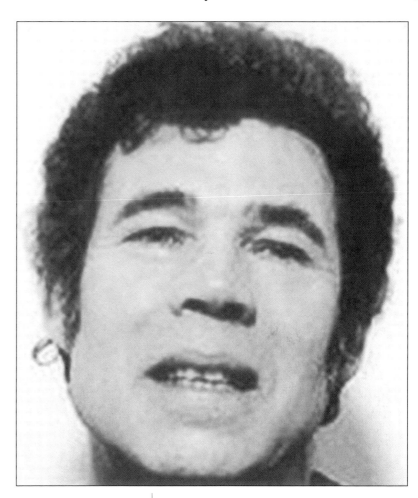

Above: *Fred West – the last photograph before his death.*

> FRED'S INTEREST IN 'NORMAL SEX' WAS MINIMAL. HE WANTED ORAL SEX, BONDAGE AND SODOMY — AT ALL HOURS OF THE DAY AND NIGHT.

goods, which he needed to maintain his home improvement projects.

The Wests took in lodgers. One of these, Shirley Robinson, 18, a former prostitute, developed a relationship with them and later became pregnant with Fred's child. Rose had also became pregnant, but by one of her black clients. Rose became uncomfortable with this situation and wanted Shirley to leave. Seven months later, Tara was born to Rose in December 1977, Shirley and her unborn baby became the next victims and were buried in the garden of Cromwell Street. Yet another baby girl, Louise, was born to the Wests in November 1978, making a total of six. Fred's daughter, Anna Marie also became pregnant by Fred, although this was terminated.

After Rose's father died in May 1979, the Wests raped, tortured and murdered their next victim, Alison

Above: *The house in Northam, Devon where Rose West lived as a child.*

Chambers who was only 17. She was also buried in the garden at Cromwell Street. The rest of the children in the West household were aware of strange happenings. They knew that their mother was a prostitute and that Anna Marie was continually raped by her father. Anna moved in with her boyfriend, so Fred made advances towards his other daughters, Heather and Mae. Heather was beaten for trying to resist her father's advances. Rose gave birth to Barry, Fred's second son in June 1980, followed by Rosemary junior, who was not Fred's, in April 1982. She also had Lucyanna in July 1983, who was half-black like Tara and Rose junior. With all these children to contend with, Rose became extremely bad tempered.

After Heather broke the silence and

WHEN HE CUT OFF HER HEAD, IT MADE A SOUND, 'A HORRIBLE NOISE... LIKE SCRUNCHING — VERY UNPLEASANT.' BUT ONCE HER HEAD WAS OFF, HE STARTED ON HER LEGS, TWISTING HER FOOT UNTIL ONE ALMIGHTY CRACK.

told her girlfriend of the abuse from her father, she too was murdered This happened after an argument with her father got out of control. Fred grabbed her round the neck, she went blue and stopped breathing. After trying to revive her, he dragged her to the bath and ran cold water over her. After taking all her clothes off and drying her, he tried to fit her in the rubbish bin. But as she did not fit, strangled her with tights just to make sure she was dead, and then cut her up into smaller pieces. Stephen, Fred's son, helped his father dig a hole in the back garden for Heather's dismembered body.

Katherine Halliday began to participate in the West's prostitution business, although this did not last long as she became very alarmed at their collection of suits, whips and chains and left abruptly.

Due to one of Fred's young rape victims talking, Detective Constable Savage, who had experience in dealing with Rena, was assigned to his case. On 6 August, 1992, Police arrived at Cromwell Street with a warrant to look for child abuse and pornography. Fred was arrested. While the Police had enough evidence to bring child abuse charges against Fred, Detective Constable Savage was curious as to the disappearance of Charmaine, Rena and Heather.

The West's children were put into care and with Fred in prison, Rose attempted suicide but failed. After rumours emerged that Heather was apparently buried under the patio, the house and garden were searched. Fred confessed to killing his daughter when human bones, other than Heather's, were found in the garden. The police began to dig the garden and it became only a matter of time before they found the first remains of a young woman, dismembered and decapitated.

Fred then told the police of the girls in the cellar, admitting to murder but not rape. In the cellar, nine sets of bones were discovered, although the police could not identify them and Fred was no help as he couldn't remember the victims.

Rena, Anna McFall and Charmaine's bodies were found, although Mary Bastholm was not.

At the joint hearing, Fred tried to console Rose, but she brushed him off, telling the police that he made her sick.

GUILTY

Fred was charged with twelve murders on December 13, 1994. After being devastated by Rose's rejection, Fred hung himself with his bedsheet on New Year's day at Winson Green Prison, Birmingham.

On October 3, 1995, Rose went to trial linking her to the murders and sadistic sexual assaults on young women. Among the witnesses were Caroline Owens, whom they had hired as a nannie in 1972, along with Anna Marie. The defence, led by Richard

AFTER BRUSHING OFF FRED, HE WROTE A LETTER SAYING THAT SHE WOULD ALWAYS BE HIS MRS WEST, THEY WOULD ALWAYS BE IN LOVE.

Ferguson QC, tried to show that Rose was unaware of what Fred was up to, and that the evidence of sexual assault was not the same as evidence of murder. But after taking the stand, the jury were left believing that she ill-treated her children and was completely dishonest.

The most dramatic evidence was given by Janet Leach, who witnessed Fred's police interviews. During these interviews, Fred had said how he had involved Rose with the murders and that Rose had murdered Charmaine and Shirley Robinson on her own. After this testimony, Janet Leach collapsed and was admitted to hospital.

It did not take the jury long to find Rose guilty of murdering Charmaine, Heather, Shirley Robinson and the other bodies all buried at Cromwell Street. With ten counts of murder, the judge sentenced Rose to life imprisonment.

Below:
Rosemary West

BRADY & HINDLEY
The Moors Murderers

Ian Brady and Myra Hindley were both obsessed with Nazi paraphernalia, pornography and sadism. Most of their victims were children whom they sexually molested before killing. These sadistic love birds would document their murderous deeds. As well as recording the screams of one of their victim's torturous end, they kept an extensive collection of photographs of the victims.

Above: *Myra Hindley*

Opposite: *Police searching Saddleworth Moor, north east of Manchester.*

Ian Brady and Myra Hindley met while woking for a chemical company in Hyde, Greater Manchester. Hindley fell in love with Brady as soon as she laid eyes on him, thinking that he was quite an intellectual as he sat reading *Mein Kampf* in German in the lunch room. Therefore Hindley was thrilled when he asked her out. They went to see a movie about the Nuremburg war crimes tribunal, and when they returned home to her grandmother's house, Brady introduced her to sex. Soon they became inseparable.

MYRA'S CHILDHOOD

Being the first child of Nellie (Hettie) and Bob Hindley, Myra was born in Gorton in the industrial district of Manchester on July 23 1942. She was raised by her mother alone, as her father served in a parachute regiment, and lived with Myra's grandmother, Ellen Maybury. This worked out well because when Myra's mother went to work, her grandmother was able to look after her.

When Myra's father, Bob, returned from the army, they bought a house just round the corner from Myra's grandmother. Bob spent most of his time in the pub when he wasn't working, as he had trouble re-adjusting to civilian life.

The Hindley's second child, Maureen, was born in August 1946. As

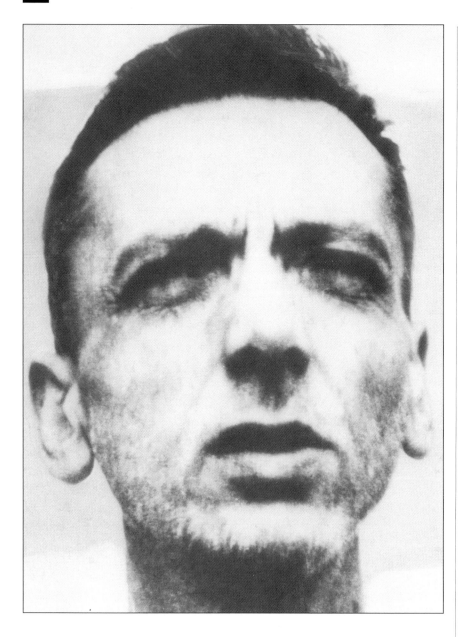

Above: *Ian Brady*

HE WAS DIFFERENT FROM ANY OF THE BOYS SHE HAD KNOWN.

both parents found this to be too much of a strain, Myra was sent to live with her grandmother. Although this meant that Myra never developed a relationship with her father, instead she enjoyed the devoted attention from her grandmother.

At the age of five, Myra started school at Peacock Street Primary School. Although regarded as a sensible and mature girl her attendance at school was poor. This led to her inability to gain the necessary grades required to attend the local grammar school. Instead, she went to Ryder Brow Secondary Modern. Although she was constantly in the 'A' stream in all her subjects her attendance was still very bad. She seemed talented at creative writing and poetry and loved sports and athletics. Myra was not considered particularly attractive and was given the nickname 'Square Arse'. She was also teased because of the shape of her nose.

During her teens, Myra became a popular babysitter, being very capable and demonstrating a genuine love of children.

Then at 15, Myra befriended a timid and fragile 13-year-old called Michael Higgins. She protected and looked after him, treating him as if he were her younger brother. She was convinced that they would be life long friends. Unfortunately he drowned in a resevoir, often used by local children as a swimming hole. This devastated Myra, made worse by her sense of guilt as she had turned down his offer of going swimming with him that day. She had been convinced that she could have saved him as she considered herself to be a very strong swimmer.

Fluctuating between depression and hysteria, Myra became inconsolable over the following weeks. She dressed in black, lit a candle in church every night for Michael and converted to his religion of Roman Catholicism. With an IQ of 107, she did not complete her O levels and left school shortly after Michael's death.

Junior clerk at an electrical engineering firm at Lawrence Scott and Electrometers, was to be her first job. Myra behaved much like any other teenager, going to dances and cafés, listening to Rock and Roll and flirting with boys. At this time, her appearence becoming more important to her, she began to wear make-up and bleach her hair in an attempt to look older.

She got engaged to Ronnie Sinclair, a local boy, on her 17th birthday. Although this apparent contentment with ordinary life did not last long, as she began to question the lifestyle to which she was supposed to conform. Myra called off the engagement.

Looking for more excitement, she applied for entrance forms to the Navy and Army, although she never actually sent them in. Another idea was to become a nannie in America. In the end she went in search of a job in London. It was two years before something new and exciting occurred. Then in January 1961 she met Ian Brady.

IAN'S CHILDHOOD

He was born Ian Stewart on January 2, 1938 in Gorbals, an area of one of the roughest slums in Glasgow. Being the illegitimate son of a single, Scottish waitress, he never knew his father except that, as his mother later told him, he was a journalist for a Glasgow newspaper and had died a few months before Ian's birth. Signing her name as Mrs. Stewart due to disapproval from society, his mother, Margaret (Peggy) Stewart was a tearoom waitress in a hotel.

Unable to afford a babysitter, his mother would often leave baby Ian at home on his own. Realising that this could not continue, she advertised for a permanent babysitter to provide the necessary attention and care that she was unable to give.

At the age of four months Ian was unofficially adopted by Mary and John Sloane, who also had another four children. Margaret would visit him every Sunday and bring gifts, but never telling him that she was his real mother. As the years went on, the visits occurred less often.

Although the Sloanes tried to provide a loving environment, Ian always felt as though he didn't belong and therefore showed no response to their attentions. He became difficult, angry and lonely resulting in him banging his head on the floor due to his temper tantrums on many occasions.

He attended Camden street Primary School and was thought to be a bright child by his teachers. But his classmates saw him as an outsider, as he was different and secretive. He was also called a 'sissy' because he didn't play sport like the others.

FAMILY, FRIENDS AND COLLEAGUES NOTICED A BIG CHANGE IN HER. AT WORK, MYRA BECAME SURLY, OVERBEARING, AGGRESSIVE AND BEGAN TO WEAR 'KINKY' CLOTHES.

When Ian was nine, he was taken for his first outing away from the Gorbals to the moors of Loch Lomond. The Sloanes had a nap after the picnic lunch. When they awoke they saw Ian about 500 yards away, standing at the top of a steep slope. They could not gain his attention as he stood there for an hour. When two of the Sloane boys finally climbed the hill to fetch him, he told them to go home without him as he wanted to be alone. But afterwards, on the bus ride home, and for the first time, he became very talkative. Being on the hillside alone seemed to fill him with a sense of strength and power as well as being a profound experience, one that would influence his future life.

Ian was accepted into Shawlands Academy at the age of eleven, a school for children with above-average intelligence. But Ian was lazy and naughty. It was not long before he started getting into trouble with the police. Also at this time his obsession with the Nazis began. He read books on the Second World War and insisted on playing German war games with his

Right: *Pauline Reade, the frst victim of Brady and Hindley's gruesome murders.*

friends.

By the time Ian reached twelve years old his mother's visits ceased. She had married Patrick Brady and moved to Manchester to be with her husband.

During the ages of thirteen to sixteen, Ian was charged with burglary and housebreaking. The court then decided that he was to be sent to live with his mother in Manchester. After meeting his stepfather for the first time, he began to use his surname of Brady which he kept permanently.

His stepfather found him a job as a porter at the local market, but Ian Brady still harboured feelings that he did not belong and looked for direction in his reading. These were books such as Dostoyevsky's *Crime and Punishment*, and sadistic titles such as the *Kiss of the Whip* and *The Torture Chamber*, which he found exciting.

Returning back to crime, Brady's next job was in a brewery. Then, arrested for aiding and abetting, he was sent to Borstal for two years. He was now 17, but as places were full, the first three months were spent in Strangeways prison in Manchester. Here he very quickly learnt to toughen up. He was soon moved to Hatfield Borstal in Yorkshire, where among other things, he ran gambling books. He also became frequently drunk while brewing his own alcohol. It wasn't long before he was sent to a much tougher Borstal in Hull Prison where he made a great effort to learn more of the criminal way of life.

In November 1957, Brady was released and after several months found work as a labourer, while studying bookkeeping. His family noticed that he had become more brooding and silent than ever before. Brady was offered the position of stock clerk with Millwards Merchandising in 1959. It was about a year later when a new secretary arrived.

THE FATAL ATTRACTION

Every night Hindley would write in her

As the weeks went past, Ian would play records of Hitler's marching songs for Myra, and encouraged her to read some of his favourite books — *Mein Kampf*, *Crime and Punishment* and *de Sade's* works.

Below: *16 Wardle Brook Avenue, the council house in East Manchester where Brady and Hindley lived*

diary of the feeling of longing that she held for Brady. They started to date and went to see *The Nuremberg Trials*. During the following weeks Hindley was happy to listen to records of Hitler's marching songs, and was encouraged to read books on crime and punishment. Having waited so long for someone like Brady, but due to her inexperience, she was unable to distinguish between what was healthy and dangerous.

Brady became Hindley's first lover and she was totally besotted, always wanting to please him. This even extended to dressing for him in the Germanic style with long boots, mini skirts and bleached hair. Brady would take pornographic pictures of her, including photographs of the two of them having sex. As Brady became increasingly outrageous and paranoid, Hindley's personality became fused with Brady's and she stopped attending church, believed as Brady had told her, that rape and murder were not wrong, and that murder was the 'supreme pleasure'.

Hindley's family noticed a big change in her personality, she had become aggressive, overbearing, secretive, hated babies, children and people and began to wear 'kinky' clothing.

Brady planned a bank robbery at the beginning of 1963, and although this was not followed through, Hindley's

blind acceptance and her willingness to go along with him seemed to cement their relationship. She took driving lessons (as Brady needed a getaway driver), joined Cheadle Rifle Club and bought two guns.

THE VICTIMS

Sixteen-year-old Pauline Reade became Hindley's and Brady's first victim on the night of July 12, 1963. Pauline had been on her way to a dance at the Railway Worker's Social Club. Enticed away by Hindley, she was never to be seen alive again.

Four months later, 12- year-old John Kilbride disappeared on November 23 from Ashton-under-Lyne.

On Tuesday June 16, 1964, 12-year-old Keith Bennett was next. As he set off to his grandmother's house which he did every Tuesday, he never arrived and was never seen alive again.

Brady and Hindley moved in with Hindley's grandmother in September of 1964. This was when Brady was first introduced to Myra's sister and her 17-year-old husband, David Smith. Brady was keen to impress Smith with his stories of criminal knowledge and theft.

The most horrifying murder was that of Lesley Anne Downey. She disappeared without trace on December 26, 1964. Lesley Anne had been gagged, stripped and sexually assaulted. She was then strangled and buried in a shallow grave up on Saddleworth Moor in Lancashire. While Lesley Anne had been tortured, Brady had photographed and recorded it all. On the tape recording, Lesley Anne can clearly be heard begging them to let her go home to her mother as she was brutally abused. The cries of the child fell on deaf ears and photographs were taken, of Lesley Anne tied down on the bed.

It was on October 7, 1965, that Brady offered Smith a practical demonstration of a murder. Edward Evans, the next victim, was a 17-year-old homosexual. Smith watched as Brady stood over Evans with a hatchet and struck him 13 times with it. As the young man let out a quiet groan, Brady hit him once more with the hatchet. As Evans lay on the ground making gurgling noises, Brady covered his head with a sheet and then wrapped a piece of electrical wire around his head. As Brady pulled the wire tighter and tighter, he kept repeatedly chanting 'You f...ing dirty bastard'. When Evan's finally stopped making any noise, Brady turned to Hindley and said, "That's it, it's the messiest yet."

CONVICTED OF MURDER

Smith was horrified and contacted the police the following morning, directing them to Brady's address. Brady and Hindley were discovered collecting a fresh corpse from the bedroom, along with a blood-covered hatchet. Brady's library of pornography, perversion and sadism were also found.

Also, a young 12-year-old girl, who had only lived doors away from Brady and Hindley, was able to recall several trips she had made with the couple to Saddleworth Moor, northeast of Manchester. After this bit of information, the authorities launched a search which uncovered the body of Lesley Anne Downey. A search of Brady's flat uncovered two left luggage tickets for Manchester Central Station. Once retrieved, the police found contained in them, nude photographs of Lesley Anne along with recordings of her torturous end and seemingly innocent snapshots of Saddleworth Moor. After another visit to the moor by the police, they discovered the body of John Kilbride.

While in custody, Brady seemed proud of his crimes, as police opened their files on eight missing persons lost over the previous four years.

Hindley and Brady were brought to trial on April 27, 1966, held at Chester Assizes. The jurors were stunned by the Downey recording as Brady

WHILE DAVID SMITH WATCHED, BRADY STOOD OVER EVANS HOLDING A HATCHET, STRUCK HIM THIRTEEN TIMES, COVERED HIS HEAD WITH A SHEET AND CONSTANTLY PULLED TIGHTER A PIECE OF ELECTRICAL WIRE THAT HE HAD WRAPPED ROUND HIS VICTIM'S NECK, CHANTING "YOU F...ING DIRTY BASTARD".

IN TWO SUITCASES FILLED WITH PORNAGRAPHIC AND SADISTIC PARAPHENALIA, NINE SEMI-PORNOGRAPHIC PHOTOGRAPHS OF LESLEY ANNE DOWNEY WERE FOUND. THESE SHOWED THE GIRL NAKED, BOUND AND GAGGED IN A VARIETY OF POSES IN MYRA HINDLEY'S BEDROOM.

described it as nothing more than 'unusual'. Throughout the trial, Brady and Hindley appeared cold and heartless as they continually attempted to blame David Smith for all the murders. Accused of the murders of Edward Evans, Lesley Anne Downey and John Kilbride, Hindley and Brady pleaded 'not guilty' to the charges brought against them. The couple had luckily escaped the death penalty by just a couple of months as 'The Murder (Abolition of the Death Penalty) Act of 1965' had just come into effect a few weeks before their arrest.

Both were convicted of the murders of Edward Evans and Lesley Anne Downey; Brady was also convicted of murdering John Kilbride, while Myra was convicted as an accessory.

Brady was sentenced to concurrent life terms on each count. Hindley received two life terms plus seven years in the Kilbride case.

Brady was transferred from prison to a maximum security hospital in November 1985, here he confessed to the Reade–Bennet murders during an interview with tabloid reporters. The

---

BOTH PLEADING 'NOT GUILTY' THROUGHOUT THE TRIAL, BRADY AND HINDLEY MADE CONTINUAL ATTEMPTS TO BLAME DAVID SMITH FOR THE MURDERS.

Below: *Police retrieving the buried body of Lesley Anne Downey, from Saddleworth Moor on 10 October 1965.*

remains of Pauline Reade were discovered on June 30, 1987. Pathologists took a month to decide how she had met her death. It was confirmed that the girl had been sexually assaulted and her throat slashed from behind. Police reopened files on 55-yearold Veronica Bondi in Manchester, and a 38-year-old prostitute, Edith Gleave from Stockport.

Myra Hindley, became a born-again Christian asking repeatedly to be let out as she had been a model prisoner. Successive Home Office ministers denied her the chance at Parole. After unconfirmed media reports that Hindley was suffering with advanced lung cancer, she eventually died in prison, at the age of 60, due to respiratory failure. Her funeral and cremation were attended only by prison officials with her final burial place remaining unmarked.

Ian Brady remains alive in the high security Ashworth Hospital on Mersey-side. After failing several attempts to legally starve himself to death, he remains on continual hunger strike being force fed through a plastic tube.

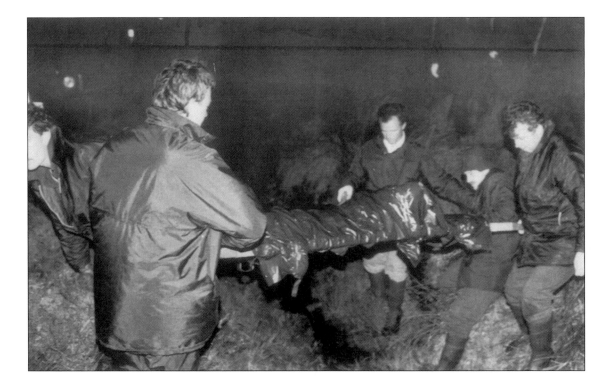

CRIMES
OF
PASSION

RUTH ELLIS
Spurned in Love

On a summer's day in 1955 a woman walked out of the condemned cell in Holloway prison to await the hangman's noose. Having shot to death a lover who had treated her appallingly, Ruth Ellis became the last woman in Britain to be executed.

For most of the year, the north London suburb of Hampstead keeps to itself on the edge of its leafy and spacious Heath. But at Easter the area's tranquillity is jovially disrupted. Outsiders flock in, as they have done for 150 years, to enjoy the fun of the fair. Lights and music flicker and boom across the green slopes, and the balmy spring air is scented with the pungent odour of fried onions from the fast food stalls.

On the evening of Easter Sunday, 10 April 1955, everything was running true to form. Downhill from the fairground, the Magdala pub in South Hill Park was packed and boisterous. Just after nine o'clock two young men parked their grey green Vauxhall Vanguard van and crossed the road to push into the saloon bar.

AS THE TWO MEN LEFT THE PUB A SMARTLY DRESSED BLONDE EMERGED FROM THE SHADOWS WITH A SMITH AND WESSON IN HER HAND

Twenty-six-year-old David Blakely and his friend Clive Gunnell had been to the fair, and were now after a quick drink before buying beer to take out to a nearby party.

As they re-emerged, neither of them noticed the slender blonde standing with her back to the wall of the pub. She was twenty-nine, her name was Ruth Ellis, and she had had a stormy relationship with Blakely which had lasted for two years. That evening, her pale, pretty face was grim behind her horn-rimmed spectacles as she called out: 'David!'

Blakely had been intent on avoiding Ruth all day. Now he ignored her. 'David!' she said again, sharply. Clive Gunnell looked up and saw that she was holding a .38 Smith and Wesson service revolver which was levelled at his friend.

David Blakely turned from the door of his van, opened his mouth, and then dropped his car keys and the bottle of beer he was holding as the first bullet slammed into his white shirt. A second bullet knocked Blakely on to his back.

'Clive!' Blakley's voice was a gurgled choke.

'Get out of the way, Clive,' said Ruth, deadly calm. She pulled the trigger again. Blakely, crawling on his stomach by now, was slammed into the tarmac. She

Leonard Crawford at Hampstead's Haverstock Hill police station, David Blakely was being declared dead on arrival at nearby New End Hospital.

When cautioned by DCS Crawford, Ruth Ellis was detached and composed. 'I am guilty,' she said. 'I am rather confused.' Then, little by little, she began to spill out her story...

Above: *Ruth had a brief and not very successful stab at modelling.*

Right: *David Blakely, Ruth Ellis's lover and eventual victim.*

positioned herself beside him, and then she fired twice more, sending fragments flying from the back of his jacket.

David Blakely lay prone and still. Ruth unfocussed from what she had done, looked Gunnell blankly in the eye, raised the pistol to her own temple, and pulled the trigger. Amazingly, the 'four-inch Smith', renowned for its reliability, did nothing.

She lowered the gun to her side and almost absent-mindedly tried the trigger again. The sixth and last bullet splintered the pavement, whined off up the road and clipped the hand of a passer-by, Mrs Gladys Kensington Yule.

Ellis and Gunnell stood facing each other. The whole bloody little drama had lasted less than ninety seconds, but those six shots were to reverberate for an unconscionable time in criminal history.

Someone had already called for the police and an ambulance when Ellis herself seemed to come out of a trance to tell a young man nearby: 'Fetch the police.'

'I am the police,' said Alan Thompson, an off-duty Hampstead officer who had been drinking in the pub. He took the pistol from her hand – inadvertently smudging latent prints, as it later proved – and led her off to await the squad car.

By the time it delivered Ruth into the hands of Detective Chief Superintendent

'FETCH THE POLICE,' SAID ELLIS TO A BYSTANDER. 'I AM THE POLICE,' REPLIED THE OFF-DUTY OFFICER AS HE TOOK THE GUN FROM HER

FROM FACTORY WORKER TO CLUB HOSTESS

It had begun a quarter of a century previously in Rhyl, North Wales, where Ruth was born the daughter of dance band musician Arthur Neilson and his wife Bertha on 9 October 1926. When Ruth was fifteen the family moved to Southwark in south London, and the girl found work in the local Oxo factory. She was ordered to take a year off work after contracting rheumatic fever. As part of her convalescence she took up dancing.

By 1943 she was working as a dance hall photographer's assistant when she met a Canadian soldier named Clare, and in September 1944, she bore him a son, christened Andria. Unfortunately Clare proved to have a wife back home, and Ruth, her mother Bertha and her older married sister Muriel were left to care for the boy.

In 1945, with the war in Europe ending and Ruth in her nineteenth year, she found another kind of career when she met Morris Conley.

Conley was a property racketeer, pimp and gangster who was to be dubbed 'Britain's biggest vice boss' by the press. But he did not attempt to draw Ruth into prostitution. Astutely, he spotted her greater potential as a club hostess.

At that time Britain's licensing laws were stringent. Pubs were permitted to open for only nine hours or less a day.

To beat the drinks ban, afternoon and late-night drinking clubs were set up, often in seedy basements and garret rooms. Usually there were rooms off the main bar where the prostitutes who were an integral part of such places could entertain their clients.

Conley owned a number of these dives in Soho, Bayswater and Kensington. Most were sleazy, but a few, like his Court Club in Duke Street near Marble Arch, catered for the raffish 'officer classes' with money to spend. He set Ruth up as hostess at the Court, and her rather tinsel good looks and natural wit were soon drawing in a fast set of hard-spending drinkers.

Ruth herself was soon earning up to £20 a week – about ten times the national average. For a time, she and her infant son lived well.

SHORT-LIVED RESPECTABILITY

Despite her lifestyle, Ruth Neilson's maternal instincts, though erratic, were strong. She yearned for respectability not only for herself but for Andria. When she met George Johnston Ellis, a forty-one-year-old-dentist with a practice in Surrey, she thought she had it within her grasp.

Ellis was a bore and a drunk, but Ruth pursued him, moved in with him and finally, in November 1950, married him.

In October 1951 the couple had a daughter, Georgina, though by then the marriage was over. Ruth now had two young children to support. After recovering from Georgina's birth, she went back to London. Morris Conley was delighted to see her, and in October 1953 he made her manageress of his Little Club in Brompton Road, Knightsbridge.

A NEW JOB AND NEW ADMIRERS

She was paid £15 per week plus commission, with a £10 per week entertainment allowance, and a rent-free two-bedroom flat above the club rooms. Even if the job lacked respectability, it

> A SINGLE MOTHER AT SEVENTEEN, RUTH TURNED TO NUDE MODELLING TO SUPPORT HERSELF AND HER CHILD

Below: *For a while, David Blakely had the money to race cars but lacked the talent to do it particularly well.*

was security of a sort. But among her first customers were two men destined to be fatal to her very existence.

Desmond Cussen was a rich and well-established businessman, with a large car and an elegant bachelor flat in Devonshire Place, near Baker Street. Aged thirty-two, he had had several minor affairs, but when he set eyes on Ruth Ellis it was love at first sight.

For her part she was fond of him – with his money and status he fitted her needs very nicely. But within hours of their first meeting a complication in the shape of a handsome young drone named David Blakely was to enter the picture.

The first time Blakely came to the Little Club he was drunk and abusive. Ruth had him thrown out, commenting: 'I hope never to see that little shit again.'

But Blakely came back to apologise, and Ruth let him buy her a drink. Within a month, Blakely had moved into Ruth's flat above the club.

David Blakely was twenty-four when he first entered Ruth Ellis's life. He had been born on 17 June 1929 in Sheffield, the fourth child of a Scottish doctor. In 1940 his parents divorced, and David's mother married a well-to-do racing driver named Humphrey Cook, who imbued his stepson with a love of his sport.

Blakely's real father had left him £7,000 – then a considerable sum. Between about 1951 and his death David was to spend all of that and more on his dream, a prototype racing car that he called the Emperor. The Emperor was probably his only real love, though Ruth Ellis learned this too late.

So Blakely moved into Ruth's rooms above the Little Club, and they began a turbulent affair. Blakely had a fiancée, Linda Dawson, the daughter of a rich Halifax millowner, whom he tried to string along for a while, but he lost her as his life became more and more centred on Ruth.

Ruth Ellis's first judgement of Blakely had in fact been the correct one. Most of his acquaintances thought him a 'little shit' and he proved it by living off his new mistress, cadging drinks from her club and openly flirting with her female customers.

The pair had violent rows, but Ruth

BLAKELY'S PROTOTYPE RACING CAR, AFFECTIONATELY KNOWN AS THE EMPEROR, WAS PROBABLY HIS ONLY REAL LOVE

tolerated Blakely's behaviour until it started driving customers away. She had a confrontation with Morris Conley about it and, favourite or no, she was fired.

Meanwhile, Desmond Cussen had proved a faithful friend to Ruth, constantly by her side whenever she felt the need of a shoulder to cry on. When Conley threw her out of her job and her flat, it was he who took her into his own apartment along with Andria – Georgina had by then been adopted. Cussen and Ellis slept together, but her benefactor was by no means possessive. He allowed her to go on seeing Blakely, and even connived at the pair sleeping in his flat.

A CYCLE OF BETRAYAL, VIOLENCE AND RECONCILIATION

In August 1954 Blakely finally broke off his engagement with Linda Dawson. Ruth thought, wrongly, that this was for her benefit. Blakely took her to Buckinghamshire and his family, but she was treated there as a London tart. And she discovered that he was in any case sleeping with other women.

One of these was Carole Findlater, wife of Anthony 'Ant' Findlater, a skilled amateur mechanic who worked on Blakely's Emperor. He and Clive Gunnell, another skilled mechanic, were almost as keen as Blakely on the expensive racing car.

After every betrayal there followed

Below: Ruth had a passion for night life.

gin-soaked acrimony, violence and finally reconciliation. But it was a punishing cycle which must have damaged Cussen almost as much as the two principals.

In any case, in January 1955 he paid for a one-bedroom service flat at 44 Egerton Gardens, Kensington. Ruth – and by tacit agreement Blakely – could now have privacy, of a sort, for their rows.

That spring, Ruth discovered she was pregnant. Her divorce from George Ellis was almost final, and Blakely was free, but when she brought up the subject of marriage his response was to beat her so badly that she miscarried. The usual boozy, tearful remorse followed, with Blakely sending a bunch of red carnations and a note of apology.

On Good Friday, 7 April, they spent what was to be their last night together. Over breakfast Blakely gave her a signed photograph proclaiming his love, and finally proposed to her. They parted with Ruth blissfully happy, and with Blakely promising to take her to drinks with the Findlaters that evening. But he failed to keep his promise.

Instead, he went alone to meet the Findlaters at the Magdala. He told them that Ruth had him trapped, that he wanted to leave her, but that he feared the consequences. And he had a sympathetic audience. Both Ant and Carole thought Ellis a grasping, vulgar woman, totally unsuitable for their friend. They suggested that Blakely stay with them for the Easter holiday.

The following morning was Easter

WHEN RUTH TOLD BLAKELY SHE WAS PREGNANT HE BEAT HER UP SO BADLY THAT SHE SUFFERED A MISCARRIAGE

Saturday, and the fair on Hampstead Heath was in full swing. Blakely, the Findlaters, Clive Gunnell and other friends spent a jovial day.

Ruth Ellis spent a distracted one. On the previous evening, she had insisted that Cussen drive her to Hampstead in search of Blakely, but she was turned away from the Findlaters' house in Tanza Road, just up from the Magdala.

Now she returned, banging vainly on the Findlaters' front door and ringing them from a telephone box nearby – only to have them hang up on her. In the afternoon she began to kick Blakely's Vanguard van, screaming at the top of her voice, and the police were called to send her away.

Finally, on Sunday evening, she took a taxi to Tanza Road, spotted Blakely and Gunnell getting into the van, and followed them to the Magdala. She had a revolver in her bag....

ARREST AND TRIAL

That, in essence, was the story Ruth Ellis told DCS Crawford. She remembered little, she said, about Sunday afternoon, other than that 'I intended to find David, and shoot him.'

And therein lay the whole case, as far as the police were concerned. Ruth Ellis had cold-bloodedly gunned down her lover in front of a pub full of witnesses, and then admitted to the crime. But where had she got the gun? Unfortunately PC Thompson, in taking the weapon from her, had accidentally

Above: *Ruth and Desmond enjoy an evening out with friends.*

appearance alienated half the jury before the evidence was heard.

As it was, the trial lasted barely two days. On 21 June the jury took just twenty-three minutes to return a verdict of guilty, and made no recommendation for mercy. Ruth Ellis was sentenced to death by hanging.

PUBLIC OUTRAGE

Back in Holloway she refused her solicitor, Victor Mishcon, permission to appeal on her behalf, though he wrote in vain to the Home Secretary begging for mercy. Instead she asked her brother, Granville, to smuggle in poison so that she could kill herself. He refused.

Granville Neilson, in fact, rightly mistrusted Ruth's story of how she had come by the fatal gun, and spent his time in a frantic search for its real owner.

Meanwhile the general public – women in particular – launched an outcry against the sentence. Letters were written to MPs and petitions were launched.

It was all to no avail. As the clock began to strike nine on the morning of 13

wiped all prints from it.

However, Ruth said that she had had the gun and ammunition for three years. It had been left with her as a pledge against a bar bill by one of her customers. The police were satisfied with her story.

So Ellis was charged with murder and removed to Holloway women's prison to await trial.

On 11 May 1955 she was arraigned at the Central Criminal Court of the Old Bailey before Mr Justice Barrie. The defence team was a distinguished and formidable one: Melford Stevenson QC, Sebag Shaw and Peter Rawlinson. Melford Stevenson asked for, and was granted, an adjournment of forty days in order to look for a precedent which would allow his client to plead guilty to manslaughter provoked by jealousy.

Unfortunately, no precedent could be found. Accordingly, when the trial proper began on 20 June, Ruth was advised to plead not guilty in the hope that her story would sway the jury to pity. But Stevenson had reckoned without Ruth's vanity.

Throughout her stay in Holloway, her main concern seems to have been that mousy roots were beginning to show through her platinum hair, and the day before her trial the Governor, Dr Charity Taylor, allowed her to bleach it. The result was that when she appeared in court she cut an impossibly glamorous figure in her smart black suit. Her lawyers were convinced that her dazzling

Right: *Mr and Mrs Neilson, Ruth Ellis's parents, leave their home in Hemel Hempstead to visit Ruth on the eve of her execution.*

July 1955, Ruth drank a last glass of brandy and walked steadfastly to the Holloway gallows.

There is no retrospective doubt that Ellis's death was a turning point in the anti-hanging campaign, though another decade was to pass before the rope was abolished competely.

THE MISSING DETAILS EMERGE

It took even longer for what seems to have been the real truth to emerge. On the night before her death, Ruth summoned Victor Mishcon to the condemned cell and dictated her account of what she said really happened on that fateful Easter Sunday.

Desmond Cussen, she said, had given her the gun. The pair had been drinking Pernod in Cussen's flat while Ruth poured out her misery. Cussen drove her and the boy Andria out to Epping Forest, where he had shown her how to load the weapon and had given her tips on aiming and firing.

Later that afternoon, after having more to drink, she had taken the loaded pistol and demanded that Cussen – not a taxi, as she had stated – drive her to the Findlaters' house in Tanza Road. From there she had made her way to the Magdala.

If this was true, what were Cussen's motives? He was certainly besotted with Ruth, lavishing money, presents and offers of marriage upon her. He had never refused her slightest whim. Perhaps he was simply going along blindly, as usual, with her wishes.

Or, as has been suggested, did he simply give her the gun, knowing that in her mood of jealous, drink-fuelled rage she would kill his rival Blakely. In which case, was he also convinced that she would be acquitted?

Desmond Cussens visited Ruth Ellis every day during her remand in Holloway prison, bringing her flowers, chocolates and other presents. But as soon as the guilty verdict was pronounced he broke all contact with her. He died twenty years after his troubled lover, in Australia, without apparently ever having told his side of the story.

Below: Huge crowds gathered outside Holloway Prison on the morning of Ruth Ellis's execution.

SAM SHEPPARD
A Travesty of Justice

A well-respected citizen is arrested for the brutal murder of his pregnant wife. Vital forensic evidence is ignored and the trial is a travesty of justice. In this, as in so many murder cases, there are no winners, only losers

Saturday, 3 July 1954 – the eve of Independence Day – was a busy one for Dr Sam Sheppard, though his wife, four-and-a-half-months pregnant Marilyn, took things rather more easily. Dr Sheppard was on call at his father's Bay View Hospital in Bay Village, Cleveland, Ohio and split his day between work and socializing with their close neighbours, Don and Nancy Ahern.

THE FATAL EVENING

The Aherns' two young sons and seven-year-old Chip Sheppard ate first, while their parents sat on the porch overlooking the lake and sipped drinks. Later the Ahern boys were sent home and Chip went to bed, after which the four adults spent a relaxed evening.

By midnight Marilyn and Sam were drowsing. The Aherns decided to go home to bed. Before leaving, Nancy Ahern locked the lakeside door of the house for Marilyn. Then she and her husband went out by the main door on to the road. Marilyn had gone upstairs to the bedroom, Sam was snoring on the sofa.

At 5.45a.m. John Spencer Houk, a businessman friend of Sheppard's who

Above: *The Sheppards' clapboard house in Bay Village, Cleveland, Ohio.*

Opposite: *Dr Sam Sheppard on his way to court.*

Below: *A detailed diagram of the Sheppard house shows the scene of the crime.*

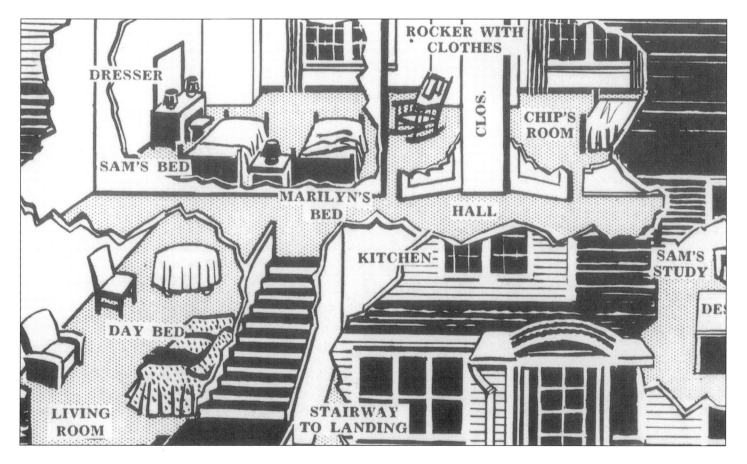

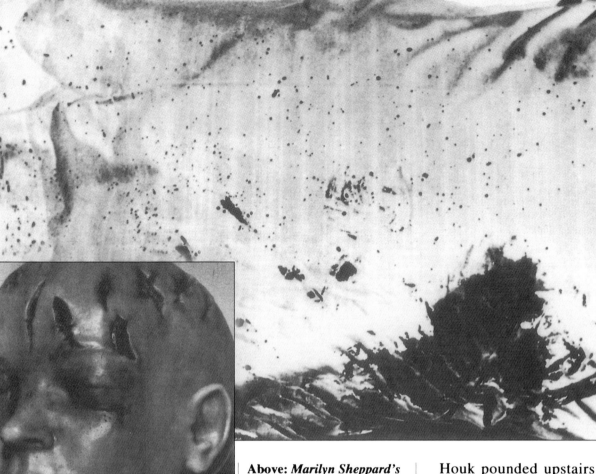

Above: *Marilyn Sheppard's blood-spattered pillow.*

Left: *A model shows the horrific wounds inflicted on Marilyn Sheppard's skull.*

was also mayor of Bay Village, was awakened by the shrilling noise of his bedside telephone. Sleepily he picked it up and heard the voice of Sam Sheppard: 'For God's sake, Spen, come quick! I think they've killed Marilyn!'

SCENES OF VIOLENCE

Houk's house was just 100 yards from that of the Sheppards. He and his wife arrived at 5.55 to a scene of chaos. The roadside door was open and Sheppard's medical bag lay inside, its contents scattered around. A desk drawer hung open, and the immediate impression was of a burglary. Sam Sheppard sat, stripped to the waist, in his den. His trousers were wet and his face was bruised. His neck was contorted with agony.

IT WAS A COSY, RELAXED, EVE-OF-INDEPENDENCE-DAY SUPPER WITH A COUPLE OF CLOSE NEIGHBOURS

Houk pounded upstairs and into the Sheppards' bedroom. Marilyn lay on her back, her legs protruding from the bottom of the bed. Her face, hair and pillow were plastered with blood from over thirty deep head wounds.

Three minutes after sunrise Patrolman Fred Drenham arrived. He was closely followed by Richard Sheppard, one of Sam's elder brothers, and his wife, and by the other brother Stephen and the local Chief of Police, John Eaton. At 6.30a.m., as police began their systematic work at the murder scene, Sam was driven by Stephen and John Eaton to Bay View Hospital for a check-up. Nurses who tended Sam were later to testify that his lips were badly cut and swollen, and his front teeth were loose.

By 9a.m. Sam had been fitted with a neck brace and was heavily sedated. He was, however, able to answer questions from the coroner of Cuyahoga County, Dr Samuel Gerber, who had already made a brief visit to the house. At 11a.m., Detectives Robert Schottke and Patrick Gareau of Cleveland Police took over the questioning.

The two detectives had already noted that there had been no signs of forced entry into the Sheppard house, and the only fingerprint was a thumb-mark which subsequently turned out to be Chip's. Sam's corduroy jacket, which the Aherns had seen him wearing the night before, was neatly folded and lying on the sofa. No bloodstained weapon had been found, and, despite the confusion, the detectives were pretty sure that the motive had not been burglary.

They were not happy that Sheppard had been taken to his family-run hospital, and they were certainly not happy with his uncorroborated story. As Schottke was to tell him: 'The evidence points very strongly at you. I don't know what my partner thinks, but I think you killed your wife.'

By that evening the murder was headline news, not merely because of its bloody drama but because it involved the Sheppards, one of Ohio's most prominent and controversial medical families.

PROMINENT MEDICAL FAMILY

Samuel Holmes Shepherd was born in Cleveland on 29 December 1923, the youngest of Dr Richard and Ethel Sheppard's three boys. Richard Sheppard was a general surgeon who was beginning to gain a reputation as an osteopath, at a time when this holistic form of medicine was little known in the United States.

Academically Sam was not particularly bright, but he had an ability for hard work which got him through his exams. In 1943, as an alternative to military service, he began to study medicine at the Western Reserve University in Cleveland, at Hanover College, Indiana, and finally at the Osteopathic School of Physicians and Surgeons in Los Angeles.

In the meantime he had met and fallen in love with Marilyn Reese, and in November 1945, when she was nineteen, the couple were married at the First Hollywood Methodist Church in Los Angeles.

In 1948 Sam graduated as a doctor of medicine, and he and his wife intended to stay in California. Sam's father, however, had that same year founded the Bay View Hospital back in Cleveland, and Sam,

---

'I DON'T KNOW WHAT MY PARTNER THINKS, BUT I THINK YOU KILLED YOUR WIFE'

Below: ***Newsmen pack the courtroom during the trial.***

---

with his two brothers, was pressured into joining the family 'firm'.

Within months, business was booming. By 1954 Bay View was one of the most prestigious hospitals in the state.

Now, despite their suspicions, the police were reluctant to arrest one of the Dr Sheppards of Bay View. As his attorney, William Corrigan, told him: 'The only way to convict yourself, Sam, is by opening your mouth.'

PRESS CAMPAIGN

There was one man, however, who was unimpressed by Sheppard's status in the community. He was Louis Benson Seltzer, editor of the *Cleveland Press*, and well known for his hard-hitting campaigns against crooked politicians and 'soft' police departments.

On 21 July, seventeen days after the killing, the *Cleveland Press* ran a splash headline: 'Why No Inquest? Do It Now, Dr Gerber.'

Dr Gerber, the fifty-seven-year-old coroner for Cuyahoga County, had felt Seltzer's righteous wrath before. The next day he called an inquest. Gerber refused witnesses the right to counsel, and when William Corrigan protested he had him thrown out to tumultuous cheers.

Above: *Police search Dr Sheppard's medical bag after the murder.*

Sam Sheppard waived his right not to give evidence, and was questioned for eight hours by Gerber. Among other things, Sheppard denied having committed adultery with a mystery woman in California named only as 'Miss X'. Finally, on 30 July, he was arrested, even before Gerber recorded his verdict that Marilyn had been murdered.

Sheppard's statement at the time of his arrest was essentially the same as he had made shortly after the crime was committed. He said that he had been awakened, as he lay on the sofa, by his wife's screams from upstairs. He refused to guess what time it might have been.

'I charged into our room and saw a form with a light garment,' he said. 'It was grappling with something or someone....'

He and this person had wrestled, until

Sheppard was knocked out from behind. When he regained his senses he saw on the floor his own police surgeon's badge – he was unpaid police surgeon for the Bay Valley force – which he normally kept in his wallet. He took Marilyn's pulse 'and felt that she was gone'.

After checking that his son Chip was still asleep and safe, Sheppard had heard a noise, ran downstairs and saw 'a form rapidly progressing somewhere'. Sheppard had chased the figure down from the porch to the lake, where he had grappled with a large man with bushy hair. The man had caught his neck in an armlock, and he had passed out.

When he came to he had woken up on his face by the water's edge. His T-shirt was missing, though he could not recollect what had happened to it.

Also missing from his wrist was his gold watch, which was later found, spattered with Marilyn's blood, in a duffle bag in the Sheppards' boat-house by the lake. This watch was to be the centre of vigorous controversy later. Sheppard had then staggered back to the house.

TRIED FOR FIRST DEGREE MURDER

The trial of Sam Sheppard on the charge of first degree murder began in the Court of Common Pleas, Cleveland, on Monday 18 October 1954. But because of delay in jury selection – many admitted that they had firm ideas on the case – it did not properly get under way until 4 November. The judge was Edward Blythin, and Sheppard pleaded Not Guilty.

The main thrust of the case against Sheppard was indicated by prosecuting counsel John Mahon in his opening address: 'The state will prove that Sheppard and Miss X talked together about divorce and marriage. No one was in that house that morning on 4 July attempting to commit a burglary. No evidence has been found that any burglar or marauder was there.'

The Aherns were called early in the trial. Don said that he had never seen the placid Sam Sheppard lose his temper, though Nancy introduced a hesitant note when she said that, though she was sure

Marilyn was very much in love with her husband, she had never been sure of Sam's feelings towards Marilyn.

Dr Samuel Gerber, the coroner, caused a sensation when he spoke of a 'blood signature' on the yellow pillowcase under Marilyn's battered head. 'In this bloodstain I could make out the impression of a surgical instrument,' he said. The instrument, he suggested, 'had two blades, each about three inches long, with serrated edges'.

No weapon of any kind had been found at the house, but, said Gerber, 'the impression could only have been made by an instrument similar to the type of surgical instrument I had in mind'. Curiously, he was not asked to specify just what the mysterious instrument was.

On 1 December came another sensation, when Miss X entered the witness box. She identified herself as Susan Hayes, a twenty-four-year-old laboratory technician who had worked at the Bay View Hospital and met Sam there in 1951.

They had begun their affair in California, after she had left Bay View to work in Los Angeles in 1954. She admitted that they had slept together, as well as making love in cars. 'He said that he loved his wife very much but not as a wife, and was thinking of getting a divorce,' she testified.

This evidence meant that Sam was not only a perjurer – he had denied adultery at the inquest – but guilty of the then criminal offence, under Ohio law, of adultery.

On the stand, Sam now admitted lying at the inquest, saying that he had done so to protect Susan Hayes rather than himself. In any case, he went on, he had never truly been in love with her, and had never discussed divorce with either her or his wife. He admitted that he had committed adultery with women other than Susan Hayes, but refused to name them.

Summing up for the prosecution, Thomas Parrino, an assistant prosecutor, said: 'If the defendant would lie under oath to protect a lady, how many lies would he utter to protect his own life?'

Corrigan's defence was, on the face of it, poor. He made no mention of one or

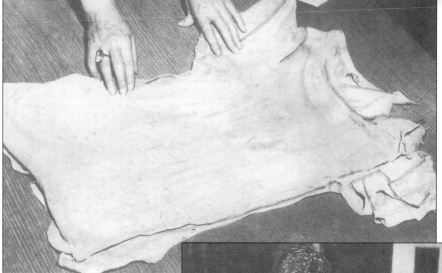

Above and right: *Police examine evidence during the investigation of the case.*

THE CORONER CAUSED A SENSATION WHEN HE SPOKE OF A 'BLOOD SIGNATURE' ON THE PILLOWCASE UNDER MARILYN'S BATTERED HEAD

IF THE DEFENDANT WOULD LIE UNDER OATH TO PROTECT A LADY, HOW MANY LIES WOULD HE UTTER TO PROTECT HIS OWN LIFE?

two curious pieces of evidence which might have helped Sam.

Tooth chippings had been found on the bedroom floor which belonged neither to Sam nor to Marilyn. There was firm evidence that Marilyn had bitten her attacker savagely, though Sheppard bore no bite marks. There was the business of the mysterious surgical instrument. And there were wool threads, found under Marilyn's nails, which matched no clothing in the house – not hers, not Sam's, not Chip's. Above all, there was the blood-spattered watch.

Instead, Corrigan took up the prosecution's sex theme and made a negative mess of it. 'Is sex the only thing in a marriage?' he asked. 'Sheppard wandered from the path of rectitude. That didn't prove he didn't love his wife, his home, or his family.'

After a briefing from Judge Blythin on the laws governing circumstantial evidence, and the difference between first and second degree murder, the jury retired. They returned on Tuesday, 21 December after over four days' deliberation. Their decision was that Sam Sheppard was guilty of second degree murder, and Judge Blythin sentenced him to life imprisonment.

After what must have been a melancholy Christmas for the Sheppard family, William Corrigan retrieved the keys of Sam's house from the police and handed them over to Dr Paul Leland Kirk. One of the country's leading forensic scientists, he had undertaken to do independent tests.

EXHAUSTIVE FORENSIC WORK

Dr Kirk began work in the Sheppards' house in January 1955, and after studying the results in his California headquarters produced a 10,000-word report three and a half months later.

Among the detailed facts examined in the report the most important was Dr Kirk's emphatic assertion that a fourth person, other than Sam, Marilyn or Chip, had been in the house on the night of the murder. Blood on the wardrobe door demonstrably did not match that of any of the Sheppards. And teeth fragments on the carpet showed that Marilyn had bitten her attacker very deeply, though, as had been shown at the trial, Sheppard bore no such scars.

Dr Kirk was able to show that whoever delivered the death blows to Marilyn would have been covered in her flying blood, but the only stain on Sam's clothing was a spot on the knee of his trousers – gained, he claimed, when he had knelt to take his wife's pulse.

Furthermore, bloodstains on the walls showed that the killer had struck with his left hand, while Sam was right-handed. The blows had undoubtedly been made with a blunt instrument such as a piece of piping, which made nonsense of the coroner's 'surgical instrument' theory.

'No actual proof of a technical nature

was ever offered indicating the guilt of the defendant,' he concluded.

Despite what seemed to be Kirk's irrefutable report, Judge Blythin refused, on 10 May 1955, to grant a retrial. Six weeks later the Ohio Court of Appeals praised 'the originality and imagination' of Dr Kirk, but nevertheless turned down an appeal for a new trial.

The following summer, on 31 May 1956, the Ohio Supreme Court upheld Sheppard's conviction by five votes to two. Hope was raised, however, by the two dissenting judges, who expressed the view that there had been little real evidence to prove Sheppard guilty, and that Judge Blythin had accepted gossip as evidence.

But on 19 December the highest judicial body in the land, the United States Supreme Court, refused to review the case on technical grounds. Again, however, doubts were expressed about the conduct of the Ohio judiciary.

A CONVICT'S CONFESSION

Sheppard's hopes were raised once more six months later, when, in June 1957 a convict named Donald Wedler, who was serving a ten-year sentence for a Florida hold-up, confessed to the murder. He claimed that he had been in Cleveland, Ohio on the day of Marilyn's killing, and after taking heroin had stolen a car and driven around looking for a house to burgle.

He had found a suitable one, a large white house on a lake front, had broken in, crept past a man asleep on a settee and gone upstairs.

A woman in an upstairs bedroom had awakened as he was preparing to rifle her dressing table, and he had beaten her repeatedly with an iron pipe. Then, as he fled downstairs, he had encountered a man, whom he had struck down with the pipe, before flinging the impromptu weapon into the lake and driving away.

The coroner was quick to point out discrepancies in the story. Sheppard had said that he was struck down from behind in the bedroom, not on the stairs, and Wedler had made no mention of a struggle in the garden by the lake. Nor was Wedler a burly man with the 'bushy'

CURIOUSLY, SHEPPARD'S LAWYER IGNORED EVIDENCE WHICH WOULD HAVE POINTED THE FINGER FIRMLY AWAY FROM HIS CLIENT

NO ACTUAL PROOF OF A TECHNICAL NATURE WAS EVER OFFERED INDICATING THE GUILT OF THE DEFENDANT

hair mentioned by Sheppard – he was slight, though he did have unruly, curly hair.

What interested Sheppard's lawyers most was the fact that a lie-detector expert who tested Wedler was quite certain that he was telling the truth, 'or what he believed to be the truth'.

Unfortunately, there were many imponderables about the Wedler story. As a heroin user, he might have been telling the truth and have confused the details, but equally he might have invented the whole thing after reading newspaper accounts of the case, and convinced his drug-addled mind that he was the murderer.

In the end, it was the plethora of newspaper speculation surrounding the original event which led to a successful appeal – but only after Sheppard had served ten years in jail. In 1961 William Corrigan died, and in his place Stephen Sheppard hired a smart, fast-talking young attorney from Boston named F. Lee Bailey.

Below: *Susan Hayes. It was revealed that she was Sam Sheppard's mistress.*

RETRIAL AT LAST

In April 1963, after a series of legal moves, Bailey lodged a petition with the US District Court, a federal rather than state body, that the case be reopened. This time he was successful. After almost a year's deliberation, Judge Carl Weinman delivered his verdict on 15 July 1964. The original trial, he said, had been a 'mockery of justice'. He ordered Sheppard to be released pending a retrial.

Lawyer F. Lee Bailey immediately swept into the attack. Quoting the exhaustive inquiry undertaken by Dr Kirk, he compared it with the muddled and pathetic attempts of the Cleveland Police, whose search for clues, he forced them to admit, had been perfunctory to a degree. Their check for fingerprints had been particularly casual. They had not even tried to get prints from the bloodstained watch found in the duffle bag, and had also ignored a key-ring and chain which accompanied it.

Bailey produced a photograph of the watch, which had blood speckles across the face such as could have been caused had Sheppard been wearing it when he battered his wife to death. But, as Bailey pointed out, there were also speckles of blood on the back of the watch and the inside of the wristband, which certainly could not have got there if he really had been wearing it under such conditions.

On 6 June, 1966, the United States Supreme Court overturned Sheppard's conviction, and he walked free.

UNANSWERED QUESTIONS

There were, of course, still questions which remained unanswered. One was the old Sherlock Holmesian puzzle of the

*Above: **Sam Sheppard
outside Ohio Supreme Court.***

'THE ANSWER TO THE
SHEPPARD CASE RIDDLE,'
WROTE A PRIVATE
DETECTIVE, 'LIES IN BAY
VILLAGE'

dog that did nothing in the night.

For if an unknown intruder had indeed broken in, why had the family dog Koko not barked a warning? Although neither police nor defendants thought fit to bring their suspicions into the open, privately they admitted that, if Sam did not kill his wife Marilyn, then it was someone who knew her, and the house, well.

As Harold Bretnall, a New York private detective hired by the Sheppard family, wrote in a report dated 1955: 'The answer to the Sheppard case riddle lies in Bay Village.' At the first trial, the jury had heard part of a statement made by Sam to detectives, in which he had said that Marilyn had 'spurned lovers – potential lovers...three that I know of and I am pretty sure more'.

Although not named at the trial, the men had, it was claimed, been identified to the investigating officers. Bretnall also claimed that a pair of Marilyn's bedroom slippers bore evidence that she had left the house during the night of 4 July 1954 while she was wearing them. 'Marilyn Sheppard was murdered by someone who was a frequent visitor to the Sheppard home,' wrote Bretnall.

The blood-speckled watch, too, posed unanswered questions. For if it had been splashed with Marilyn's blood, it must surely have been lying on the bedside table when she was killed – when it should have been downstairs on her husband's wrist. Did he come to bed, leaving his corduroy jacket downstairs, place his watch on the bedside table and batter his wife to death?

Or did he come to bed, take off his watch, hear an intruder, put on his trousers to investigate, get himself laid out – and then inexplicably lie to the police about his movements?

FURTHER TRAGEDY

One thing was sure: Marilyn's death and Sam Sheppard's ruined career were not the only tragedies involved in the drama. Sam's mother Edith was deeply shocked by the event, and took an overdose of sleeping pills during the first trial. She recovered at the family hospital.

But on 17 January 1955, soon after her youngest son was convicted of murder, she shot herself. Eleven days later Sam's father, Dr Richard Sheppard, died at the age of sixty-five of a bleeding gastric ulcer. Almost exactly eight years after Mrs Sheppard's suicide, Marilyn's father, Thomas Reese, also shot himself.

Soon after his release, Sam married Ariane Tebbenjohanne, who had supported his cause. In December 1967, after a vigorous fight to regain his medical licence, it was granted, and Sheppard joined the staff of the Youngstown Osteopathic Hospital, Ohio. His appointment lasted a year, until a malpractice claim was made against the hospital. The insurance company refused to pay out until Sam resigned.

On the day of his resignation, 3 December 1968, Sheppard was sued for divorce by Ariane. She claimed that she had suffered mental and physical cruelty at the hands of 'that maniac'.

Sheppard had authorized a ghost-written autobiography entitled *Endure and Conquer*, but most of the proceeds went to pay F. Lee Bailey's legal fees. While fighting once more to re-establish his medical career, he took up wrestling. In October 1969 he married his manager's daughter, a twenty-year-old named Colleen Strickland.

For a while his wrestling career and the third marriage seemed to prosper, but Sheppard was consuming heavier and heavier amounts of vodka. On 5 April 1970 he died of liver failure.

ORGANIZED CRIME

THE KRAY TWINS
A Lethal Double-Act

From playground bullies via the boxing ring, East End twins Reggie and Ronnie Kray went on to build a gangland empire the like of which London had never seen before. 'The Firm' allowed no liberties to be taken, and was feared by all

On 24 October 1933 twin boys were born to Mrs Violet Kray of 178 Vallance Road, Bethnal Green. She named them Reginald and Ronald.

The twins grew up in London's East End, surrounded by street traders, boxers and petty criminals. Fighting was a way of life for children in Bethnal Green. But Reggie and Ronnie seemed to derive enormous pleasure out of terrifying and hurting other human beings.

BOXERS

At fourteen they found another, more acceptable outlet for their violent tendencies – boxing.

Both lads showed real promise as amateurs, but demonstrated a completely different approach to the sport, a difference which was reflected in their personalities as men. Reggie was a skilful

Above: *'I gotta horse!' Ronnie Kray, with minder, poses briefly as a racehorse owner.*

Opposite: *At 18 years of age, Reggie and Ronnie Kray were successful young boxers with two years of professional experience behind them. Their styles were very different, however: Reggie was a skilled fighter, but Ronnie won his matches by vicious slugging.*

Left: *The twins were adored by their mother Vi, for whom they could do no wrong. But their career in boxing soon came to an end when they were put on probation for beating up a police constable.*

Above: *To the end of her life Vi kept her faith in her sons. They are seen together here with the twins' grandfather, who had also been a professional boxer, outside her modest East End house in Vallance Road.*

IN BOXING AS IN LIFE, RONNIE WAS A HARD AND FEARLESS SLUGGER

and resourceful boxer, whereas Ronnie was a slugger, totally fearless and vicious. The net result of these contrasting styles, however, was the same. They both won every fight.

At sixteen the twins turned professional and maintained their unbeaten record until their careers were brought to an abrupt halt. They both got into a street fight during which they beat up a police constable.

They were let off with a probationary sentence. But fight managers dislike boxers with a reputation for violence outside the ring, since any serious conviction usually costs a fighter his licence.

The next watershed in the Krays' young lives came in March 1952, when they were called up to do their National Service. They had no intention of spending two years in the Royal Fusiliers and made that immediately and absolutely clear. The boys absconded and were back at Vallance Road for tea after a mere six hours of army service.

They were arrested, escaped, arrested again and escaped again. They continued their running battle with the army for more than a year before the Royal Fusiliers gave up on them. After spending nine months in a military prison at Shepton Mallet they were given a dishonourable discharge.

MANAGEMENT PROSPECTS

When they were released in 1953, the twins went straight back to the East End.

While they considered their career prospects, the twins established semi-residence in the Regal Billiard Hall in the Mile End Road. It was a seedy, down-at-heel place which had become a popular hang-out for small-time criminals.

Around the time the Krays arrived at the Regal, there was a sudden outbreak of violence and vandalism. The twins never seemed to be directly involved, but there were fights every night, and there were anonymous threats to burn the place down.

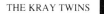

ASPIRATION 'UP WEST'

By 1955, the Firm was the established power through Hackney and Mile End to Walthamstow. And they were starting to make real money.

But the twins had their sights set on bigger things. Reggie wanted the 'good life', the wealth that West End crime offered, and Ronnie craved the kudos that came with being a big-time gangland boss.

Ronnie spent most of his time planning elaborate deals and alliances which would establish the Firm 'up West', but none of them ever quite worked out. The Krays were too wild and too dangerous for the established West End gangs to deal with. They closed ranks and shut the twins out.

This frustrated Ronnie, and the more frustrated he became, the more violent his thinking became. He grew increasingly paranoid and psychotic, toting his guns in public and threatening to 'do' people all the time.

Ronnie finally had his chance to use his gun for real when a young docker tried to cheat one of the Firm's associates. The docker gave Ronnie some lip, and Ronnie promptly shot him in the leg.

Everyone in the East End, including

The manager eventually left and the twins approached the owners with an offer. They would pay the owners £5 a week to take the hall over. The owners accepted, the Krays became managers, and the violence and vandalism stopped as abruptly as it had started.

Reggie, who proved an astute businessman, set about renovating and redecorating the Regal, and before long it was becoming a successful commercial concern.

It also continued to serve as a meeting point for local criminals, but now the Krays offered them a genuine service. There were lock-up cubicles under the seats for thieves' tools, and stolen goods could be stashed round the back. The Krays received a cut of every job planned or executed from their premises.

The billiard hall was now making good money, and the Krays were supplementing this with extortion. Clubs, billiard halls, unlicensed gambling dens and illicit bookmakers from Bethnal Green and Mile End were soon paying a 'pension' to 'the Firm', as the Kray gang was now known.

Despite their growing reputation, however, the Krays still had no real power. Each section of the East End had its own 'guv'nor', and the twins hadn't yet achieved 'guv'nor' status.

However, their activities were causing some displeasure with these established gang bosses. There were a number of bloody showdowns and, despite being outnumbered and outgunned by their rivals, the twins always seemed to come out on top.

Above: *From the Regal Billiard Hall in London's Mile End Road, the Kray twins soon moved on to bigger and better enterprises. At a charity evening in the Kentucky Club, they line up for a photograph with brother Charles (behind Ronnie, right).*

Right: *The psychopathic Ronnie was a practising homosexual, but Reggie did not resemble his twin brother in this respect. Here he escorts long-standing girl-friend Frances Shea in Vallance Road.*

the police, knew that the Firm were responsible for the shooting, and after a few hours they picked up a man they believed to be Ronnie Kray and put him into an identification parade.

'Yes, but I'm not Ronald Kray,' said the man in the line-up. 'I'm Reggie Kray. I can prove it – and, what's more, I can prove I wasn't anywhere near where this bloke says he was shot.' The police, angry and embarrassed, had no option but to free Reggie with an apology.

OUT FOR REVENGE

The police, who do not like to be bested, now had it in for the Krays. Their chance to nail one of them came the following year, in 1956.

Terry Martin, a street trader from Stepney, had been taking 'extreme liberties', and Ronnie decided that he needed 'teaching a lesson'. He dragged Martin out of the Britannia pub in Watney Street, slashed him twice on the head with a bayonet, stabbed him in the shoulder and then kicked him unconscious.

Ronnie was being driven home in his new black Buick when police picked him up. They found a crowbar and a bayonet in the car and when they asked how he got blood on his shirt, Ronnie shrugged. 'I 'ad a nose bleed, di'n' I?'

Ronnie was found guilty of grievous

Above: *Reggie eventually married Frances Shea. He looks on as best man Ronnie kisses the bride.*

DESPITE THE BAYONET FOUND IN HIS CAR, RONNIE CASUALLY TOLD THE POLICE HIS BLOODSTAINED SHIRT WAS CAUSED BY A NOSE BLEED

---

bodily harm and sentenced to three years' imprisonment.

It was the first time since they were born that the twins had been separated for more than a few days at a time, and most East End pundits said it would be the end of the Firm.

They were wrong. Reggie, freed from his brother's manic influence, not only continued to run the gang's illegal activities but also embarked on several legitimate enterprises. He rented an empty shop in Bow Road with his older brother Charles and converted it into a drinking club, the Double R – in honour of himself and his absent brother.

The club was a huge success, not only

Left: *Bride and groom and best man pose for the camera at the wedding reception.*

Right: *All for one and one for all: the twins and brother Charles affirm their family ties.*

with local villains but also with certain members of the entertainment and sporting fraternities who considered it was chic to rub shoulders with the criminal element.

INSANITY

In prison, Ronnie Kray soon showed signs of severe mental illness. He became paranoid and depressed and complained of 'hearing voices'. He couldn't sleep, and wouldn't eat because he was convinced that he was being poisoned.

He was transferred to the psychiatric wing of Winchester Prison for observation. There he was put on sedatives and showed some signs of improvement until the morning he received news that his favourite auntie, Rose, had died of cancer.

By that evening Ronnie was totally incoherent and had to be strapped into a straitjacket for his own protection. The following day, doctors at Winchester certified Ronald Kray as legally insane.

Ronnie was transferred to Long Grove Hospital near Epsom where he received the very best psychiatric treatment. He was diagnosed as a paranoid schizophrenic.

Doctors treated his illness with a new wonder drug called Stematol. Within days Ronnie was stabilized and was showing marked signs of improvement.

But he was still technically insane which meant that, despite the fact that he had only a year of his sentence to serve, the authorities could detain him indefinitely.

Alarmed by this prospect, Reggie Kray decided something had to be done to rectify the situation. He drove up to Long Grove, switched clothes with his brother and took his place in the hospital while Ronnie walked to freedom.

On the run, Ronnie was taken to see a top Harley Street psychiatrist who, not knowing his patient's true identity, pronounced him sane.

But Ronald Kray was most certainly not sane. Without close medical supervision, his condition deteriorated rapidly. Even Reggie was eventually forced to face the fact that his brother needed professional help. So he did the

Above: *Although Reggie was cleverer and more responsible than his brother, he was constantly influenced by Ronnie, dressing like him and following him in his pose as a big-time gangster.*

RONNIE KRAY, IN COMMON WITH HIS HERO AL CAPONE AND THE BOSTON STRANGLER, WAS A PARANOID SCHIZOPHRENIC

---

unthinkable. He called the police.

Ronnie was returned not to hospital, but to jail to complete his sentence. He was no longer technically insane, so the ploy had worked. He was released in the spring of 1959.

CLEVER BUSINESS MOVES

During Ronnie's absence, Reggie and Charles Kray had proved extremely shrewd. They had moved away from street violence and consolidated their section of the East End by negotiation, albeit with underlying menace. They had also formed a loose partnership with one of the big-time West End bosses, Billy Hill. Hill had recently gone into semi-retirement but retained extensive interests in the West End, particularly illicit gambling, and he had needed someone to look after the show.

In the mid-fifties, gambling fever had hit London. Illegal casinos had become a major industry which was almost completely controlled by the underworld. Even high-society 'chemin de fer' parties at their secret Belgravia and Mayfair addresses were paying a 'fee' to the Mob to ensure that their sport continued uninterrupted.

Hill had introduced Reggie and Charles Kray to several of these parties where they acted as minders. It was a good source of income and, more important, it gave them contacts and a presence in the West End.

Parliament was on the verge of legalizing gambling, a move which was intended to legitimize the industry and to remove the criminal element from it. Reggie Kray, however, reckoned it would be just like Las Vegas – a licence to print money.

The casinos would have to be run by someone, and who better than the men who already knew the ropes, men like Reggie Kray? All he had to do was keep his nose clean and grab the opportunity when it came along. The only problem was Ronnie. He was now back on the scene, paranoid and hostile, toting guns and talking about 'doing' people.

Ironically, it was Ronnie's thuggery that eventually got the Krays their first solid stake in the West End. He had been putting pressure on racketeer landlord Peter Rachman to pay protection.

Rachman was too clever to let himself get on that particular treadmill, but knew he would have to do something to get Ronnie off his back. So he negotiated a deal which gave the Krays an interest in Esmerelda's Barn, a newly licensed casino in Belgravia's Wilton Place.

In addition to this, the Krays established themselves as 'security consultants' to other casinos in Mayfair, Chelsea and Knightsbridge, some thirty in all, each paying £150 a week for the benefit of the Firm's expertise.

By 1962, the American Mafia had started to buy stakes in some of the smarter casinos and the Krays established themselves as the Mob's London minders.

Despite Ronnie's ongoing lunacy, Reggie continued with his efforts to smarten up the Krays' image. He opened a new, plusher club in the East End, and became actively involved in a whole range of charitable works – old folks' homes, cancer appeals and boys' clubs.

By this time a certain policeman, Detective Inspector Leonard 'Nipper' Read was starting to take an unhealthy interest in the Kray twins and their Firm.

Below and bottom: *As the twins' influence grew 'up West', so did their ambition to rub shoulders with showbiz personalities such as film star Judy Garland or actress Barbara Windsor.*

LAUNDRYMEN TO THE MOB

By 1965, business was booming for the twins. They had their casinos and clubs and their protection racket, and they were involved in large-scale fraud.

Then, in April, they were approached by one of their American Mafia contacts, Angelo Bruno, to launder $55,000 worth of stolen bearer bonds. They were part of a $2 million consignment of bonds that the Mafia was holding in New York. If the Krays did well, they could act as the exclusive Mafia fence in London.

The whole idea appealed to the Firm – particularly to Ronnie, whose dream of being a big-time Mob boss seemed finally to be becoming a reality. The Firm bought the first shipment of bonds at a quarter of their face value and found, with the help of a crooked merchant banker, Alan Cooper, no trouble in disposing of them. Things had never looked better.

ORGY OF VIOLENCE

But soon people started 'taking liberties' again, and Ronnie couldn't stand for that. The target of his displeasure on this occasion was one George Cornell, an enforcer for the rival Richardson gang.

On 9 March 1966, Ronnie slipped his 9mm Mauser automatic into his shoulder holster, collected henchman Ian Barrie, and told 'Scotch' Jack Dickson to drive them down to one of Cornell's hangouts, a pub called the Blind Begger.

When they arrived, Cornell was sitting perched on a stool at the far end of the bar, drinking a beer with a couple of friends.

'Well, look who's here!' said Cornell, smiling. But his smile soon evaporated as Barrie fired two warning shots into the ceiling. Ronnie Kray never spoke. He raised his Mauser and shot Cornell through the head. The massive 9mm shell exploded his skull and he died instantly.

When the police arrived at the Blind Begger, nobody had seen anything. The identity of George Cornell's killer,

Above: *An unlikely pairing. The homosexual Ronnie in conversation with Christine Keeler, central character in the sex-and-security scandal involving War Minister John Profumo and Russian spy Ivanov in 1963.*

IN THE EARLY SIXTIES THE KRAYS MADE THEIR FIRST CONTACTS WITH THE US MAFIA - WHICH WOULD PROVE VERY USEFUL LATER

JACK 'THE HAT' McVITIE HAD DONE MUCH TO IRK THE TWINS, BUT HIS ONE SUICIDAL ERROR WAS TO CALL RONNIE A 'FAT POOF'

however, was the worst-kept secret in the East End. And among those who were fully aware of his identity was Detective Inspector 'Nipper' Read.

Rather than lying low after the murder of Cornell, Ronnie seemed to have his taste for violence heightened and he embarked on an orgy of maiming and killing.

All reason seemed to leave the twins at this point in time. Perhaps their most bizarre escapade involved Frank 'Mad Axe Man' Mitchell.

Mitchell, an old friend of Ronnie's, was serving a thirty-two-year sentence in Dartmoor for robbery with violence.

On 12 December 1966 they had him snatched from a working party on the moor. A massive manhunt ensued and the Krays hid Mitchell in a friend's flat in Barking. But it wasn't long before the twins regretted taking Mitchell on. His incessant, child-like demands on them became intolerable. He, too, would have to be taught a lesson.

On Christmas Eve, Reggie Kray told Mitchell that he was going to be moved down to a safe house for the holiday. At 8.30 p.m., he was bundled into the back of a van which sped off down Barking Road. Frank Mitchell was never seen again.

THE KILLING OF JACK 'THE HAT'

The Firm was falling apart at the seams, but desertion from the ranks was rare. Deemed a 'diabolical liberty', it was dealt with appropriately.

One exception was Jack 'The Hat' McVitie, a strong-arm man who had worked with the Krays at various times over the years. He was definitely a liberty-taker. He had taken money from Reggie for a contract killing and then bungled it. He had threatened the twins behind their back. And, worst of all, he had described Ronnie as a 'fat poof'.

The twins agreed that McVitie must be punished. At Ronnie's insistence, Reggie would be the one to mete out that punishment.

McVitie was lured to a basement flat in Stoke Newington with the promise of a lively party. Arriving at the flat just before midnight, he demanded: 'Where's all the birds and all the booze?'

As Ronnie Kray got up to greet him from the sofa, Reggie stepped out from behind the door, aimed a .32 automatic at McVitie's head and pulled the trigger.

The gun jammed and Reggie threw himself at his hapless victim. Ronnie watched the ensuing struggle, egging his brother on with hysterical screams. McVitie broke free and dived through a window, but Reggie caught his legs and dragged him back into the room and plunged a carving knife into his face, chest and stomach. He slid on to the floor and died in an ocean of his own blood.

Like Mitchell and the others, McVitie's body was spirited away and never found. But again the East End underworld and the police, notably Detective Inspector 'Nipper' Read, were well aware of what had happened and who was responsible.

GUNNING FOR THE TWINS

'Nipper' Read was a textbook detective. Hard-working, methodical and totally dedicated, he was a five-foot-seven terrier who had his teeth into the Krays and wasn't about to let go.

After the McVitie murder Read was assigned a team of fourteen detectives and set up an undercover operation in an anonymous block of government offices south of the Thames. Their sole task was to build a case against the Kray twins.

Read knew that any attempt to convict the Krays of a specific crime was doomed to failure. They were too powerful and too well organized. They could intimidate witnesses and threaten jurors. They had the money to retain top lawyers and pay others to take the blame or provide them with an alibi.

Above: *After the murder of George Cornell the Kray twins were held for questioning by the police for 36 hours, before returning to Vallance Road to give an informal press conference.*

'I HATE THE SIGHT OF BLOOD,' SAID ONE MAN WHO REFUSED TO TESTIFY AGAINST THE KRAYS. 'PARTICULARLY MY OWN'

Left: *Reggie leaves the Central Criminal Court (the 'Old Bailey') in 1965, after successfully evading charges of extortion with menaces.*

No – if Read was to get them, he would have to persuade one or more of their past victims to testify against them.

Read made a list of thirty people whom the Krays had maimed or robbed over the past decade. Then he and his team went about the laborious process of questioning them all.

As well as making countless enquiries in London, detectives travelled to Scotland, Canada, Belgium, Spain and the United States.

They were met with a wall of silence. The reason for people's reticence was not hard to understand. In the words of one potential witness whom the Krays had maimed and ruined, but was reluctant to talk: 'I hate the sight of blood, particularly my own.'

Evidence might have been slow in materializing, but 'Nipper' Read and his team did start to accumulate information, first from Leslie Payne, the Krays' erstwhile business manager, and later from Alan Cooper, the merchant banker who had fenced the Mafia's bearer bonds.

The police were gradually building up a complete picture of the Firm's activities. But they still didn't have any hard evidence which they could take in front of a jury.

Six months passed and the investigation had stalled. Read, however, felt confident that, if the Krays and their associates were all safely behind bars, reluctant witnesses would summon up the

So Read went all out to get the two men. Hart was the first to be caught. The police found him hiding in a caravan with his girlfriend. He gave them no trouble and confessed to everything.

Three days later they picked up Barrie in Mile End. He was drunk, broke and frightened. He, too, told the police everything they wanted to know.

With the threat of a Kray reprisal force removed, the whole situation changed. Conmen, club owners and racketeers suddenly got their memories back. When the trial opened on 6 July, long-forgotten victims, accomplices saving their own skins, and eye-witnesses all trooped through the witness box.

The death blow for the Krays came, however, with the appearance of the barmaid from the Blind Beggar. Previously she had been too frightened to identify Ronnie after the shooting of George Cornell. Now she said she was absolutely certain that it had been Ronnie Kray who had fired the fatal shot.

The defence made a brave attempt at discrediting the witnesses, but the barmaid's story stuck, and the Krays were effectively finished.

The twins were arrogant and defiant throughout the long trial, but even they must have realized that the verdict was a foregone conclusion. They were found guilty of the murders of Cornell and McVitie and sentenced to life imprisonment, '...which,' Mr Justice Melford Stevenson said, 'I recommend should not be less than thirty years.' If his wishes were respected, the Kray twins would be sixty-four before they were released.

It would be easy to write off Reggie and Ronnie Kray as a couple of vicious East End thugs. They certainly were that, but they were much more besides. They were professionals of violence who operated on a scale previously unknown in Britain.

The odds against their rise to power were enormous. They were both mentally unstable and had no education or finesse. Yet they came closer to building a crime empire on the lines of Al Capone than any other criminal organization that London has ever known. They were truly dangerous men on the grand scale.

courage to come forward.

He would have to arrest and charge the Krays before he had finished preparing his case. It was a massive gamble, but Read was rapidly running out of options.

At 6a.m. on 9 May 1968, sixty police officers descended on twenty-four separate addresses across London. 'Nipper' Read had his revolver drawn as his men broke down the door of Braithwaite House, where the twins each had a flat.

He needn't have worried. Both men were sound asleep, Reggie with a girl from Walthamstow, Ronnie with a fair-haired teenage boy from Bethnal Green.

FIGHT TO THE FINISH

The twins were charged with murder, extortion and sundry other offences, and were remanded in Brixton Jail.

Read had only a few weeks before the preliminary hearings in which to persuade witnesses to talk and thereby clinch his case. His job wasn't made any easier by the fact that two of the firm, Ronnie Hart and Ian Barrie were still on the loose.

Because the twins were still on remand and technically innocent, they were allowed as many visitors as they wanted. It was therefore easy for them to pass messages to their fugitive henchmen, who in turn could continue to intimidate witnesses.

Above: The picture of innocence, Ronnie and Reggie sip tea while answering journalists' questions after their 36-hour detention.

AL CAPONE
Public Enemy No. One

Neither a Mafioso nor even a Sicilian, by the age of twenty-six Al Capone had connived and murdered his way to become the biggest gangland boss in the most lawless city in America. But what was the truth and how much was legend?

For most people the very mention of organized crime conjures up a whole range of vivid images – the roaring twenties, Chicago, bootleg whiskey, speakeasies and, of course, Al Capone.

It is not that Chicago, or even America, ever had a monopoly on organized crime, it is merely the very public nature of its criminals which is so evocative. Gangsters with colourful nicknames like 'Pretty Boy' Floyd, 'Legs' Diamond, 'Machine Gun' Jack McGurn and Al 'Scarface' Capone, captured the public imagination and became a part of criminal folklore.

THE YOUNG BROOKLYN IMMIGRANT

Contrary to popular myth, Al Capone was never a member of the Mafia. He wasn't even a Sicilian. He hated Sicilians and spent most of his active years at loggerheads with various branches of the Mob. Capone was a gangster pure and simple, a racketeer whose only loyalty was to himself and his immediate family.

Born in Brooklyn in 1899, Alphonse was the fourth son of Gabriele and Teresa Capone, a Neapolitan couple who had emigrated from Italy some six years earlier. As a teenager, Al ran with the

Opposite: *From a flashy teenage thug, Capone rapidly grew into a portly, conservatively-dressed figure who could have been taken for a successful middle-aged businessman.*

Below: *Capone's career as a big-time mobster lasted a mere six years, but in that time he acquired all the trappings and habits of a rich man.*

murderous Five Points gang which was led by fellow-Italian and partner-to-be John Torrio.

He had his first brush with the Mafia when he was fifteen. The Black Hand, a Mafia murder squad, had been extorting money from his father. Capone hunted down the two men responsible and shot them dead. Torrio was impressed by the young man's nerve and ruthless efficiency. Six years later, in 1919, when Torrio was in the process of building his bootlegging empire in Chicago, he remembered the name of Al Capone.

Torrio had been in Chicago for about five years when the Volsted Act was passed and America went dry. The country developed an immediate and insatiable thirst which organized crime was ready and willing to slake. In Chicago, drinkers were supplied by one of a dozen big gangs, each with its own clearly defined territory.

Torrio's gang controlled the South Side of the city and soon teamed up with the Irish Druggan-Lake gang who supplied the inner West Side. The North Side of Chicago was the territory of Dion O'Banion, a florist and failed safe-cracker, who had a flower shop opposite the Holy Name Cathedral.

O'Banion could have made a legitimate income by supplying floral tributes to the victims of gangland slayings. Instead he teamed up with two Polish Catholics, George 'Bugs' Moran and Hymie Weiss. Together, these three were the biggest challenge to Torrio's pre-eminence in the city.

The other important gang were the Gennas who controlled the West Side. These six brothers from Marsala in Sicily were the most ruthless of all the Chicago gangsters; they didn't only kill for gain and self-protection – they killed for fun.

In the first year of Prohibition, there was comparatively little trouble between the rival gangs. There was more than enough business for everyone, and most of the gangsters' energy was devoted to maintaining supply to meet the enormous demand.

By 1920, however, things were getting better organized and some of the smaller gangs were looking to expand their territories. The O'Donnell gang from the

Above: *Chicago was no place to bring up his children, said Capone, and in 1928, after an unsuccessful attempt to settle in California, he purchased a magnificent house on Palm Island, Miami.*

IMPRESSED BY THE TEENAGE CAPONE'S STYLE, WHEN GANG LEADER TORRIO STARTED BOOTLEGGING HE TOOK HIM ON AS A PARTNER

South Side started hijacking Torrio's beer trucks and smashing up his speakeasies. Torrio retaliated by killing several of O'Donnell's drivers. Elsewhere in the city, other gangs were at each others' throats.

Torrio could see the way things were going and decided that, if he was to fulfil his ambition and have overall control of Chicago, he would need to import some extra muscle. So he called up Al Capone, now twenty-one and a lieutenant in the Five Points gang, and made him an offer he couldn't refuse: 25 per cent of existing turnover and 50 per cent of all new business.

In the early days of the partnership Capone did the killing for both himself and Torrio. One of his first victims was a small-time crook called Joe Howard. Howard had ideas above his station and one night hijacked two of Torrio's booze trucks. The following evening, Joe was having a drink in his neighbourhood bar. Capone walked in with a broad grin on his face. It was happy hour.

preferred to sit back and pick his moment.

In late October 1924, the O'Banion gang hijacked a large shipment of the Gennas' Canadian whiskey. They swore revenge. 'To hell with them Sicilians,' O'Banion said to reporters. A war was in the offing and this was just the situation Torrio and Capone had been waiting for.

WAR BREAKS OUT IN CHICAGO

On 4 November O'Banion was in the back room of his florist's when he heard someone come into the shop. He went out to welcome three customers.

Six shots rang out, the last of which exploded into O'Banion's left cheek. He sprawled back into his flower display as his assassins made good their escape. When the police arrived at the shop, Dion O'Banion was dead.

Torrio, Capone and the Genna brothers were all questioned by the police, but all had satisfactory explanations as to their whereabouts at the time of the killing. The street outside O'Banion's shop had been crowded, yet no one had seen anything. Faced with the customary wall of silence, the coroner was forced to bring in a finding of 'unlawful killing at the hands of a person or persons unknown'.

The tradition of lavish funerals for American gangsters started with O'Banion. His body lay 'in state' at the undertaker's for three days. A contemporary report describes the scene: 'Silver angels stood at the head and feet with their heads bowed in the light of ten candles that burned in solid golden candlesticks they held in their hands. Beneath the casket, on a marble slab that supports its glory, is the inscription: "Suffer the little children to come unto me." And over it all the perfume of flowers.'

At the funeral, mounted police kept order as the cortege of gangsters rolled slowly through the streets of Chicago, followed by twenty-six trucks of flowers, valued at more than $50,000. Among the floral tributes was a basket of red roses with a card which read, 'From Al'.

Both Capone and Torrio solemnly attended the funeral, but no one was

'Hi, Al,' Joe said, sticking out his hand. Capone fired six shots into his body at point-blank range, and Howard fell to the bar-room floor with a smile of welcome still on his face. The police immediately put out an arrest warrant on Capone, but had to release him when all the eye-witnesses developed amnesia.

By the end of 1923, Capone had gained control of the middle-class Chicago suburb of Cicero and made it his personal headquarters. By a combination of bribery and intimidation, he had the entire administration in his pocket – mayor, town clerk and town attorney. So backed, he was free to do whatever he liked. His illegal casinos and brothels and bars were open day and night.

By this time Torrio and Capone were each making in excess of $100,000 a week, but they were still a long way from gaining absolute control of the city. The O'Banion gang and the Gennas still controlled the North and West sides. Capone was in favour of all-out war to eliminate the competition; Torrio

> CAPONE WALKED INTO THE BAR AND FIRED SIX SHOTS INTO HOWARD AT CLOSE RANGE. IT WAS HAPPY HOUR

> BENEATH GANGLAND CHIEF O'BANION'S FUNERAL CASKET WAS THE INSCRIPTION: 'SUFFER THE LITTLE CHILDREN TO COME UNTO ME'

fooled – least of all Hymie Weiss, O'Banion's most trusted lieutenant and the new boss of his organization. Weiss was a cold-blooded killer who had devised a method of assassination in which the victim was seated in the front passenger seat of the car with his killer directly behind him. He was then shot in the back of the head. After such a murder, Weiss would calmly say that his victim had been 'taken for a ride'. And so the expression became part of modern parlance.

Weiss, who was genuinely heartbroken by O'Banion's death – observers described him as crying like a baby, swore to get his revenge. Days later Capone's car was machine-gunned. Al escaped unhurt, but two weeks later John Torrio was gunned down in front of his wife by another O'Banion man, Bugs Moran.

Torrio recovered from his wounds, but only weeks later he was jailed for nine months for operating a brewery. Badly shaken by Moran's attack, he had steel screens fitted to the windows of his cell and hired three extra deputy sheriffs to stand sentry.

On his release in October 1925, he announced that he was leaving Chicago, which he described as being 'too violent'. The fact is, at the age of forty-eight, Johnnie Torrio had lost his nerve. This was a game for young men, and the young man on the spot was Al Capone.

THE KING IS DEAD – LONG LIVE THE KING!

So, at the age of 26, Al Capone inherited the entire Torrio empire. His promotion to unrivalled boss of Chicago was helped by the demise of the six Genna brothers. Angelo, Mike and Antonio were killed in separate gun battles within the space of six weeks. The three surviving brothers fled to their home town of Marsala in Sicily. While there is no evidence to connect Capone with the killings, he made no secret of his pleasure at the Gennas' departure.

The Sicilians might have been out of the way, but Hymie Weiss wasn't finished yet. His second attempt on Capone's life was anything but subtle,

Above and right:
14 February 1929. At 10.30 a.m., while Al established an alibi in Miami, six members of Bugs Moran's gang were shot down in a Chicago garage by Capone's men disguised as policemen.

and highlighted the level of lawlessness that existed in Chicago in 1925. In broad daylight, eight carloads of gunmen made an assault on Capone's Cicero headquarters, the Hawthorne Inn, firing more than a thousand rounds into the building in a matter of seconds.

Again Capone escaped unscathed and, with customary largesse, paid $10,000 out of his own pocket to save the sight of a woman who had been injured in the cross-fire. Capone had overlooked the first attempt on his life by the North Side gang, considering it legitimate revenge for the killing of their boss Dion O'Banion. Now he had had enough.

On 11 October 1926, Weiss was machine-gunned to death on the steps of Holy Name Cathedral.

Now only Bugs Moran was left alive to challenge Capone's absolute control of Chicago. And Moran could wait. Ten days after the execution of Weiss, Capone chaired a meeting of Chicago gang bosses to negotiate a peaceful division of Cook County: 'We're a bunch of saps to be killing each other,' he postulated.

For a while after that the peace held and there were no gangland slayings. Everyone was making a fortune, and none more than Al Capone. His turnover was truly astonishing. In Cook County he controlled ten thousand speakeasies, each purchasing an average of six barrels of beer a week costing a total of $3.5 million. In addition they were each buying two cases of liquor at $90, making another $1.8 million. (Beer was costing Capone about $5 a barrel to make, and liquor about $20 a case.) Added to all this, Capone had his other rackets – gambling and vice – which contributed to a grand total of about $6.5 million per week.

He had huge overheads, of course, not least of which was his illicit payroll. Everyone was on the take in Chicago, from humble patrolmen to the city's mayor 'Big Bill' Thompson, whose 1927 re-election campaign Capone financed to the tune of $260,000. It is estimated that his annual graft bill to the police, judges and politicians came to more than $30 million.

Capone was no longer the flashy, loud-mouthed thug that arrived in Chicago in 1919. He was now an immaculately tailored, even conservative figure, sporting hand-made silk shirts and solitaire diamond tie-pins. Despite the fact that he was still only twenty-six, he gave the impression of being a successful, middle-aged businessman.

Capone's public image was important to him, and he was given to ostentatious displays of generosity. He paid for church roofs to be restored; he gave $10,000 to Pennsylvania's striking miners and,

during the Depression, he opened a string of soup kitchens and contributed more than $2 million of his own money to help down-and-outs.

Everyone in Chicago knew that Al Capone was a bootlegger, and most of them didn't care. To the vast majority of ordinary people Prohibition was a nonsense anyway, so bootlegging wasn't a real crime. He had become a success story, a working-class hero.

THE ST VALENTINE'S DAY MASSACRE

By 1928 Al Capone felt secure enough about his hold on Chicago to spend time away from the city. He was a devoted family man, who wanted his dependants to benefit from his vast wealth. Chicago was no place to bring up children, he said, and so he set about looking for a suitable second home away from the turmoil of the big city.

He quite liked the look of California, but California didn't like the look of him and summarily booted him out. Next he tried Florida and, despite the violent objections of honest citizens, managed to procure a magnificent house on Palm Island, Miami.

Capone spent Christmas and the New Year of 1929 in his new home. He had a lot to be thankful for. He was not yet thirty, had amassed a vast fortune and was the undisputed boss of America's

Above: When Herbert Hoover was elected President of the United States in 1929, he named Capone as his prime target in an attack on lawlessness. The mobster was finally indicted on a charge of income tax evasion. Here seated with his lawyers, he looks confident of a successful outcome to the hearing.

second city. Unfortunately for Capone, one man didn't quite see it like that.

Bugs Moran had neither forgotten nor forgiven the murder of his two associates Dion O'Banion and Hymie Weiss. He decided to take advantage of Capone's absence to make him pay. With his North Side gang Moran regularly hijacked Capone's liquor shipments and then started to move in on some of his other legitimate businesses, notably dog racing and dry cleaning.

Capone may have been in Florida, but his finger was very much on the pulse. He heard all about Moran's activities and decided that they had to stop. Over the telephone he instructed Jake Guzik, his most trusted aide in Chicago, to 'take care' of Moran. The time and method of execution were discussed in minute detail, and on 14 February 1929 Capone made a point of keeping an appointment in Miami with a city official. He wanted a watertight alibi for that particular Valentine's Day.

At 10.30 a.m., as Al Capone was trying to explain to the Miami official where he had got the money to buy his Palm Island home, six of Moran's men were waiting for a truckload of hijacked whiskey in a garage on Chicago's North Clark Street. They were Frank and Peter Gusenberg, Moran's top executioners; James Clark, a Sioux Indian and Moran's brother-in-law; Al Weinshank, his accountant; Adam Heyer, his business manager; and Johnny May, a burglar and safe cracker. There was also a seventh man, whose presence has never been satisfactorily explained – an optician called Dr Richard Schwimmer. Moran himself should have been there, but had been delayed.

Shortly after 10.30 Mrs Max Landesman of 2124 North Clark Street heard shots from the garage next door. She looked out of the window and saw a man leaving the garage and getting into a large touring car. From the flat below, Miss Josephine Morin saw two men, apparently under arrest, come out of the garage with their hands up. They were followed by two uniformed police officers. All four of them got into a black Cadillac and drove off.

Mrs Landesman hurried over to the

garage, pushed open the door and saw seven men sprawled on the floor, blood streaming from their bodies. Minutes later Sergeant Tom Loftus arrived on the scene with a dozen other officers. Only one of the victims, Frank Gusenberg, was conscious, and Loftus tried to persuade him to say who had done the shootings. Gusenberg declined to comment and was shipped to hospital along with the other six victims, all of whom were pronounced dead on arrival.

Loftus maintained a vigil at Gusenberg's bedside but, true to the gangster's code of honour, he died three hours later without revealing anything.

Moran had arrived on Clark Street fifteen minutes late, and, seeing the police cars outside the garage, assumed that there had been a raid, and promptly left. Later, when he heard about the massacre, he said: 'Only Capone kills like that!'

The police were of the same opinion. So they picked up Capone's top killer, 'Machine Gun' Jack McGurn. McGurn claimed to have been with his girlfriend at the time of the killings. He was indicted for perjury, but married his girl so that the police could not force her to testify against him. Other Capone men were questioned, but soon released for lack of evidence.

In the end, no one was ever charged in connection with the St Valentine's Day massacre. But no one was in any doubt that it was carried out on the direct orders of Al Capone from the safety of his Florida retreat.

Even though Moran had survived, Capone returned to Chicago confident that he had finally crushed any opposition to his authority. Instead he found that two of his own lieutenants, John Scalise and Albert Anselmi, had been conspiring to take over the Outfit. Al invited them, along with other gang members, to a meeting at a restaurant in Hammond, Indiana. Capone was his usual jovial self until halfway through the meal, at which point he rounded on the two conspirators: 'I understand you want my job,' he said. 'Well, here it is!' and promptly clubbed them both to death with a baseball bat. It was a salutary lesson to the assembled diners.

Early in his career, Capone was known for his surgical use of violence. It was never used gratuitously – only as a tool to protect himself and to promote his business interests. This was no longer the case. Anyone who incurred his displeasure – policemen, politicians, journalists – could expect to be summarily dispatched.

'GET CAPONE!'

In March 1929, Herbert Hoover was inaugurated President of the United States. He came to office primed with a promise to tackle lawlessness in America, and he named Al Capone as his primary target.

By May of that year, Capone was feeling the heat. There were rumours of a massive contract out on his life. Some said it had been taken out by Bugs Moran, others that it was the families of Scalise and Anselmi. Whatever the truth, Capone decided it would be wise to get out of circulation for a while and, rather than going to Florida, he contrived to have himself arrested for a minor firearms offence in Philadelphia. He was expecting to get a jail sentence of thirty days, but in the event he was sent to prison for a year. Capone was initially horrified, but he soon adapted to the situation. His status was such that he was able to continue running his Chicago

> WHEN BUGS MORAN HEARD ABOUT THE MASSACRE WHICH HE HAD SO NARROWLY ESCAPED, HE EXCLAIMED: 'ONLY CAPONE KILLS LIKE THAT!'

> FACED WITH A 'COLONELS' REVOLT', CAPONE INVITED THE MISCREANTS TO DINNER AND THEN CLUBBED THEM TO DEATH WITH A BASEBALL BAT

Below: *Matters are not going so well in the hearing in Chicago Federal Court in October 1931, and Capone looks grimly concerned as his financial affairs are brought out into the light.*

Right: *The style of elaborate gangster funerals in Chicago was set by that of Dion O'Banion.*

empire from his prison cell with the minimum of inconvenience.

While Capone was in prison, the new administration in Washington were devising ways to keep him there for ever. President Hoover discussed a variety of approaches with his various agencies – the Prohibition Bureau, the Justice Department's Federal Bureau of Investigation (FBI) and the Treasury Department. Their brief was simple. Get Al Capone any way you can.

The Justice Department set about destroying Capone's booze empire by brute force. In the space of six months they raided and wrecked thirty of his breweries and seized fifty of his heavy trucks. But this was no more than an annoyance for Capone.

In Washington it was the Treasury that really took the Capone challenge on board. Their Special Intelligence Unit sent top investigator Frank Wilson to Chicago to look at Al Capone's books.

Wilson had already enjoyed spectacular success jailing gangsters who had escaped conviction for years. Among his victims were Frank Nitti, Capone's deputy; Jack Guzik, his accountant; and Capone's brother, Ralph. They had received prison terms of between eighteen months and five years. But Al Capone himself would prove tougher for Wilson than his associates.

Capone had never filed a tax return in his life. This was not a crime, so long as he did not earn more than $5000 in any given year. It was Frank Wilson's job to prove that he had. Considering Capone's lavish lifestyle, this might appear to have been a simple matter. It wasn't. Capone had no bank accounts in his own name and all his assets were listed to third parties.

Wilson and his team started a detailed probe into Capone's personal spending. They found that in the three-year period 1926-29 he had purchased more than $25,000 worth of furniture for his homes in Chicago and Florida. He had spent $7000 on suits and $40,000 on telephone calls. In all the Treasury men unearthed $165,000 worth of taxable spending. They could have gone to court with that, and they would probably have secured a conviction, which would have jailed Capone for about three years. But that wasn't good enough. Wilson had been told to go for broke.

After months sniffing around Chicago, Wilson managed to persuade some of Capone's casino employees to turn state's evidence. Now he had Al where they wanted him. He was charged with failing to pay tax on $1 million in the years from 1925 to 1929 and, while this was a fraction of Capone's true income, it could still mean thirty years in a federal prison.

Capone's attorneys initially struck a deal with the prosecution – if Capone pleaded guilty, he would receive a sentence of not more than two and a half years. Judge Wilkerson, however, was outraged by this and threw it out. Capone withdrew his plea and elected to go to trial.

His associates immediately set about bribing or threatening members of the jury, but this was discovered and, at the very last minute, a new jury was sworn in. They heard stories of Capone's extravagant lifestyle – a lifestyle he could not possibly have supported on the $450 a month he claimed to earn – and on 24 October they returned a verdict of guilty on all charges. He was sentenced to eleven years and fined $50,000, the most severe sentence ever imposed for a tax offence.

Capone was sent to Cook County jail pending an appeal and when that failed, in May 1932, he was shipped to Atlanta Federal Penitentiary. A year later he became one of the first convicts to take up residence at Alcatraz in San Francisco Bay. He emerged from there in 1939 a physical and mental wreck. He was still only thirty-eight years old.

Capone had been diagnosed as suffering from syphilis shortly after his imprisonment in 1931. The disease had now reached its tertiary stage, and his brain was being eaten up. After his release he returned to his home on Palm Island, Florida where he lived for another seven years, increasingly mad, surrounded by his adoring family.

In 1947 he suffered a fatal brain haemorrhage. He was forty-eight years old. His body was shipped back to Chicago and buried in an elaborate mausoleum in Mount Olivet cemetery.

Above left: *The trial concluded, Capone is led away from Chicago Federal Court on 24 October 1931 to begin his eleven-year sentence.*

Left: *Guarded by a US Marshall, Al Capone puts a brave face on his defeat as he is taken by train to Atlanta Federal Penitentiary.*

CARELESS THIEVES
Great Train Robbery

It was called the 'robbery of the century', yet when thieves audaciously robbed a mail train of 22.5 million they were unbelievably careless in concealing the evidence. The law was draconian, but the public secretly admired them.

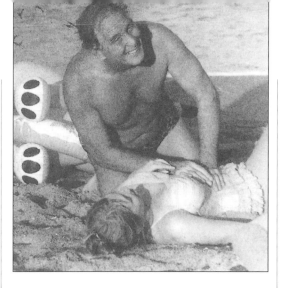

Shortly after 2a.m. on Thursday, 8 August 1963, the Glasgow to London mail train was nearing the end of its journey. As it passed through Leighton Buzzard in Bedfordshire, half an hour should have seen it safely into Euston. It wasn't to be, however.

A few miles further down the line, the driver, forty-eight-year-old Jack Mills, spotted an amber signal. He slowed the big diesel and prepared to stop. A mile on, at Sears Crossing, he was faced with a red light and pulled to a halt.

Mills sent his fireman, David Whitby, down the line to phone ahead for information. Within a matter of seconds, however, Mills found himself confronted by a gang of masked men clambering into his cab.

He tried to fight them off but was coshed into submission, as the biggest and most audacious robbery in history began. Half an hour later the train had been divided, moved and relieved of 128 mail sacks containing more than £2.5 million in used banknotes.

Left: Train robber Ronald Biggs may have been a fugitive in Brazil, but he was seldom out of the public eye. In 1980 he appeared in the film Honeymoon as a swimmer who rescued German actress Dolly Dollar from drowning.

Opposite: Ronnie Biggs, one of the instigators of the 'robbery of the century'.

Below: Post Office workers lean out from the robbed train as the police start their search for clues.

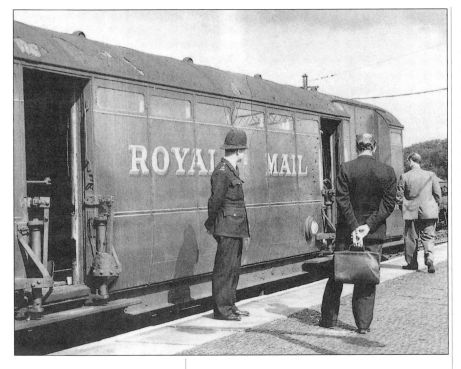

Above: Forensic experts inspect the Royal Mail van from which the 128 mail sacks were taken.

THE LOCAL POLICE SOON REALIZED THAT THIS CRIME WAS FAR TOO MAJOR FOR THEIR OWN RESOURCES, AND CALLED IN SCOTLAND YARD

FEW CLUES TO START WITH

By the time Detective Superintendent Malcolm Fewtrell, head of the Buckinghamshire CID arrived, the robbers and their spoils were long gone. Fewtrell, a seasoned professional, started routine investigative procedures, gathering physical evidence and interviewing the eighty-odd people who had been on the train.

But no one, not even Mills, Whitby or the post office sorters from whose HVP (high-value packages) coach the mail sacks had been taken, could give Fewtrell anything to go on.

It was soon obvious to Fewtrell that he was not dealing with any ordinary crime. This robbery was the work of a highly organized team, and the investigation would be on a scale far beyond the meagre resouces of his force. After consulting with his Chief Constable, he elected to 'call the Yard' - to ask for the assistance of the Metropolitan CID.

Later that day, Fewtrell attended a meeting at the headquarters of the Post Office. Present were Post Office officials including their own senior investigator, Frank Cook, and George Hatherill deputy chief of CID at Scotland Yard: together with a team of detectives.

Cook told the police that, in his estimation, the haul from the robbery might well be in excess of £3 million. The police for their part could give little comfort to the Post Office. All they could say for certain was that approximately fifteen men had been involved in the robbery, and that the fireman, David Whitby, had noticed an army lorry parked on the Bridego Bridge where the robbery took place.

Right: Five days after the robbery, police discovered the deserted Leatherslade farmhouse where the gang had hidden out and divided their loot.

Hatherill agreed to send two of his most able detectives - Gerald McArthur and Jack Prichard - down to Buckinghamshire to assist the local police with their enquiries. The two men returned to Aylesbury with Fewtrell that night.

The three detectives had to try and put themselves in the robbers' shoes. What would they do immediately after the robbery? A total of 128 mail sacks would not be easy to hide or transport for long distances without attracting attention.

The police decided that the robbers would hole up somewhere near the scene of the crime and distribute the money at their leisure, partly because one of the robbers had ordered the men in the HVP coach not to move for 'half an hour'. This suggested that the gang had a safe haven within half an hour's drive from the scene of the crime.

It was a guess, but they decided to back it with all their resources. Every policeman from Buckinghamshire and neighbouring forces was mobilized in a search of barges, houses and barns in a thirty-mile radius of Bridego Bridge.

So far the police were spot on. The perpetrators of the Great Train Robbery were holed up some twenty miles from Bridego Bridge at Leatherslade Farm. They had purchased it through a nominee, some weeks earlier, specifically for this purpose.

The robbery itself had gone like clockwork. The only minor hitch had been Mills, the train driver, who had offered token resistance. The haul, something over £2.5 million, had been less than they had expected. But even after they had paid their German backers a million for financing the robbery, each member of the seventeen-strong gang had received £90,OOO, a huge sum of money in 1963. All in all, no one was complaining.

TWO GANGS WITH COMBINED TALENTS

The robbery, which had been almost a year in the planning, was the work of not one but two London-based gangs or 'firms'. The first firm, the men who conceived the idea and did most of the ground work, consisted of Buster Edwards, Gordon Goody, Charlie Wilson, Bruce Reynolds, John Daly, Jimmy White, Ronnie Biggs and Jimmy Hussey.

They were a loose-knit team of thieves who had worked together over the years on numerous occasions with a varied degree of success.

In January 1963, Buster Edwards and Gordon Goody were approached by a friend, Brian Field, a crooked solicitor's clerk who had worked for them in the past. He claimed to have information for them about a huge shipment of cash which was theirs for the taking.

Field introduced them to an Irishman (whose name is still unknown) who told them about the high-value-package coach which made up part of the overnight mail train from Glasgow to London. It was on this coach that the banks sent all their surplus cash down to London.

Above: *Roy James, known as 'the weasel', was arrested in December after a chase over the roof of this house in a mews in St John's Wood, north London.*

EVEN AFTER PAYING THEIR GERMAN BACKERS, THERE WAS A SMALL FORTUNE LEFT FOR DIVISION AMONG THE GANG

Above: In the summer of 1965, after serving little more than a year of his sentence, Ronald Biggs escaped from Wandsworth Prison. More than 150 armed police surrounded Winterford House in Surrey when told he was hiding out there, but a six-hour search revealed no trace of him.

NORMALLY THE TRAIN CARRIED SOME SIXTY MAIL SACKS, BUT AFTER A BANK HOLIDAY THERE WERE THREE TIMES AS MANY

PANIC AND DISARRAY QUICKLY SET IN, AND THE GANG LEFT VALUABLE INFORMATION AT LEATHERSLADE FARM FOR THE POLICE TO FIND

Normally the coach would carry about sixty bags, the Irishman told them, but if they timed their raid to follow a bank holiday they might find upwards of two hundred, each holding about £25,000, a total haul in excess of £5 million.

Edwards and Goody were incredulous. But they assured the Irishman that if such a robbery was possible, they had the team to pull it off. They arranged a meeting with Bruce Reynolds and Charlie Wilson.

All four of them were torn between euphoria and scepticism. Before they went any further, they had to check that their informant was himself well informed.

So they staked out Euston station and saw for themselves HVP sacks being offloaded from the night mail train. There was no doubt that the prize was there.

The only way the job could be done, they decided, was to stop the train on the track, separate the engine and the HVP coach from the main body of the train, and ransack it at their leisure. The trouble was, how do you stop a train at a predetermined spot

Buster Edwards had a solution to the problem. He had heard of a south London firm, headed by one Thomas Wisbey, which had been robbing trains on the London to Brighton line for a couple of years. They had an expert who knew how to tamper with the signalling system.

Buster approached the rival gang boss and, after a period of intense haggling, terms were agreed. Wisbey would let them have his man, Roger Cordrey, as long as Wisbey himself and his partner Bob Welsh were included in the robbery as full partners.

And so the team to rob the mail train started to take shape, and the preparations began: researching a suitable location for the ambush, buying a hide-out, instructing various members of the gang in their specific tasks, and rehearsing the ambush in the most minute detail.

And now it had all paid off. The Great Train Robbers were sitting in Leatherslade Farm with more than £2.5 million in used notes.

That team of faces, already known to the police, would soon be known to the world at large. The first piece of bad news for the robbers came over the radio in the form of a public appeal by the police. They were asking for information on strange goings-on in remote dwellings, and they wanted to know about movements of army vehicles.

This presented the robbers with two problems. They had originally planned to stay at Leatherslade Farm until the

Left: *Charlie Wilson escaped from Winson Green prison in August 1964. In January 1967 he was recaptured in Montreal, Canada, and was brought back to Britain by Detective Chief Superintendent Butler.*

Below: *For more than five years Bruce Reynolds was a wanted man. Eventually, in November 1968, police found him in this rented house in Torquay.*

Fewtrell and McArthur dashed to the farm. After a cursory glance they ordered that the whole area be cordoned off in readiness for the forensic team.

In London, Butler and his team had compiled a list of possible suspects to be pulled in for questioning. The bulk of the gang's names appeared on that list.

Roger Cordrey, the signals expert, was the first to be picked up. The local police found him in Bournemouth along with £141,000 in used notes, money which he found extremely difficult to explain.

The next break for the police came on Friday, 16 August. A man called John Ahern was taking a stroll in the woods near Dorking in Surrey when he came upon a briefcase, a holdall and a camelskin bag containing no less than £100,900. More important, a receipt was found made out by a German restaurant in the name of Herr and Frau Field.

Sunday night and then disperse the money using the army truck and two army Land Rovers. This was now clearly out of the question.

For the first time they were in a state of disarray and, from this point on, it was effectively every man for himself. They cleared up the farm as best they could, burning clothes and mailsacks, but in their haste to get away they were forced to leave the job half done. The various members of the gang returned to their homes and jobs in London, unaware they had left a plethora of clues for their pursuers.

THE INVESTIGATION TAKES OFF

Once the scale of the robbery was appreciated, Scotland Yard decided to beef up its support for the investigation. They brought in Chief Superintendent Tommy Butler to head up the London end. Butler would prove the downfall of many of the Train Robbers.

The first mention of Leatherslade Farm came from a cowman called John Maris on Monday, 12 August. In outbuildings the police found an army lorry and the two Land Rovers. Once inside the farm proper, half-burnt mailsacks and money wrappers left them in no doubt that they found the hide-out.

Fewtrell and McArthur knew that one Brian Field, a solicitor's clerk, had acted for several of their suspects, including Buster Edwards and Gordon Goody. They also knew that the company for which Field worked had acted in the purchase of Leatherslade Farm. They went to his home and questioned him but did not arrest him - yet.

The following day, more money - £30,440 - was found in an old caravan in the Dorking Woods by Surrey Police. Fingerprints in the caravan matched those on file for Jimmy White. At Leatherslade Farm fingerprint experts were also doing well. They had identified the prints of Charlie Wilson and Bruce Reynolds. Wilson was picked up within a few hours, but Reynolds had gone to ground .

On Thursday, 22 August local police arrested Gordon Goody in Leicester where he was having dinner with a girlfriend. They questioned him and then released him for lack of evidence.

Ronnie Biggs was next. He was pulled in on 4 September, and three days later they brought in Jim Hussey for questioning. Thomas Wisbey was questioned, released and then rearrested.

PLAYING A WAITING GAME

By the middle of September the police were fairly certain they had a complete picture of who had robbed the mail train, but Tommy Butler was in no particular hurry to

Above: Ronald Biggs hid out in Australia, where he worked as a carpenter, until a new spate of publicity forced him to flee to Brazil. Here police search his baggage, left behind in a Melbourne motel.

ROY JAMES WAS FINALLY ARRESTED AFTER A SPECTACULAR ROOFTOP CHASE IN LONDON

Right: Chief Superintendent John Slipper and Inspector Peter Jones return to Gatwick Airport in February 1974, foiled in their attempt to repatriate Ronald Biggs.

find them. He reckoned that, by playing the waiting game, he stood a better chance of catching them with some of the money.

However, Butler decided it was time to pull in Brian Field. He charged him with conspiring to rob a mail train and for being an accessory after the fact.

Police efforts were now on two fronts. The Flying Squad were trying to track down Buster Edwards, Bruce Reynolds, John Daly, Roy James and Jimmy White. The forensic team were building up a case against them and the men already in custody, trying to tie them to the scene of the crime. It was thanks to this work that they felt confident enough to rearrest Gordon Goody on 3 October.

Over the next few weeks, Butler and his men arrested Bob Welsh and John Daly. They ran Roy James to ground in the St John's Wood area of London and, after a spectacular rooftop chase, took him into custody and charged him.

By the end of the year, nine of the sixteen men who had been at Bridego Bridge were in jail awaiting trial. Bruce Reynolds, Buster Edwards and Jimmy White were still on the run, while the other four had been overlooked or released for lack of evidence.

With no prospect of an early arrest of the three fugitives, the authorities decided to press ahead with the trial of the others.

SHOW TRIAL

The trial began on 20 January 1964. All the accused pleaded not guilty to all charges except for Roger Cordrey. He pleaded guilty to robbery and was removed from the dock to await sentence, while the trial of the others continued.

Only Mr W. Raeburn QC, counsel for John Daly, was successful in persuading Mr Justice Davies that his client had no case to answer. Daly walked from the court a free man. The jury returned with a guilty verdict on all the others.

On Wednesday, 15 April the convicted prisoners were brought to court to be sentenced. Mr Justice Edmund Davies called first for Roger Cordrey. The judge told him that he would take into consideration his guilty plea and the fact that his share of the stolen money had been recovered, and would reduce his sentence accordingly. 'In respect of the four counts you must go to prison for concurrent terms of twenty years.' There was a moment's stunned silence from the court, and then a gasp. Journalists and barristers were astounded by the severity of the sentence. If this was Mr Justice Davies's idea of leniency, what would the others get?

One by one the guilty men faced the bench: Ronnie Biggs: thirty years, Thomas Wisbey: thirty years, Bob Welsh, Jim Hussey and Roy James: thirty years, Brian Field: twenty-five years. The convicted men were whisked off to various prisons around the country, where the true horror of their situation sank in. Even with full remission, most of them would not be released for at least twenty years.

EXPATRIATES

To the gang members still on the loose, news of the sentences was no less shattering. Any idea they may have had about turning themselves in evaporated. Bruce Reynolds sneaked out of the country in August 1964, Buster Edwards spent a short time in Germany having plastic surgery before leaving for Mexico City in March 1965.

In the same month that Reynolds fled to France, Charlie Wilson was sprung from Winson Green prison in Birmingham. He too was smuggled out of the country and headed for the South of France. Less than a year later, Ronnie Biggs escaped from Wandsworth and flew to Australia via Paris. By 1967, Edwards, Wilson and Reynolds had all been rearrested.

Ronnie Biggs was now the only gang member still at large. In 1969 he fled from Australia to Brazil, which had no extradition treaty with the United Kingdom, and went about making himself into an international superstar. He hosted parties, made film appearances and even recorded a track with the *Sex Pistols*. Ronnie eventually returned to Britain on Monday 7 May 2001, ending an amazing 35 years on the run. He was met by police, immediately arrested and transported to Belmarsh Prison, where, despite rapidly failing health, he remains to this day.

Above: *Ronnie Biggs with Miss Brazil.*

BRINK'S-MAT
Robbers Strike Gold

It was almost by chance that the trio of vicious armed robbers realized they had struck gold. Their getaway van drove off groaning under the weight of three tons of bullion. Yet the biggest haul in criminal history proved harder to track down than a needle in a haystack.

A t 6.25 on the morning of Saturday, November 26, 1983, a group of men were gathered outside Unit 7, a warehouse on the Heathrow International Trading Estate in Hounslow, London.

Despite its unprepossessing appearance, Unit 7 is one of the world's biggest safes. It is used by Brink's-Mat, Britain's leading security company, to store hugely valuable cargoes of precious metals, currency, bonds, jewels, fine art and other high-risk consignments en-route for Heathrow International Airport.

The ground floor of the building is a huge vault containing three safes. Above this are the manager's office, a radio room, a common room and a locker room for the thirty or so guards who usually work from the building.

At precisely 6.30 Michael Scouse, the senior duty guard and 'keyman', unlocked the unit, leaving the rest of the crew outside. He switched off the alarm system, then returned to the main door. He allowed the other men to enter and locked the door again from the inside.

Scouse reset the alarms and went up to the office. He was joined by Robin Risley, the crew leader for the day. Risley knew the men had been brought in specially for a bullion run. Scouse looked through his bills of lading. 'It's gold. Three tons. Gatwick airport for the Far East via Cathay Pacific Airways. It's got to be there by 8 a.m.'

Risley walked over to the common room, where the rest of the crew were warming themselves up with cups of tea. They were discussing the run when the doorbell rang. It had to be Tony Black, late as usual. The guards heard Scouse go down the stairs to let him in. Seconds later, Black walked into the common room. The 31-one-year-old guard looked pale and drawn as he glanced around the room. He muttered that he needed to go to the toilet, and then went back downstairs.

A couple of minutes later, the guards heard footsteps returning. They paid no attention until a voice bellowed out, 'Get on the floor or you're fucking dead!'

A figure appeared in the doorway of the common roof. He was about 5ft 8in, dressed in a black blazer and black trousers. His face was covered with a canary-yellow balaclava and he brandished a 9mm Browning automatic.

The guards, immobilized by fear, failed to react quickly enough for the intruder's satisfaction. Without a word, he pistol-whipped one of them, sending him crashing to the floor. The other guards quickly dropped to the floor.

Above: *The police arrive at Unit 7 of the Brink's-Mat warehouse on the morning of November 26, 1983.*

Opposite: *Even when the thieves were in prison, the police still had to track down the loot, like these bars of bullion found in Kenneth Noye's garage.*

Left: *When Detective Constable John Fordham was stabbed to death by Kenneth Noye in January 1985, dozens of plain clothes police combed the house and grounds in search for the missing gold.*

THE SECURITY TEAM HAD BEEN BROUGHT IN SPECIALLY FOR A BULLION RUN TO GATWICK AIRPORT

'Lie still and keep quiet,' the intruder said in a Cockney accent. As he spoke, two other masked men rushed into the room. Soon the gang had handcuffed all four guards. They also taped their legs together and placed cotton bags, secured with drawstrings, over their heads.

In the radio room, Michael Scouse was suffering a similar ordeal. After letting in the late arrival, Tony Black, Scouse had returned to the radio room. Seconds later he had found himself confronted by two masked men brandishing handguns.

'Are you Scouse?' a voice asked. Scouse nodded and a knife sliced through the front of his jeans. Petrol was poured down his front and over his genitals.

'You'd better do as I say, or I'll put a match to the petrol and a bullet through your head. You have two numbers . . . What are they?'

With a gun pressed under his chin, Scouse was in no mood for heroics. He shouted the numbers: '94-45-57-85'.

That combination opened the vault door. But there were several other lines of defence which needed to be neutralized before the intruders could reach their treasure.

They were fully conversant with the sophisticated arrangement of silent alarms, combinations and time locks. And they knew exactly what authority Scouse had as shift supervisor. There was no way to bluff them, so Scouse had no option but to lead them through the maze of defences.

As the robbers stepped into the vault, their attention was immediately focused on the three safes at the far end of the room. They totally ignored the stacks of small boxes, bound with metal straps, which littered the floor. They didn't know, and Scouse wasn't about to tell them, that these were the real treasure. Each of these inconspicuous little boxes contained a gold ingot. Together they were worth more than £25 million.

Scouse explained to the gang leader that he couldn't open the safes alone. He had the keys, but only Robin Risley knew that day's combination. Risley was dragged down to the vault and was told to enter the relevant numbers.

Risley was in a panic. The safe numbers had just been changed and he had barely committed them to memory. As he fumbled with the dials, the intruders became increasingly impatient. As

Risley continued to struggle with the locks and pleaded with the Cockney, another member of the gang asked Scouse what was in the boxes. Scouse, realizing that it was the only chance to save Risley and probably himself, told him that they contained bullion.

The man ripped open one of the boxes and saw that Scouse was telling the truth. Immediately the gang lost interest in Risley and the safes, and turned their attention to shifting the

Below: *John Palmer, a jeweller in Bath, was acquitted at the Old Bailey in 1987 on charges of handling gold from the Brink's-Mat robbery, and was presented with a congratulatory 'All Gold' Easter egg by the press.*

three tons of gold into the loading bay.

The gang leader asked Scouse how the shutter doors to the loading bay opened. Scouse replied that that was Tony Black's job. The leader went back upstairs. 'Which one of you is Black?' he asked. Black, who was lying in a pool of petrol on the office floor, identified himself and was frog-marched into the radio room at knifepoint. He opened the shutter doors by remote control, and a van drove into the warehouse.

Fifteen minutes later the same van drove out again, suspension groaning under the weight of £26 million worth of gold, the biggest haul in criminal history.

Within minutes of Michael Scouse freeing himself and raising the alarm, the Flying Squad were at the scene of the robbery. The investigation was headed by Commander Frank Cater.

From the outset, Cater had no doubt that this was an inside job. The most obvious suspects were the guards. They had all been taken to the casualty department of Ashford Hospital. The pistol-whipped Peter Bentley was treated for head wounds, and Scouse and Risley were suffering from petrol burns. The other men were unhurt.

By 10 a.m., all six men were being grilled by Cater and his team at Hounslow police station.

PRIME SUSPECT

The most obvious suspects, because of their special knowledge and responsibilities, were Scouse and Risley. But, as the morning wore on and more information about the six men came into the incident room, another name caught Cater's eye.

Anthony John Black stuck out like a sore thumb. He did not have a criminal record himself, but his common-law brother-in-law, Brian Robinson, was well known to the police.

Despite the fact that he was sure that Black was the man he was after, Commander Cater elected to send him home along with the other guards. At 8 a.m.

on Sunday, 4 December, more than a week after the raid, detectives arrived simultaneously at the homes of all six guards and invited them down to Hounslow police station for further questioning. Five of the guards were asked to go over their statements again. It was all routine.

Tony Black, however, was given the full treatment. His interrogation, led by Detective Inspector Tony Brightwell, lasted more than six hours as they went over his statement again and again in minute detail.

Then Detective Sergeant Alan Branch dropped his bombshell. He looked Black straight in the eye and asked, 'What does your brother-in-law think about the robbery?'

The fact that the police knew about his connection with Brian Robinson obviously shook Black, but he was not ready to fold yet. The game of cat and mouse lasted until 3 p.m. the following day. The police piled more and more pressure on the prisoner and he was obviously getting ready to crack.

'Can I have a cup of tea?' Black asked.

Detective Sergeant Nicholas Benwell left the interview room and returned with a plastic cup from the vending machine. Black took a sip and looked up.

'Where do I start?' he asked.

MOLE TURNS GRASS

When Tony Black decided to talk, he talked with a vengeance. It took Sergeant Benwell more than eight hours to take down his statement. He explained how he had been approached by his sister's common-law husband, Brian Robinson, to provide inside information about shipments, security arrangements, the layout of the warehouse and details of personnel and procedures. Black admitted that on the day of the robbery, he had let the gang into the warehouse.

According to Black, Robinson had two accomplices. One was a man in his

---

> BLACK WAS ALLOWED HOME, NOT REALIZING THAT THE POLICE WERE CONVINCED HE HAD BEEN IN ON THE ROBBERY

> THE SECURITY GUARD HAD PROVIDED THE ROBBERS WITH PHOTOGRAPHS, KEYS AND DETAILED INFORMATION

Below: *John Palmer's house outside Bath. Armed police raided the house on the morning after the death of DC Fordham, but found Palmer and his wife had left for a holiday in the Canary Islands.*

---

early thirties called Mick. The other was a giant of a man who went by the name of Tony.

Shortly after Black finished his statement, Detective Sergeant Branch came into the interview room with two files containing mugshots of known associates of Brian Robinson. Black leafed through the photographs and did not hesitate in identifying two of them – Tony White and Mick McAvoy.

Having broken every rule in the criminal code book, Tony Black was taken back to his cell.

At 6.30 the following morning, Tuesday December 6, the Flying Squad picked up Robinson, McAvoy and White. The three men were taken to separate police stations well away from Hounslow. Robinson was polite but firm in his denial of any wrongdoing, and provided the police with a detailed alibi for the day of the robbery. White was aggressive and blunt. McAvoy would say nothing without his lawyer being present.

Under normal circumstances, Frank Cater knew that breaking the three men down would take time. He decided to take a short cut. He showed them Tony Black's statement. White was the first

Robinson, Mick McAvoy and Tony White. Black's testimony lasted almost three days and was frequently interrupted by catcalls and abuse from the public gallery. Nobody, it seems, likes a grass.

Since identity parades and forensic evidence had proved inconclusive, the prosecution's case rested almost totally on Black's evidence. In the cases of Brian Robinson and Mick McAvoy, this proved insufficient to convince the jury of their guilt. But Tony White, who claimed the police had tricked and coerced him into his confession, was found not guilty.

The Judge warned Robinson and McAvoy that he had no choice but to impose a heavy sentence of 25 years' imprisonment.

ONGOING INVESTIGATION

For the police, the matter did not end with the conviction of Black, Robinson and McAvoy. There was still the small matter of £26 million in gold bullion to be accounted for.

The police used their vast network of criminal intelligence to narrow down the field in their hunt for the Brink's-Mat haul. They came up with a list of names, known associates of Robinson and White. This list included Kenneth Noye, a Kent businessman and property dealer with a considerable criminal pedigree.

After months of investigation, Cater became convinced that Noye was the main link in an elaborate chain through which the Brink's-Mat bullion was being channelled. It went from Noye to his friend Brian Reader and on to Garth Chappell, John Palmer and Scadlynn Ltd, a bullion dealer in Bristol.

The police's main problem was that if they moved in on any member of that chain, the others would be alerted and go to ground. In the short term it was decided to keep the key players under surveillance. Detective Chief Superintendent Brian Boyce, who had taken over the Brink's-Mat case, was sure

to capitulate. He admitted being a party to the robbery and wanted to explore the possibility of doing a deal. At the end of the interview, however, White refused to sign his statement and he would later withdraw his admission of guilt at his trial.

Brian Robinson realized that, in the light of Black's testimony, his position was hopeless. He admitted that he had helped set up the robbery but denied being involved in the execution of the crime itself.

McAvoy stuck to his tactic of silence until he too had read Black's statement, at which point he folded completely.

There would be no deal for McAvoy or White, but there certainly was for Tony Black. On February 17, 1984, Black – the 'Golden Mole' – stood trial at the Old Bailey. In less than an hour he was arraigned, tried and sentenced to six years' imprisonment. This meant that, with full remission and parole, he would serve no more than two years.

Black's next appearance in court was at the Old Bailey in October 1984 – not as the accused but as the chief prosecution witness in the trials of Brian

Above: *The makeshift smelting shack found in the grounds of John Palmer's house. Inside, police discovered a foundry crucible and lifting gear, and in the house itself they came across two ingots of gold, still warm.*

that at least part of the bullion was being stored at Hollywood Cottage, Noye's Kent mansion.

THE WAITING GAME GOES TRAGICALLY WRONG

By January 1985 Boyce was getting ready to move in. The round-the-clock observation on Hollywood Cottage was intensified. On the evening of Thursday January 10, Detective Constables John Fordham and Neil Murphy of the elite C11 surveillance team were sent into the grounds of the house for close observation. Seconds later, three Rottweilers leapt out of the dark.

Murphy made a dash for the perimeter fence. Once safely in the road, he waited for his partner. Detective Constable Fordham never materialized.

Almost half an hour elapsed before Detective Constables David Manning and John Childs went into the grounds of Hollywood Cottage to look for their missing colleague. Almost immediately they saw Fordham lying on his back, with the Rottweilers pulling at his clothes. Standing over the fallen policeman was Kenneth Noye, pointing a shotgun at him.

Manning whipped out his warrant card and shouted, 'I am a police officer.' He walked over to where Fordham was lying and immediately saw blood oozing from his chest and stomach. 'He's done me,' Fordham gasped. 'He's stabbed me.'

Noye was dragged off, and charged with malicious wounding, a charge which had to be changed to murder a few hours later. With the tragic loss of Detective Constable Fordham, the nature of the police operation became public and Boyce had to move quickly.

Within an hour of the stabbing, police raided the home of Brian Reader and discovered almost £70,000 in new £50 notes along with several lumps of yellow-coloured metal. They took these away, together with notebooks, diaries and address books – anything which would help establish Reader's

> ONCE IN POSSESSION OF THE GOLD, CHAPPELL WOULD RESMELT IT, MIXING IT WITH COPPER TO HIDE ITS PURITY. SCADLYNN WOULD THEN SELL IT ON THE OPEN MARKET AS SCRAP.

connection with other members of the bullion chain.

The search of Hollywood Cottage and its grounds did provide ample evidence that Kenneth Noye was involved in the Brink's-Mat robbery. In a shallow gully beside the garage wall, they found eleven gold bars, weighing some 13kg and worth something in excess of £100,000.

Nearly 50 officers sealed off the village of Litton, home of Garth Chappell. Inside Chappell's home they discovered a briefcase containing £12,500 in £50 notes. Armed police raided John Palmer's house. Palmer was not there. Three guests at the house informed police that Mr and Mrs Palmer had left the day before with their children for a three-week holiday in the Canary Islands. In the grounds of the house, police found a makeshift smelter. In the house itself they discovered two gold ingots, still warm, along with a selection of firearms, and a large quantity of cash.

It took months for the detectives to piece everything together. As they had suspected, the gold had been passed from Noye to Reader and from him to Chappell. Chappell had paid Reader for each shipment in £50 notes, and Reader had paid Noye.

Once in possession of the gold, Chappell would resmelt it, mixing it with copper to hide its purity. Scadlynn would then sell it on the open market as scrap. In the space of six months, Chappell had managed to dispose of about half of the Brink's-Mat haul – some £13 million worth of gold.

Noye was jailed for thirteen years and fined £250,000. Chappell received ten years and a £200,000 fine. Reader was sentenced to ten years, and John Palmer, who returned from Spain voluntarily, was found not guilty.

CRIMES
OF
TERROR

SEPTEMBER 11
World Trade Center

On September 11, 2001, terrorists unleashed a shocking air assault on America's military and financial powers by hijacking four commercial jets and then crashing them into the World Trade Center in New York, the Pentagon and the Pennsylvania countryside.

It was the most dramatic attack on American soil since Pearl Harbor and caused the most incredible scenes of chaos and carnage. With the estimated death toll at over 5,300, this was definitely one of the most devastating terrorist operations in American history.

HIJACKED PLANES

The terrorists hijacked four California-bound planes from three airports on the Eastern Seaboard. The planes were loaded with the maximum amount of fuel, which suggested a well-financed and well-co-ordinated plan. The planes were identified as American Airlines flight #11 and United Airlines flight #175 both flying from Boston, Massachusetts to Los Angeles, California. There were a total of 157 people on board the two planes.

At 8.45 a.m. the first hijacked passenger jet, Flight #11, crashes into the north tower of the 110-storey World Trade Center, tearing a gaping hole in the building and setting it on fire.

As if this wasn't horrifying enough, at precisely 9.03 a.m. the second hijacked airliner, Flight #175, crashes

Above: *The second plane hits the south tower of the World Trade Center.*

THE WORLD TRADE CENTER'S NORTH TOWER COLLAPSES FROM THE TOP DOWN AS IF IT WERE BEING PEELED APART, RELEASING A TREMENDOUS CLOUD OF DEBRIS AND SMOKE.

into the south tower of the World Trade Center and explodes – both buildings are now burning. They had ripped a blazing path through the Defence Department, bringing the domestic air traffic system to a halt and plunging the whole nation into an unparalleled state of panic.

Immediately the Federal Aviation Administration shut down all New York City area airports, halting all flight operations for the first time in US history. The Port Authority of New York and New Jersey ordered that all bridges and tunnels in the New York area were to be closed.

President Bush put US military forces, both at home and abroad, on their highest state of alert, and navy

Above: *Firefighters attempting to put out the blaze at The Pentagon.*

In a grim address to the nation, President Bush condemned the attacks as a failed attempt to frighten the United States and promised a relentless hunt to find those responsible. 'We will make no distinction,' he said, 'between the terrorists who committed these acts and those who harbour them.' Bush also promised that America would continue to function 'without interruption'.

Below: *The collapse of the south tower at the World Trade Center.*

warships were deployed along both coasts for air defence.

The horrors of the attack, however, were not yet over. At 9:43 a.m. American Airlines Flight #77 out of Dulles International Airport, ripped through the newly renovated walls of the Pentagon – perhaps the world's most secure office building.

Evacuation of The Pentagon and the White House began immediately.

At 10:05 a.m. the south tower of the World Trade Center collapses, plummeting into the streets below. A massive cloud of dust and debris forms and slowly drifts away from the building. At the same time as the collapse of the tower, a fourth jet, Flight #93, is reported to have crashed 80 miles southeast of Pittsburgh, shortly after it was hijacked and turned in the direction of Washington.

None of the 266 people aboard the four planes survived. There were even more horrific casualties in the World Trade Center and the Pentagon, which together provided office space for more than 70,000 people.

The spectacular collapse of the historic twin towers and another not so famous skyscraper during the rescue operations caused even more bloodshed. At least 300 New York firefighters and 85 police officers lost their lives.

GROUND ZERO

The site of destruction became known as 'Ground Zero'. The extent of the devastation, even the limited view of it that could be seen from outside the perimeter, was a horrifying sign of just how evil mankind can be. However, you could also see many signs of the good side of humanity, in the numerous outpourings of love and support for the victims and their families that surrounded the site. You could see the tributes everywhere – in the yard of a describe the place as clean, the cleanup of the World Trade Center site is now complete. What was just a pile of jagged, knotted steel and concrete, is now a hole, a neatly squared-off, rectangular cavity of 16 acres.

One prominent reminder of the scale of the disaster that engulfed New York on that fatal day was the remains of 'The Sphere' which stood in the fountain. This was once the centrepiece of World Trade Center plaza.

The search for bodies has now officially been called off.

Above: *Recovering the body of the firefighter's chaplain from the Ground Zero site.*

church near the site, and along the fence surrounding the area. There were signs, posters, greeting cards, dolls, stuffed animals, flowers and numerous other messages and items indicating that people all over the world cared about the people who died in this tragedy. It seemed to show the sheer determination of the people to stand up against the terrorists.

Though it may never feel right to

> THE GRIM AND EXHAUSTING TASK OF CARTING AWAY THE RUINS OF THE WORLD TRADE CENTER TOOK MONTHS AND A BILLION DOLLARS — AND FINISHED UNDER BUDGET AND AHEAD OF SCHEDULE.

WHO IS RESPONSIBLE?

Although no one claimed responsibility for the attacks on September 11, federal officials said they suspect the involvement of Islamic extremists with links to fugitive terrorist Osama bin Laden. Bin Laden has been implicated in the 1998 bombings of two US embassies in Africa and several other attacks. There is also a lot of evidence implicating bin Laden's militant network in the attack. Politicians from both parties predicted a major and immediate escalation in America's worldwide war against terrorism.

Following the cataclysmic events of September 11, the US authorities were quick to name Osama bin Laden as their prime suspect. The reasons for their suspicions were many, and the evidence collected during the ensuing investigation seemed to support their theory.

Although the evidence seemed compelling, at least two people weren't convinced. Milt Beardon, a former CIA agent who spent time in Afghanistan advising the mujahedeen during their fight against the Soviets,

'My prime suspect is Osama bin Laden because he was indicating he was going to do this, he was calling for the killing of Americans just recently and he had the capability, so why wouldn't we suspect him — we'd have to be crazy.'

Professor Bard O'Neil from the National War College in Washington

told ABC's Sunday programme that the attacks may have been the work of Shi'ite Muslims because the hijackers on the aircraft that crashed outside Philadelphia were described as wearing 'red head bands,' an adornment known to date back to the formation of the Shi'ite sect. While Pakistani journalist, Hamid Mir, also doubts that bin Laden was behind the September 11 attacks, saying the terrorist leader did not have the resources to pull it off.

Despite these doubts, another piece of information provided a chilling insight into what was to come. While recording a segment for the CBS *60 Minutes* programme, the show's producer George Creel, was travelling in a car with Khaled Kodja, a known bin Laden associate, when Kodja told him:

'America is a very vulnerable country, you are a very open country. I tell you, your White House is your most vulnerable target. It would be very simple to just get it. It is not difficult. It takes only one or two lives to have it, it's not difficult. We have people like this.'

Although the world intelligence community has been aware of bin Laden and his al-Qaeda network for some time, no one was able to predict where and when he would strike next. The organization is not only more sophisticated than past terrorist groups, but it is controlled and financed by a man who has dedicated most of his adult life to fighting a jihad against anyone he sees as an 'enemy of Islam', particularly America.

FROM A LARGE FAMILY

Osama bin Laden (Usamah bin Muhammad bin Awad bin Ladin) was born in 1957 or 1958 in Riyadh, Saudi Arabia. He was the seventh son in a family of 52 children.

His father, Sheik Mohammed Awad bin Laden, was a poor, uneducated

Above: *Osama bin Laden*

labourer from Hadramout in South Yemen who worked as a porter in Jeddah. In 1930, the elder bin Laden started his own construction business, which became so successful that his family grew to be known as 'the wealthiest non-royal family in the kingdom.'

Bin Laden tops the FBI's most wanted terrorist list and, until recently, has been living in exile under the protection of Afghanistan's Taliban regime. Since the collapse of the Taliban regime, he has been in hiding. Though his current whereabouts are unknown, most reports indicate that, if alive, bin Laden is probably in Afghanistan.

Although the September 11 attacks shocked the world with their audacity and far-reaching repercussions, one positive factor remains. A large percentage of the world's population was united in a collective resolve to never let it happen again. Perhaps, at least in this case, some good will come out of it and the thousands of victims will not have died in vain.

THE BIGGEST AL-QAEDA CATCH

The arrest and interrogation of Khalid Sheikh Mohammed is the biggest catch yet in the global hunt for al-Qaeda suspects. Western security sources say they have no doubts that Khalid played a major role as al-Qaeda's operational commander in the September 11 attacks.

Kuwaiti-born Mohammed was one of three al-Qaeda suspects detained in the city of Rawalpindi near the Pakistani capital Islamabad as part of Pakistan's support for US President George W. Bush's war on terror.

Nobody but a few Pakistani intelligence agents had heard of Khalid until a 1,200lb bomb of fertilizer, petrol and hydrogen exploded in the underground car part of the World Trade Center in New York on February 26, 1993. This attack, which killed six people and injured more than 1,000, was Khalid's spectacular debut in international terrorism.

Chilling details have begun to emerge regarding Khalid's alleged activities since September 11. He is reported to have commanded Richard Reid, the shoe-bomber now serving life in an American prison for attempting to blow up a US aircraft over the Atlantic. Jose Padilla, who was arrested in Chicago last June on suspicion of planning a 'dirty bomb' attack, is said to have been another one of his protégés. Attacks on an Israeli aircraft, bombings on the USS Cole in Yemen and a hotel in Kenya last October were planned by him, according to reports. He has also played an important role inspiring and fostering ties with Asian terrorist groups, particularly those responsible for the Bali bombings.

Witnesses in Pakistan are also reported to have confessed that Khalid personally killed Daniel Pearl, the Wall Street Journal reporter who was kidnapped in Karachi last year.

Some of America's most senior politicians are already saying that the normal rules governing the torture of terror suspects, should be set aside because Sheikh Mohammed is the repository of so much important information.

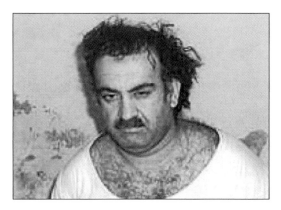

Left: *Khalid Sheikh Mohammed following his arrest.*

Sheikh Mohammed has already disclosed the names and descriptions of about a dozen key al-Qaeda operatives believed to be plotting terrorist attacks on American and other Western interests. He has also filled in important gaps in what U.S. intelligence knows about al-Qaeda's practices.

WAR ON TERRORISM

Following September 11, America justifiably declared a 'War on Terror' against all terrorists and the countries which harboured them. They also vowed to hunt down those in possession of weapons of mass destruction. Intelligence in this field led them directly to Iraq.

After many months of threats and a long military build-up, the United States finally attacked Iraq on Thursday, March 20, 2003. The war faced strong opposition from France, Germany, Russia, China and the great majority of UN member states as well as world public opinion. The combined military ground force of the US and the UK was around 300,000, and they encountered stiff Iraqi resistance.

THE REASONS BEHIND THE WAR

Iraq posed as a threat mainly because of the Iraqi regime's own actions. It had a history of aggression and also a continual drive towards an arsenal of terror. One of the conditions for ending the Persian Gulf War (1990–1991), was that the Iraqi regime was required to destroy all its weapons of mass destruction, to cease production of such weapons, and finally to stop all support for terrorist groups. However, the Iraqi regime continued to violate all of these obligations. It was still considered to possess and produce chemical and biological weapons, and was thought to be also seeking nuclear weapons. It was known to give shelter and support

"THE FUNDAMENTAL PROBLEM WITH IRAQ REMAINS THE NATURE OF THE REGIME ITSELF. SADDAM HUSSEIN IS A HOMICIDAL DICTATOR WHO IS ADDICTED TO WEAPONS OF MASS DESTRUCTION"
President George Bush

to terrorists, and practised terror against its own people.

After the attack on September 11, America started to feel vulnerable. They resolved to fight the war against terrorism, to confront every threat, from whatever source, that could bring sudden terror and suffering to their country.

It is a known fact that Iraq and the al Qaeda terrorist network share a common enemy – the United States of America. Iraqi and al Qaeda connections are known to go back more than a decade, and some of the al Qaeda leaders who fled Afghanistan went to Iraq. Not only has Iraq willingly harboured these terrorists, it is also known they also trained al Qaeda members in bomb-making, poisons and deadly gases.

The United States knew that on any given day Iraq could provide a biological or chemical weapon to a terrorist group or individual terrorist, leaving America open to attack.

Below: *The statue of Saddam Hussein, in Paradise Square, is set on fire amidst cheers from the Iraqi civilians. This enabled it to be brought crashing down as the world watched on (left).*

THE TYRANT

While there are many dangers in the world, it was thought that the threat from Iraq was the strongest due to the fact that their weapons of mass destruction were controlled by a murderous tyrant who had already used chemical weapons to kills thousands of people – Saddam Hussein. This same tyrant had tried to dominate the Middle East, had invaded and brutally occupied a small neighbour, had struck other nations without any prior warning and had led a burtal regime of terror and suffering against his own people. He was also known to hold an unrelenting hostility towards the United States. Saddam Hussein was considered to be a homicidal dictator who was addicted to weapons of mass destruction.

THE ATTACK

The attack on Iraq began at around 5.30 a.m. on March 20, 2003 when the United States launched 'Operation Iraqi Freedom'. The attack was an attempt to target Saddam Hussein and other Iraqi leaders, using air strikes and ground troops which entered the country by crossing southern Iraq from Kuwait. The following day the major phase of the war began with heavy aerial attacks on Baghdad and other cities. There was also fighting in the north of the country, with some reports that it involved US Special Forces. During the day, a number of oil wells – seven, according to the British

A ♠

SADDAM HUSAYN AL-TIKRITI
President

♠ A

Left: *In the aftermath of the war, with many members of the Iraqi regime still evading capture, the US issued a set of playing cards, depicting the faces of those that the coalition forces still had to 'pursue, capture and kill'. Saddam Hussein was the ace of spades.*

THE GUNFIRE GREW LOUDER, UNTIL CLUSTERS OF BULLETS SWARMED INTO THE AIR AMID GRENADE BURSTS. IN THE MAIN STREET OF BAGHDAD, CARS CRASHED INTO ONE ANOTHER IN THE ENSUING CHAOS.

---

government – were reported to be on fire. According to the British government, two of the fires were extinguished by special firefighting troops. The Iraqi government denied that oil wells had been set on fire, saying that it had set fire to oil-filled trenches as a defensive measure against airstrikes.

By March 23 USA and British forces succeeded in taking the airport outside of Basra, and were in battle with Iraqi forces for control of the city itself. On April 9 Baghdad fell to US forces. Some Iraqis cheered in the streets after American infantrymen seized deserted Ba'ath Party ministries and pulled down a huge iron statue of Saddam Hussein, ending his brutal 24-year rule of Iraq.

The looting and unrest, especially in major cities Baghdad and Basra became a very serious issue. In Baghdad, with the notable exception of the Oil Ministry, which was guarded by American troops, the majority of government and public buildings were totally plundered. On April 13, Tikrit, the home town of Saddam Hussein, and the last town not under control of the coalition, was taken by American marines.

Left: *The Iraqi people celebrate the capture of their ousted dictator.*

Above: *Fear and terror still reign in Iraq even after Saddam's capture. Here, a car burns at the entrance to one of the police stations in Basra, southern Iraq, hit by an explosion only hours after 3 car bombs had already killed 60 people and wounded a further 100.*

Below: *Saddam Hussein after his capture.*

With the fall of the Tikrit region, the coalition partners declared the war effectively over on April 15.

CAPTURE OF SADDAM HUSSEIN

On Saturday, December 13, 2003, US troops converged on a two-room mud hut, squatting between two houses on a Tigris farm near the village of Ad-Dawr. One room, which appeared to serve as a bedroom, was in disarray with clothes strewn about the place. Inside the hut, dirt and a rug covered the entryway to a subterranean hideaway. The US troops had finally caught up with the man who had eluded them for many months. Saddam Hussein's last hiding place was a miserable 8-foot hole dug in the mud. Although Saddam was armed with a pistol, he showed no resistance during his capture. The former dictator of Iraq appeared tired and disoriented when he was pulled from his hiding place, which was found to contain arms and around $750,000 in cash. The US proudly declared 'We got him', and paraded the once proud man, now unkempt and with a scraggy beard, around in front of a world audience.

The assumption that the capture of Saddam Hussein would solve all the problems surrounding Iraq soon seemed to lose its credence. Violence on the streets, and attacks against coalition forces continued with the same ferocity and fatalities that they had prior to Saddam's capture. Saddam, the pathetic, bedraggled man, living in a hole in the ground with only three guns and some cash, certainly was not the powerful figure behind the resistance forces in Iraq. The fact that he probably had very little control or influence is a disturbing and significant fact as it raises the question as to whether these were insurgents vying for power, or Iraqis demonstrating their continued hatred and aggression towards the US?

THE TERROR CONTINUES
Bali and Madrid

In spite of the West's efforts to counter terrorism, the attacks continue . . .

BALI

The Indonesian island of Bali was rocked by two explosions on October 12, 2002. It was the worst incident ever to occur on this normally peaceful island, and the repercussions had a major impact on the lives of the people of Bali. At 11.05 p.m. October 12, an electronically triggered bomb ripped through Paddy's Bar, forcing the injured out into the street. About ten to fifteen seconds later, a second much more powerful car bomb concealed in a white Mitsubishi van, exploded in front of the Sari Club. Windows throughout the town were blown out. Scenes of horror and panic inside and outside the bars followed, with many acts of individual heroism. The final death toll was 202, the majority of them holidaymakers in their 20s and 30s who were in the two bars. Hundreds more people suffered horrific burns and other injuries. The largest group among those killed were holidaymakers from Australia. The Bali bombing is sometimes called 'Australia's September 11' because of the large number of its citizens killed in the attack.

The organisation claiming responsibility for the bombing was Jemaah Islamiyah, an Islamist group linked to the al Qaeda network. On April 30, 2003, the first charges relating to the Bali bombings were made against Amrozi bin Haji Nurhasyim, known as Amrozi, for allegedly buying the explosives and the van used in the bombings. On August 8 he was found guilty and sentenced to death by shooting.

Left: *Searching Bali rubble.* Below: *Madrid train explosion.*

MADRID

At the height of Madrid's morning rush hour, on Thursday, March 11, 2004, ten terrorist bombs tore through trains and stations all along the commuter line. It killed more than 191 people and wounded over 2,000 and was timed to take place before the weekend's general elections.

Panicked commuters abandoned their bags and their shoes as they trampled each other to escape the train terminal at Atocha. Some people, in their panic, fled into dark, dangerous tunnels at the station, which was a bustling hub for subway, commuter and long-distance trains, just south of Madrid's famous Prado Museum.

The explosives that were used in the blasts were a type of dynamite that was normally used by the ETA Basque separatist group. However, only eleven days after the atrocity in the Spanish capital, ties started to emerge between a key suspect in the bombing and Islamic militants elsewhere in Europe and North Africa. It pointed towards a widening web of organizations that may have direct links to al Qaeda.

The suspected ringleader of the Madrid bombings, Serhane ben Abdelmajid Fakhet, blew himself up along with four other suspects, during a police raid. Spain has provisionally charged fifteen suspects in connection with the blasts, six of whom have been charged with multiple counts of murder, and nine accused of collaborating with, or belonging to, a terrorist organization.

TIMOTHY McVEIGH
The Oklahoma Bomber

It was April 19, 1995 – a perfect, sun-drenched spring morning in Oklahoma. A yellow Ryder Rental truck carefully made its way through the streets of downtown Oklahoma City. Just after 9 am, the truck pulled into a parking area outside the Alfred P. Murrah building and the driver stepped down from the trucks cab and casually walked away. A few minutes later, at 9.02, all hell broke loose as the trucks deadly 4000-pound cargo blasted the government building with enough force to shatter one third of the seven-story structure to bits

Above: *Timothy McVeigh as a child*

GLASS, CONCRETE, AND STEEL RAINED DOWN. INDISCRIMINATELY MIXED IN THE SMOULDERING RUBBLE WERE ADULTS AND CHILDREN —ALIVE AND DEAD.

Timothy McVeigh was born on April 23, 1968 in Pendleton, New York, and grew up in a rural community. He was the middle one of three children, and the only boy.

His father worked at a nearby General Motors manufacturing plant and his mother worked for a travel agency. His parents marriage was rather stormy and they separated for a third and final time in 1984.

Timothy's school classmates remember him as small, thin and quiet. He became involved in the normal school functions – football, track, extra-curricular activities – but usually dropped out shortly after joining them. He was shy, did not have a girlfriend, and in reality was somewhat of a loner.

McVeigh graduated from high school in June, 1986 and in the autumn, entered a two-year business college course. He attended for only a short time, during which time McVeigh lived at home with his father, and worked at a Burger King and drove dilapidated, old cars.

In 1987 he got a pistol permit from Niagara County and a job in Buffalo as a guard on an armoured car. A co-worker recalls that McVeigh owned numerous firearms and had a survivalist philosophy – a tendency to stockpile weapons and food in preparation for what he believed to be the imminent breakdown of society. In 1988 McVeigh and a friend bought 10 acres of rural land and used it as a shooting range.

JOINING THE ARMY

McVeigh enlisted in the Army in Buffalo in May 1988, and went through basic training at Fort Benning, Georgia. After basic training, his unit was transferred to Fort Riley, Kansas, and became part of the Army's 1st Infantry Division.

McVeigh had finally found his calling. The Army was everything he wanted in life, and more. When he joined, he was no leader, but an eager follower. There was discipline, a sense of order, and all the training a man could want in survivalist techniques. Most of all, there was an endless supply of weapons, and instruction on how to use and maintain them.

McVeigh became a gunner on a Bradley Fighting Vehicle. He was promoted to corporal, sergeant, then platoon leader. Fellow soldiers recalled that McVeigh was very interested in military stuff, kept his own personal collection of firearms and constantly cleaned and maintained them. Other soldiers went into town to look for entertainment or companionship but McVeigh stayed on base and cleaned his guns. During his time in the Army, he also read and recommended to others *The Turner Diaries* – a racist, anti-Semitic novel about a soldier in an underground army. A former roommate said that McVeigh would panic at the prospect of the government taking away peoples' guns, but that he was not a racist and was basically indifferent to racial matters.

While at Fort Riley, McVeigh re-enlisted in the Army. He aspired to be a member of the Special Forces and in 1990 was accepted into a three-week school to assess his potential for joining that elite unit. He had barely begun to prepare himself physically for Special Forces training when, in January 1991, the 1st Infantry Division was sent to participate in the Persian Gulf War. As a gunnery sergeant, McVeigh was in action during late February, 1991. Pursuing his desire of joining the Special Forces, he left the Persian Gulf early and went to Fort Bragg, North Carolina, where he took a battery of IQ, personality and aptitude tests to qualify for Special Forces. However, his participation in the Persian Gulf War had left him no time to prepare himself physically for the demands of Special Forces training. McVeigh was unable to endure a 90-minute march with a 45-pound pack, and he withdrew from the programme after two days.

This disappointing experience left him facing years of active service due to his re-enlistment at Fort Riley. The Army was downsizing however, and after 3$^{1}/_{2}$

One of McVeigh's favourite films was the 1984 Patrick Swayze epic 'Red Dawn'. It follows a group of small town teens' conversion to guerilla fighters when a foreign army invades America.

Left: *Sgt. Timothy James McVeigh*

years of service, McVeigh took the offer of an early discharge and got out of the military in the autumn of 1991.

OUT OF THE SERVICE

By January 1992, at the age of 24, McVeigh was back where he had started, living with his father in Pendleton, New York, driving an old car and working as a security guard.

In January 1993 McVeigh left Pendleton, and began to travel, moving himself and his belongings about in a

Left: *Timothy McVeigh, top centre, with his platoon, Fort Benning, Georgia, 1988.*

series of battered old cars. He lived in cheap motels and caravan parks, but also stayed with two Army buddies, Michael Fortier in Kingman, Arizona, and Terry Nichols in Decker, Michigan from time to time.

McVeigh travelled to Waco, Texas during the March-April 1993 standoff between the Branch Davidians and federal agents, and was said to have been angry about what he saw. He sold firearms at a gun show in Arizona and was heard to remark on one weapon's ability to shoot down an ATF helicopter.

Although both Arizona and Michigan are host to militant anti-tax, anti-government, survivalist and racist groups, there is no evidence that McVeigh ever belonged to any extremist groups. He advertised to sell a weapon in what is described as a virulently anti-Semitic publication. After renting a Ryder truck that has been linked to the Oklahoma City bombing, McVeigh telephoned a religious community that preached white supremacy, but no one there can remember knowing him or talking to him. His only known affiliations are as a registered Republican in his New York days, and as a member of the National Rifle Association while he was in the Army.

CHANGES IN THE GUN LAW

On September 13, 1994, the gun shows that McVeigh attended had become sombre occasions. New laws had been passed to stop the manufacture of many types of weaponry, including a range of semi-automatic rifles and handguns. Gun traders and buyers alike were outraged to learn the government was controlling their 'right to bear arms'.

To McVeigh, it also meant his livelihood had become endangered. He had been buying weapons under his own name and charging a brokerage fee to other buyers – those who didn't want their names on government forms.

Paranoia rose on rumours that owners would be subject to surprise

HOMEGROWN TERRORISM HAD ARRIVED WITH A VENGEANCE, AND THE TERRORIST WAS THE KID NEXT DOOR – AND HE WAS CRUISING AWAY FROM THE CARNAGE – DOWN INTERSTATE 35.

searches of their homes and businesses. McVeigh decided that action could no longer be postponed. From the Nichols home in Marion, Kansas, he wrote to Fortier. He insisted that the time had come for action, and he wanted Fortier to join him and Terry Nichols in their protest. Imitating *The Turner Diaries*, they planned to blow up a federal building. McVeigh cautioned Fortier against telling his wife Lori – but this was an instruction Fortier ignored. Furthermore, Fortier said he would never be part of the plan.

Undeterred, McVeigh and Nichols took advice from various bomb-building manuals. They followed the recipe and stockpiled their materials – bought under the alias 'Mike Havens' – in rented storage sheds. The recipe also called for other ingredients like blasting caps and liquid nitro methane, which they stole – but that's not the only thing they stole.

To pay for their despicable enterprise, Nichols robbed gun collector Roger Moore at gunpoint. Moore claimed the thief had taken a variety of guns, gold, silver and jewels – about sixty thousand dollars' worth. Nichols also stole Moore's van to transport the loot. When police made a list of visitors to the ranch, McVeigh's name was on it.

Earlier, McVeigh and Nichols travelled to the Fortier's Kingman home and stashed the stolen explosives in a nearby storage shed McVeigh had rented. When Fortier saw the explosives, McVeigh explained his plan. He stayed with the Fortiers, and while there, he designed his bomb. He showed Lori – using soup cans – how the drums he planned on using, could be arranged for maximum impact.

McVeigh wanted a rocket fuel called anhydrous hydrazine for his bomb. He phoned around the country to find some, but its expense made it impossible for him to obtain. So he settled on a satisfactory equivalent – nitro methane. In the course of trying to locate volatile fuels, McVeigh had phoned from the Fortiers, knowing full well his calls could be traced to the Fortier's telephone number – and the calling card he bought under the alias, Darel Bridges.

In mid-October 1994, McVeigh's plans were suddenly complicated, when he received news that his grandfather had died. He headed home to Pendleton, New York. There, he helped sort out his grandfather's estate and further poisoned his younger sister against the government.

While McVeigh was in Pendleton, he was unable to reach Terry Nichols. The co-conspirator had gone to the Philippines to see his current wife and baby daughter. But before he left, he visited his son and first wife Lana Padilla. He left her a few items including a sealed package, telling her it was to be opened only in the event of him never returning, but she opened it anyway. Included in its contents was a letter detailing the location of a plastic bag he'd hidden in Padilla's home. It contained a letter to McVeigh telling him he was now on his own – along with twenty thousand dollars. There was also a combination to Nichols' storage locker. When she opened the shed, she found some of the spoils of the Moore robbery.

In mid-December 1994, McVeigh and the Fortiers met in McVeigh's room at the Mojave Motel in Kingman, Arizona. There, he had Lori giftwrap boxes containing blasting caps in Christmas paper. He then promised Fortier a cache of weapons from the Moore robbery if he would accompany McVeigh back to Kansas. On the way, McVeigh drove through Oklahoma City to show Fortier the building he intended to bomb, and the route he would take to walk away from the building before the blast. They parted.

The getaway car would be his 1977 yellow Marquis since his other car had been damaged in an accident. The plan was for Nichols to follow the car in his truck and, after McVeigh parked it away from the bombsite, they would drive back to Kansas. The night before the bombing, they left the Marquis

TERRY NICHOLS WAS BITTER, SEEING MCVEIGH AS HAVING BULLIED HIM INTO PARTICIPATING IN THE BOMB PLOT. SENTENCED FOR LIFE FOR HIS PART IN THE BOMBING, HE HAS — SO FAR — ESCAPED THE DEATH PENALTY. OKLAHOMA WANTED TO TRY HIM ON STATE MURDER CHARGES, BUT HIS LAWYERS ARGUED HE CAN'T BE CHARGED TWICE FOR THE SAME CRIME.

Below: *An FBI agent comforts a weeping man whose loved one is still trapped in the rubble of the bombed Murrah building.*

after McVeigh removed the licence plate and left a note on it saying it needed a battery. Then, they drove away and Nichols dropped him off at his motel.

The next afternoon, McVeigh picked up the Ryder truck and parked it at the Dreamland Motel for the night. The following morning he drove it to the Herington storage unit. When Nichols finally arrived – late – they piled the bomb components in the truck and drove to Geary Lake to mix the bomb. When they had finished, Nichols went home and McVeigh stayed with the lethal Ryder vehicle.

He parked in a gravel parking lot for the night and waited for the dawn – and the drive to his target. He was dressed for the mission in his favourite T-shirt. On the front was a picture of Abraham Lincoln with the motto *sic semper tyrannis*, the words Booth shouted before he shot Lincoln. The translation: 'Thus ever to tyrants'.

On the back of the T-shirt was a tree

with blood dripping from the branches. It read, 'The tree of liberty must be refreshed from time to time with the blood of patriots and tyrants'.

Like his role model in *The Turner Diaries*, he headed for a federal building where he was convinced ATF agents were working. There, the people of Oklahoma City would pay a terrible price for McVeigh's compulsive and irrational paranoia.

Around 9:03 a.m., just after parents dropped their children off at day care at the Murrah Federal Building in downtown Oklahoma City, the unthinkable happened. A massive bomb inside the rental truck exploded, blowing half of the nine-storey building into oblivion.

A stunned nation watched as the bodies of men, women and children were pulled from the rubble for nearly two weeks. When the smoke cleared and the exhausted rescue workers packed up and left, 168 people were dead, including 19 children and hundreds more wounded.

THE ARREST

McVeigh was finally arrested on the basis of a traffic violation and the charge of carrying a weapon. McVeigh's yellow Mercury was left on the side of the highway and was not impounded.

Between April 19, 1995, and April 21, 1995, federal law enforcement officials traced a Vehicle Identification Number appearing upon the axle of the truck believed to have carried the bomb to a Ryder rental truck dealership in Junction City, Kansas. The FBI prepared a composite drawing of 'unidentified subject #1' based upon descriptions provided by witnesses at the Ryder rental dealership. By showing the composite drawing to employees at various motels in Junction City, Kansas, the FBI determined that the drawing resembled a man named Timothy McVeigh that had been a guest at the Dreamland Motel in Junction City from April 14-18, 1995. On checking their records it then came

> 'I EXPLAIN HEREIN WHY I BOMBED THE MURRAH FEDERAL BUILDING IN OKLAHOMA CITY. I EXPLAIN THIS NOT FOR PUBLICITY, NOR SEEKING TO WIN AN ARGUMENT OF RIGHT OR WRONG. I EXPLAIN SO THAT THE RECORD IS CLEAR AS TO MY THINKING AND MOTIVATION IN BOMBING A GOVERNMENT INSTALLATION.'
> (LETTER WRITTEN BY MCVEIGH)

to light that a man named Timothy McVeigh was in custody in the Noble County Jail in Perry, Oklahoma, facing state misdemeanor charges.

THE SENTENCE

It was a trial fraught with pitfalls and tough decisions for U.S. District Judge Richard P. Matsch, who maintained strict control in his Denver courtroom. McVeigh was deemed responsible for the blast that killed 168 people – the worst terrorist attack ever on American soil until September 11, 2001.

Timothy McVeigh was found guilty of bombing the Oklahoma City federal building on April 19, 1995. During a separate phase of the trial, jurors condemned the 29-year-old Gulf War veteran to die by lethal injection.

Convicted Oklahoma City bomber Timothy McVeigh was put to death by lethal injectionon at 7.14 a.m. on Monday, June 11. He is the first federal prisoner to be executed in 38 years.

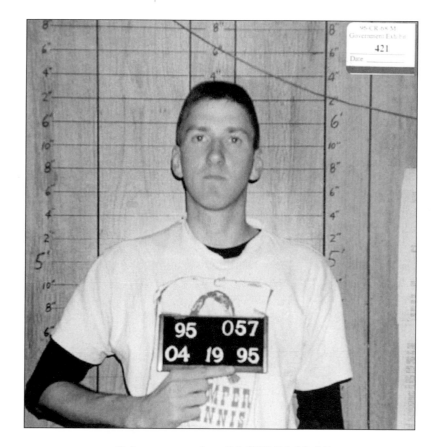

Prisoner number 95 057 04 19 95.

ILICH RAMIREZ SANCHEZ
Carlos the Jackal

'Carlos' is one of the best known 'revolutionary terrorists' in the history of modern insurgent movements. He reportedly has worked for Mohamar Qaddaffi of Libya, Saddam Hussein of Iraq, President Assad of Syria, Fidel Castro of Cuba, George Habash and the Popular Front for the Liberation of Palestine (PFLP), the Italian Red Brigade, Columbia's M-19 Movement, the Baader-Meinholf Gang, and any number of other 'Communist and Socialist' employers.

Left: *Carlos at the age of sixteen*

HIS RESUME IS ALMOST UNPARALLELED IN THE EXPLOITS OF TERRORISTS OF THE LAST THREE DECADES. ACCORDING TO ANTI-TERRORIST ANALYSTS, THE ONLY INTERNATIONAL TERRORIST OF GREATER REPUTE IS PROBABLY ABU NIDAL(SABRI BANNA).

Carlos was born in Caracas, Venezuela, on October 12, 1949. His mother, Elba Maria Sánchez had planned to give him a Christian name in keeping with her strong Catholic beliefs. José Altagracia Ramírez Navas, the boy's father, however, had other ideas. As a devout Marxist, he insisted that his first son should be named after his hero, Vladimir Ilich Ulyanov or Lenin, as he was better known. Stubbornly ignoring his wife's protests, José registered his son as Ilich Ramírez Sánchez.

Ironically, in his youth, José had entered a Catholic seminary with the intention of becoming a priest. However, after completing only three years of study, he declared himself an atheist and returned home to the town of Michelena in Tachira. Determined that Ilich would not waste his life pursuing Christian ideals, José taught his son the Marxist beliefs.

Carlos, a 1969 graduate of Moscow's Patrice Lamumba University, had been tied to 'Communist revolutionary movements' since the age of fourteen, when he became a member of the Communist party in Venezuela. His father, a wealthy Venezuelan Communist party leader, was dedicated to Leninist/Marxist theory and practice. In his teens, Carlos was allegedly given guerrilla training in Cuba, and by the age of twenty, had moved to Jordan and was being trained in weapons and explosive usage by hard-core members of the PFLP commando. Soon after, he began what has turned out to be an infamous career as an international 'pay for hire' terrorist.

THE POPULAR FRONT

In July 1970 Ilich travelled to the Middle East. His first stop was Beirut where he arrived unannounced at the office of Bassam Abu-Sharif, the unofficial 'recruiting officer' for the Popular Front. Abu-Sharif was impressed with the passion of Ilich's convictions and made arrangements for him to start his training. According to subsequent investigations, it was at that first meeting that Ilich was given the name that, in the years to come, would strike terror throughout the world. From that day forward, Ilich was known only as 'Carlos'

Within weeks of the meeting, Carlos went to a Palestinian training camp in the hills north of Amman, Jordan to begin training in the handling of weapons and explosives. Carlos longed for real action and, in the final week of his training, he got his wish. Israeli jets bombed an adjoining camp and killed a member of Yasser Arafat's personal guard. Keen to move on to 'more exciting' pursuits, Carlos contacted Abou Semir, a senior member of the Popular Front, and was sent to an advanced commando training camp.

BLACK SEPTEMBER

On September 6, 1970, the Popular Front, acting on the instructions of Dr Wadi Haddad, carried out one of the most memorable hijackings in history. They began with the simultaneous diversion to Jordan of a Swissair DC-8 and a TWA Boeing 707, which was followed six days later by the hijacking

EDWARD HEATH'S GOVERNMENT IN LONDON HAD ALREADY CONCLUDED THAT RESCUING THE HOSTAGES WAS NOT FEASIBLE, AND BEHIND THE SCENES BRITAIN BEGAN TO NEGOTIATE WITH THE HIJACKERS, THROUGH BOTH OFFICIAL AND ITS OWN SECRET CHANNELS.

of a BOAC VC-10. The aircraft were forced to land at Dawson Field, 30 miles from Amman, which was quickly renamed Revolutionary Airport. Meanwhile another Popular Front hijack team, which had failed to board an El Al plane, managed to hijack a Pan Am Boeing 747 to Cairo and blow it up, while the media recorded the incident for a gasping world audience. The resulting conflict was dubbed 'Black September' and was to become Carlos's first taste of real warfare.

THE PLAYBOY

Carlos was appointed as the Popular Front's representative in London. His task was to ingratiate himself into British society and draw up a list of 'high profile' targets that would either be murdered or kidnapped. Carlos was sent to another training camp to learn the 'finer points' of terrorism and by February 1971, Carlos was considered ready for his appointment. He travelled to London to be reunited with his family. With his mother's help, he quickly slipped back into the 'cocktail-party set' and developed his playboy habits.

He attended the University of London to study economics and later took Russian language courses at Central London Polytechnic, all part of his carefully planned façade. His Popular Front contact in London was Mohamed Bouria, an Algerian who, as one of Haddad's most loyal followers, was responsible for European operations. In search of targets, Carlos read English newspapers selecting any prominent citizens who were either Jewish or had Israeli sympathies. Once he had created his list, he went to great pains to learn as much about his targets as he could, including home addresses, telephone numbers, nicknames and as many personal details as he could glean. His list of names included famous film identities, entertainers politicians and prominent business figures.

Above: *The Popular Front demanded the release of Fedayeen (members of the Palestinian movement) imprisoned in Germany, Switzerland and Israel.*

By December 1971, he had compiled a detailed list containing hundreds of names. It was during this time that his early career as an undercover terrorist was almost terminated. Acting on a tip-off, members of Scotland Yard's Special Branch raided the house in Walpole Street, Chelsea, where he lived with his mother, but after searching the house, found nothing of an incriminating nature. They were led to believe that Carlos was linked to a cache of illegal weapons that had been seized in a previous raid at the house of one of his friends. Incredibly, a fake Italian passport bearing a picture of Carlos was found in the raid but the police considered it unimportant. Apart from being placed under surveillance for several days after the raid, the police left him alone. The family later moved to a new apartment in Kensington.

During February 1972, while Carlos languished in London, one of Haddad's teams was hijacking a Lufthansa airliner to Aden. One of the 172 passengers taken hostage was Joseph Kennedy, son of the late Robert Kennedy. Following a short period of negotiations, Kennedy and the other hostages were released safely after the West German government paid a $5,000,000 ransom. The following May, Haddad sent three members of the Japanese Red Army to carry out a brutal attack at Tel Aviv's Lod airport. After arriving at the airport, the three men retrieved automatic weapons and grenades from their luggage and opened fire on the crowd. By the time the firing had stopped, 23 travellers were dead and another 76 were wounded.

MARIA TOBON

Maria Nydia Romero de Tobon was an attractive, 37-year-old Colombian divorcee who moved to London following her divorce to resume her University studies. She was not only attracted to Carlos's Latin American charm and impeccable manners, but

IN THIS MURKY WORLD WHERE ESPIONAGE, TERRORISM AND INTERNATIONAL POLITICS MEET, LITTLE IS EVER KNOWN FOR CERTAIN.

Below: *The first floor flat at Phillimore Court, Kensington, which was occupied by Ilich Ramirez Sanchez during his period in London.*

also became enamoured by his passion for politics. Nydia, whose grandfather had founded the Colombian Liberal Party, was a revolutionary at heart and was won over by Carlos and the fervour he showed for his cause. Some months later, Carlos successfully recruited Nydia and enlisted her aid in securing a string of safe houses for visiting envoys.

At one point she posed as the wife of Antonio Dagues-Bouvier, the Ecuadorian guerrilla who had supposedly trained Carlos in Cuba, and rented three apartments in central London. Her other duties included transporting documents and funds. Carlos would later tell investigators that he and Dagues-Bouvier had, at that time, carried out several 'missions' against selected targets. No record has ever been found of any such events having taken place. The general belief is that

Carlos's time in London was largely one of inactivity, while in other parts of the world; Haddad had selected others to play his deadly games.

TERRORIST ACTIVITIES

It is thought that by early 1972, Carlos was fighting and learning combat tactics in a guerrilla war against King Hussein, in Jordan. It is also possible that 'The Jackal' had begun acting as an intelligence agent or informer for the KGB.

By 1973, however, his terrorist activities had begun in earnest. He has publicly admitted to his 1973 assassination attempt on a British Millionaire named Joseph Edward Sieff, who was a well-known Jewish businessman and owner of the Marks and Spencer stores in London. Within the next two years, he was involved in the takeover of the French Embassy at the Hague, the killing of two French Intelligence agents for which he has been recently captured, and a 1976 takeover/ kidnapping of OPEC oil ministers in Vienna, Austria. Later in 1976, he was involved in a Skyjacking, that led to the now famous Entebbe raid by Israeli commandos.

In the late seventies and early eighties, Carlos was blamed for any number of skyjackings, bombings and machine gun/grenade attacks on British, French and Israeli targets. He became a master of disguises and was known to have obtained any number of false identities, complete with passports and credit cards. Adding to his reputation as a 'terrorist master-mind' was the fact that, even if no real evidence could be produced to link him to an atrocity, it was often blamed on him, out of convenience or ineptitude. Carlos was described as 'a ruthless terrorist who operates with cold-blooded, surgical precision', according to Ahmed Zaki Yamani. Acclaimed by some as a 'professional killer' with 'cool, deliberate actions', he has also been described by others as a 'bumbling psychotic who shoots people in the face, and is

Above: *Joseph Edward Sieff, 68, was one of the most successful and influential Jewish businessmen in London, and was Carlos's first victim.*

extremely lucky'. Whatever way you look at it, Carlos seemed to revel in the limelight of his deadly performance.

In 1982 and 1983, Carlos was suspected of several bombings in Paris, France, resulting in deaths of at least 13 people and the wounding of 150 more. In the mid-1980s, it is believed that he may have also participated in the planning and execution of several operations against Israel, operating out of Syria and Lebanon. He is also reported to have consulted with Col. Mohammar Qaddaffi and even Saddam Hussein, during their conflicts with the United States.

CARLOS THE PRISONER

Nothing was heard of Carlos during the late 1980s and there were even reports of his death. Unconfirmed reports have placed him in Mexico, Columbia, Damascus and Syria during recent years. However, on Friday, December 12, 1997, Carlos was led into a courtroom in the Palais de Justice and placed in the dock. Over the next eight days, Carlos tried every tactic he could think of to counter the prosecutions case against him. On December 23, 1997, after three hours and 48 minutes of deliberation, the jury returned with their verdict, guilty on all counts, the sentence – life imprisonment. Ironically, the death sentence that Carlos should have received for his crimes had been abolished years earlier by President Francois Mitterrand, the same man who had ordered his agents to find Carlos and kill him.

To this day Carlos is held in the maximum-security wing of Le Sante prison. He is allowed few visitors and spends his time reading, writing and watching television.

One thing is certain, the man who began life as Ilich Ramirez Sanchez and named himself Carlos the Jackal, is now known by a less flamboyant title. In Le Sante he is known simply as 'Detainee 872686/X' and probably will be for the rest of his life.